Sex and Virtue

CATHOLIC MORAL THOUGHT

General Editor: Romanus Cessario, O.P.

Sex and Virtue

An Introduction to Sexual Ethics

John S. Grabowski

The Catholic University of America Press

Washington, D.C.

The paper used in this publication meets the minimum requirements of American National Standards for Information Science—Permanence of Paper for Printed Library materials, ANSI Z39.48-1984.

∞

LIBRARY OF CONGRESS CATALOGING-IN-PUBLICATION DATA
Grabowski, John S.
    Sex and virtue : an introduction to sexual ethics / John S. Grabowski.
        p. cm. — (Catholic moral thought)
    Includes bibliographical references.
    ISBN 0-8132-1345-2 (cloth : alk. paper) —
    ISBN 0-8132-1346-0 (pbk. : alk. paper)
        1. Sex—Religious aspects—Catholic Church. 2. Sexual ethics. 3. Catholic Church—Doctrines. I. Title. II. Series.
    BX1795.S48 G73 2004
    241'.66—dc21
    2002015319

Contents

Acknowledgments

The Assumption of Mary, like all Marian doctrines, not only further reveals the mystery of Christ but sheds light on the dignity and destiny of all of the redeemed as well. For her flesh, born to human parents through sexual union, now lives in the presence of the Triune God. Such is the destiny of all men and women united to her Son in faith and love, whether married, single, or celibate. This book is a reflection on learning how to live well and love well as a body person in the hope of sharing the beatitude she now enjoys.

Portions of Chapter 2 previously appeared in *Église et Théologie*. Portions of Chapter 4 previously appeared in *The Living Light*. I am grateful for the permission given by these two fine publications to reuse and rework some of that material.

Many persons have contributed to this project. I am indebted to Amy Vineyard Ekeh, Ted Whapham, and Aaron Massey for invaluable research and editorial assistance. My daughter, Rachel Grabowski, generously helped to check Latin references in Migne's *Patrologia Latina* and also provided needed perspective ("Dad, do you know that St. Augustine wrote way too much?"). I am grateful to the members of the Missouri Valley Association of Catholic Theologians, particularly its president, Dr. Lawrence J. Welch, for helpful feedback and suggestions on portions of this work presented at its annual meetings. I have also benefitted from generous and helpful criticism by Dr. William E. May of the John Paul II Institute for Studies on Marriage and Family and Dr. Paul J. Wadell of St. Norbert's College who reviewed this work for The Catholic University of America Press. I am particularly indebted to Dr. David McGonagle of The Catholic University of America Press and Fr. Romanus Cessario, O.P., the general editor of this series, for taking the initiative to organize this series, for the invitation to contribute to it, and for their encouragement and suggestions about my manuscript along the way. Finally, I am grateful for the support and encouragement of my

wife, Claire, from whom I have learned more about virtue and friendship than anything gained through my work over eleven years of teaching moral theology.

Washington, D.C.
August 15, 2002
Feast of the Assumption

Introduction

The Second Vatican Council (Vatican II) in its decree on priestly formation called for the renewal of moral theology. In particular, Vatican II specified that moral theology needed "livelier contact with the mystery of Christ" and should be "more thoroughly nourished by scriptural teaching."[1] The decades following Vatican II have seen a variety of responses to this call. Among these treatments one often finds disagreement not only on specific moral questions, but on the very sources and methods to be used in moral reasoning.

How, then, can one begin to discern what constitutes authentic renewal in moral theology? One way to approach this question is to ask what prompted the Second Vatican Council fathers to issue this summons. What were the characteristics of Catholic moral theology prior to Vatican II that required change or renewal?

Historical analysis has shown that the Catholic moral thought of the manuals (the textbooks that dominated Catholic moral theology between the Council of Trent and the Second Vatican Council) was characterized by a focus on law and sin.[2] The moral life was conceived of as a series of largely unrelated acts that were judged to be good or bad on the basis of law. This judgment could take place interiorly in one's con-

---

1. Second Vatican Council, Decree on Priestly Formation, *Optatum totius*, no. 16. The citation is from *The Documents of Vatican II*, ed. Walter M. Abbott, S.J. (Piscataway, N.J.: New Century Publishers, 1966), 452. Subsequent references to Council documents will be to this edition.

2. See John Mahoney, S.J., *The Making of Moral Theology: A Study of the Roman Catholic Tradition* (Oxford, U.K.: Clarendon Press, 1987), 224–58; and Servais Pinckaers, O.P., *The Sources of Christian Ethics*, trans. Mary Thomas Noble, O.P. (Washington, D.C.: The Catholic University of America Press, 1995), 254–79, 327–53. Pinckaers, in particular, traces these tendencies to the corruption of Thomistic categories by nominalism (see pp. 240–53). For a helpful overview of the casuist systems to which this outlook gave birth, see Romanus Cessario, O.P., *An Introduction to Moral Theology*, Catholic Moral Thought Series 1 (Washington, D.C.: The Catholic University of America Press, 2001), 229–42.

science or exteriorly in the domain of human acts, but in both arenas the question of morality concerned what bearing relevant moral laws (whether natural, divine positive, or ecclesiastical) had on the matter at hand. Hence Catholic moral thinking between the Council of Trent and Vatican II was heavily legalistic and act-centered. Little attention was given to the *person* and to his or her own moral growth and development. Scripture was often employed to provide isolated authoritative laws abstracted from their place in the history of salvation (e.g., the Ten Commandments) or "proof texts" to embellish conclusions reached by other means. The moral life thus considered was not well integrated with the mystery of salvation.

Given this historical backdrop, Vatican II's summons becomes more clear. There are at least three marks of authentic renewal that can be gleaned from Vatican II's teaching. First, genuine renewal within moral theology requires its immersion within the teaching of Scripture, the study of which is "the soul of sacred theology."[3] But Scripture is also integral to the experience of Christian moral living. For it is Scripture, along with the sacraments, that affords the primary contact for believers with the person and the mystery of Christ in their lives of faith.[4] This contact with the person of Christ is especially intense in prayerful reading of the text, either in the context of personal or of liturgical worship. Thus the assimilation of Scripture in careful study and prayerful reflection is at the heart of an authentic renewal of moral theology and Christian living.[5]

Second, authentic renewal also necessitates greater focus on the human person (vs. a preoccupation with human acts) who is fully revealed

3. Dogmatic Constitution on Divine Revelation, *Dei verbum*, no. 24. The citation is from *Documents of Vatican II*, 127.

4. Cf. *Dei verbum*, no. 21. It is significant that the first part of Pope John Paul II's landmark encyclical on moral theology *Veritatis splendor* (nos. 6–27) is an extended mediation on Jesus' dialogue with the Rich Young Man in Matthew 19. The treatment of the elements of fundamental moral theology that follow (freedom and law, conscience and truth, fundamental choice, sin, and human acts) are thus placed upon a biblical foundation in the form of Christ's call to discipleship.

5. On the importance of prayerful reading of Scripture by all the faithful as key to genuine renewal of Christian living and moral theology, see Pinckaers, *Sources of Christian Ethics*, 316–23.

by Christ.[6] As *Gaudium et spes*, Vatican II's Pastoral Constitution on the Church, notes:

The truth is that only in the mystery of the incarnate Word does the mystery of Man take on light . . . Christ, the final Adam, by the mystery of the Father and his love, fully reveals man to himself and makes his supreme calling clear.[7]

The "livelier contact with the mystery of Christ" called for in post-conciliar moral theology necessarily brings the human person created for and redeemed by him into sharper focus. As the Incarnate Son of God, Jesus Christ is the concrete "answer" to perennial human questions about goodness and morality.[8]

Third, this focus on the human person redeemed by Christ and called to communion with the Trinity requires an account of how a person can grow in moral goodness or holiness.[9] It is not enough to offer juridical criteria for analyzing isolated acts that are unconnected from one another and the person who authors them. Rather, one must consider the role human acts play in the *moral becoming* of the person. While human finitude means that there are real limits to the freedom men and women possess, they still possess the ability to define themselves as moral beings through their freely chosen behaviors and attitudes. That

6. On the need for a Christological and biblical basis for the renewal of moral theology called for by the Council, see Livio Melina, "Moral Theology and the Ecclesial Sense: Points for a Theological 'Re-Dimensioning' of Morality," *Communio* 19 (1992): 67–93.

7. Pastoral Constitution on the Church, *Gaudium et spes*, no. 22. The citation is from *Documents of Vatican II*, 220. For a more complete consideration of theological anthropology as the starting point for moral theology, see Cessario, *Introduction to Moral Theology*, 4–8, 22–38.

8. Cf. *Veritatis splendor*, nos. 6–8. For a more complete account of the Christological basis of the moral life and the virtues, see Livio Melina, *Sharing in Christ's Virtues: For a Renewal of Moral Theology in Light of "Veritatis Splendor*," trans. William E. May (Washington, D.C.: The Catholic University of America Press, 2001).

9. "In Jesus Christ and in his Spirit, the Christian is a 'new creation,' a child of God; by his actions he shows his likeness or unlikeness to the image of the Son who is the first born among many bretheren (cf. Rom 8:29), he lives out his fidelity or infidelity to the gift of the Spirit, and he opens or closes himself to eternal life, to the communion of vision, love and happiness with God the Father, Son and Holy Spirit" (*Vertiatis splendor*, no. 73). The citation is from the Vatican translation (Boston: St. Paul's Books and Media, 1993), 92.

is, human beings create for themselves a specific moral character through their free choices and actions.

There have been a number of attempts to recover this focus on the moral dynamism of the human person in postconciliar theology. Fundamental option theory has attempted to balance the previous focus on specific acts with an account of the deep transcendental freedom of the person vis-à-vis God and the moral goodness expressed through the whole of his or her life.[10] However, the relationship between this transcendental freedom and concrete human actions is sometimes less than clear, and, in some articulations of the theory, seems to undercut the possibility of mortal sin.[11]

A better account of the dynamic interplay between moral character and specific moral choices is provided by the recent revival of virtue language and theory. The last two decades have witnessed an explosion of studies in philosophy, ethics, and theology on this topic by a host of scholars, as well as a resurgence of popular interest.[12] Insofar as virtue can uphold the importance of specific moral actions as both illustrating and shaping moral character without reducing the whole of morality to isolated acts, it can make an important and positive contribution to the renewal of moral theology for which Vatican II called. Further, historical study has shown that such an approach better reflects the understanding of morality found in early Christianity and among the great Scholastic doctors of the High Middle Ages.[13] Because premodern

10. Scholars who have contributed to the development and articulation of this theory include Karl Rahner, S.J., Bernard Häring, Josef Fuchs, S.J., and Timothy O'Connell. For a summary and overview of the theory, see Richard Gula, S.S., *Reason Informed by Faith: Foundations of Christian Morality* (New York: Paulist Press, 1989), 75–83.

11. On the problems of some versions of the theory, see William E. May, *An Introduction to Moral Theology* (Huntington, Ind.: Our Sunday Visitor Press, 1990). Cf. *Veritatis splendor*, nos. 67–68.

12. In the area of moral philosophy, this would include the works of Alasdair MacIntyre and Yves Simon. In the theological arena, this would include the works of Christian ethicists such as Stanley Hauerwas and Gilbert Meilaender, as well as Catholic moral theologians such as Servais Pinckaers, O.P., Benedict Ashley, O.P., Romanus Cessario, O.P., Jean Porter, and Paul Wadell. As a barometer of popular interest, one might point to the success of William J. Bennett's *Book of Virtues: A Treasury of Great Moral Stories* (New York: Simon & Schuster, 1993).

13. See esp. Pinckaers, *Sources of Christian Ethics*, 195–239. It should be noted that Pinckaers also finds a basis for the prominence of virtue-based teaching in early Christianity

moral theology was not divorced from soteriology and spirituality, its moral vision was more closely connected with "the mystery of Christ" and the life of faith. Likewise, a recovery of virtue theory can offer a wider and more theologically fruitful vision of the moral life.

In spite of the plethora of studies on virtue language in its historical context and prospects for its contemporary application, there is further work to be done in this area. Namely, there is need for the application of virtue theory to specific branches of moral theology. This application is one goal of the series of which this present volume is a part.

The specific task of this book is to undertake a systematic application of biblical and virtue-based categories to the topic of sexuality in the hope of contributing to the ongoing renewal of moral theology sparked by the Second Vatican Council. While such a project has been partially begun by others such as Lisa Sowle Cahill, this study will attempt to recover basic biblical themes (i.e., covenant, beatitude, and discipleship) other than those on which she has focused (i.e., community and identification with the marginalized) and to give more weight to virtue itself rather than to human goods and empirical experience in an account of human flourishing.[14] This study will therefore contend that the biblical theology of covenant fidelity wedded to an account of chastity as an integral part of human flourishing can provide a suitable framework for a Christian approach to issues of sexuality in a contemporary context.

In order to establish this thesis, it will be necessary to examine a number of issues: the current historical setting regarding attitudes and practices concerning sexuality; key biblical, historical, and contempo-

---

within the New Testament in the teaching of Paul and the patristic interpretation of the Sermon on the Mount (see pp. 104–67).

14. In her early work Cahill emphasized the theme of community in biblical sexual ethics. See *Between the Sexes: Foundations for a Christian Ethics of Sexuality* (Philadelphia: Fortress Press, 1985). Her more recent work has supplemented this with an emphasis on identification with the marginalized. See *Sex, Gender, and Christian Ethics*, New Studies in Christian Ethics 5 (Cambridge, U.K.: Cambridge University Press, 1996). It is in this latter work that she identifies her work more closely with an Aristotlelian-Thomistic account of human flourishing. An overall difficulty with these works is that Cahill's revisionist commitments place her at odds with the Church's tradition and teaching on issues such as the morality of contraception, homogenital sex, and reproductive technologies.

rary resources for articulating a virtue-based approach to sexual ethics; current issues with which such an approach must wrestle; and some description of how to foster growth in moral virtue, particularly chastity.

Because the acquisition of virtue takes place within specific historical and cultural contexts, Chapter 1 will examine the current understanding of sexuality in Western culture, using the United States as a case in point. It will explore the tension experienced by large numbers of contemporary first-world Catholics in trying to relate the phenomenon of sexuality to their faith. These Catholics live in a culture that prizes individual autonomy and valorizes sexual expression as integral to personal fulfillment, yet they are confronted by authoritative Church teachings often perceived as hostile to such values and divorced from their own experience. Further, in the wake of the controversy over *Humanae vitae* and subsequent scandals, many preachers and religious educators in the Church have stopped addressing the subject of sexuality altogether. But in historical perspective, Paul VI's encyclical was but the spark that ignited the powder keg created by centuries of envisioning morality as a struggle between freedom and law.

Building on the work of recent biblical scholarship on covenant, Chapter 2 will locate the foundation for a biblical understanding of sexual union in its being a gesture that recalls and enacts a couple's covenantal pledge to one another. This understanding, which emerges from the second creation account of Genesis, is enlarged by its juxtaposition with Israel's covenant with Yahweh in later pentateuchal traditions and prophetic theology. It is transposed to a new theological context by the New Testament, which uses the mutual submission of husband and wife and their "one flesh" union as a "mystery" signifying the relationship of Christ and the Church (see Eph 5:21–33). This understanding of sex as a covenantal reality will be briefly traced through the church's liturgical and sacramental tradition.

Chapter 3 will consider other key biblical themes that can be used to frame an understanding of sexuality. Chief among these are Jesus' preaching of the Kingdom of God, the invitation to discipleship, the teaching of the Sermon on the Mount (particularly the Beatitudes), and New Testament descriptions of Christian character. Some implications of overlaying these varied themes on the covenantal motif of the previous chapter will be developed in the form of a contemporary sketch of a spirituality of sexuality within marriage.

The recovery of an ethic of virtue, particularly chastity, from various historical settings and in light of some contemporary impulses, will be the aim of Chapter 4. Early Christianity, while offering no systematic account of morality, nevertheless does offer a focus on beatitude that transcends individual discussions of chastity carried on in the midst of the evolving disciplines of sexual renunciation, marriage, and penance. Aquinas's work in the High Middle Ages provides a systematic approach that integrates a discussion of human nature into a larger theological account of virtue. Modern psychology and philosophical personalism can provide further nuances in understanding the acquisition and expression of this virtue in a contemporary context.

Chapter 5 examines the human person as a sexual being—as *male* or *female.* The changing social and political status of women and the rise of feminist theory has raised fundamental questions as to how to properly account for both the equality and the differences of women and men. This study will locate the equality of the sexes in their possession of a shared human nature, while arguing that sexual difference may be understood as a fundamental relation constitutive of personhood. Chapter 5 will also consider some fundamental threats to the dignity of women and men as sexual beings, such as pornography, casual and commercial sex, sexual harassment, sexual abuse, and sexual violence.

There are other pressing contemporary issues beyond the effort to articulate the equal dignity of the sexes and to oppose those things that undermine it. There is also the widespread view that regards sex in terms of pleasure and individual fulfillment unconnected to any form of covenantal commitment. Further, there is the contemporary suspicion of fertility, which sees it as a biological constraint or a danger to a planet with a growing population and limited resources. Such views are antithetical to the thrust of the Church's tradition. Chapter 6 notes the primacy of the procreative purpose of sex within this tradition and how this can be integrated with the self-donation made possible through chastity. It will also focus on particular ethical questions regarding marital sexuality and practices that can foster conjugal chastity.

Chapter 7, the final chapter, considers issues of education in human sexuality. How does one avoid simply lapsing into the legalism of the past centuries of moral thought, while at the same time avoiding the relativism in which contemporary culture is awash? A focus on virtue and character can indeed provide a mean between these equally unhealthy extremes. While rules have a place in education in sexuality, these are but an initial stage in the interiorization of values necessary to human sexual flourishing. Equally or perhaps more important is the presentation of a compelling vision of human sexuality in the light of Christian faith that can provide a viable alternative to dominant cultural ideologies that trivialize sex and concrete practices that can enable growth in moral freedom. Such a vision in turn must be internalized both individually and communally through specific practices that shape moral action.

Sex and Virtue

CHAPTER I

Clashing Symbols
Sex, Conscience, and Authority

Before examining biblical and historical sources that can be used to shape a contemporary sexual ethic, some attention must be given to the actual cultural situation to which such an ethic is addressed. This is necessary for a number of reasons.

First, it is important to attend to the context in which biblical teaching can be received and heard. While it is reductionist to totally identify the teaching of Scripture with one's own cultural horizon and experience, modern hermeneutical theory has made it clear that one's cultural horizon and experience does impact the reading of the biblical text. Therefore some awareness of this horizon, along with appropriate use of critical methods, can serve to guard against various forms of *eisegesis*, reading one's own ideas and presuppositions into the text.[1] In this way some awareness of the cultural matrix in which it is received can aid in the hearing and reception of God's word in Scripture.

Second, unlike other more abstract forms of moral theory, a virtue-based approach is ordered to actual praxis in specific historical situations. This means that one must attend to the actual cultural setting, symbols, and social attitudes that might impact the development of specific kinds of excellence that are integral to human flourishing. In this case, it means paying attention to the intellectual and cultural forces that have shaped contemporary attitudes toward sexuality.

Third, a certain historical perspective can shed some light not simply on the complex confluence of current cultural ideas that shape a perception of sexuality, but also on the equally complicated and often contentious debates about ethics to which they have given rise. Arguments

1. This topic will be considered more fully at the beginning of Chapter 2.

about sexual morality may not be new, but the last thirty years have witnessed debates of unprecedented scope and intensity. These have taken place not simply within the Catholic Church, but in many Christian churches and in other religious traditions as well.

This chapter will examine current cultural attitudes about sexuality and their impact particularly on Catholic Christians. The focus of this examination will be on the experience of Catholics in Western industrialized nations, using the United States as a case in point.[2] It will be argued that many such Catholics experience a kind of "disconnect" between their faith and the experience of sexuality, shaped as it is by cultural symbols and attitudes. The roots of this alienation can be traced to a number of sources: the powerful and diverse influences that have shaped Western and U.S attitudes toward sexuality; the controversy surrounding Pope Paul VI's encyclical *Humanae vitae;* and the entrenched legalism of the Catholic moral tradition in the modern period which this controversy exposed.

I. The Experience of Alienation

Numerous studies, polls, and surveys highlight the fact that there is a disturbing gap between official Catholic teaching regarding sexuality and the actual beliefs and practice of large numbers of the baptized.[3] This is not simply true of the contentious issue of birth regulation, but also of other issues such as extramarital sex, homogenital activity, the use of reproductive technologies such as artificial insemination or in vitro fertilization, and even abortion.[4] These findings are true not only

2. It is undoubtedly true that the validity of these assertions would have to be qualified somewhat in terms of their application for other (even Western) societies. However, the dominance of the United States's economy and the widespread influence of its political institutions at the close of the twentieth century have undoubtedly contributed to the export of American culture and attitudes to other parts of the globe.

3. On this divergence, see George Gallup Jr. and Jim Castelli, *The American Catholic People* (Garden City, N.Y.: Doubleday, 1987); William D'Antonio, James Davidson, Dean Hoge, and Ruth Wallace, *American Catholic Laity* (Kansas City, Mo.: Sheed & Ward, 1989); and Andrew M. Greeley, *Religious Change in America* (Cambridge, Mass.: Harvard University Press, 1989), and "Sex and the Single Catholic: The Decline of an Ethic," *America* 167 (Nov. 7, 1992): 342–47.

4. On the issue of premarital sex, see Greeley, "Sex and the Single Catholic"; and

in the United States: they have correlates in European countries increasingly impacted by secularism.[5] This divergence has led some observers to speak of a kind of "moral schism" in which increasing numbers of disenchanted laity and even pastors, while not publically rejecting Church teaching, consign it to irrelevance by ignoring it.[6]

There are a number of observations that should be made about this data. First, it should be noted that some of these surveys are not careful in distinguishing practicing from nonpracticing Catholics. Hence the voices of those who have not prayed or been near a church in years are given equal weight with those who seek to live their faith on a daily basis. Second, it is undoubtedly true that such results can be distorted by bias in the way in which the questions are asked or the way in which the data is compiled. Third, often buried in the analysis of such results are genuinely positive signs that are not given equal attention.[7]

Nevertheless, such cautions aside, the basic point remains: there is a

Larry R. Pedersen and Gregory V. Donnenwerth, "Secularization and the Influence of Religion on Beliefs about Premarital Sex," *Social Forces* 75 (1997): 1071–88. In regard to homosexuality, see, e.g., Andrew K. T. Yip, "Dare to Differ: Gay and Lesbian Catholics' Assessment of Official Catholic Positions on Sexuality," *Sociology of Religion* 58 (1997): 165–80. On the divergence between Catholic teaching and social attitudes toward reproductive technologies, see John G. Deedy, "Five Medical Dilemmas that Might Scare You to Death," *U.S. Catholic* 53 (April 1988): 6–14. On the issue of abortion, see Michael R. Welch, David C. Leege, and James C. Cavendish, "Attitudes toward Abortion among U.S. Catholics: Another Case of Symbolic Politics?," *Social Science Quarterly* 76, no. 1 (1995): 142–57.

5. On changing moral values within European countries, see Loek Halman, "Is There a Moral Decline? A Cross National Inquiry into Morality in Contemporary Society," *International Social Science Journal* 47 (1995): 419–39. Halman, basing his work on the European Values Studies of 1981 and 1990, argues that there is no evidence of a widespread adoption of an "anything goes" morality in most European nations. However, his research does find large-scale increase in moral lenience and sexual permissiveness due to the decline of religion in the West and a move to a "personal" as opposed to an "institutional" morality. On the phenomenon of secularization in Europe, see Mattei Dogan, "The Decline of Religious Beliefs in Western Europe," *International Journal of Social Science* 47 (1995): 405–18.

6. See Frans Böckle, *"Humanae vitae* als Pruefstein des wahren Glaubens? Zur kirchenpolitischen Dimensionen moraltheologischer Fragen," *Stimmen der Zeit* 115 (1990): 3–16.

7. Thus some of the same surveys have found that in spite of allegedly "oppressive" official teaching, married Catholics have very positive views of sexuality. See Andrew M. Greeley, "Sex and the Married Catholic: The Shadow of St. Augustine," *America* 167

large and perhaps growing disjunct between magisterial teaching and the belief and practice of many Catholics in the area of sexuality. Even many committed members of the faithful find themselves wrestling with little success in trying to reconcile their own experience and convictions regarding sexuality with what they know of official Church teaching. The result is a kind of alienation in that these Christians cannot relate the very fundamental experience of their sexuality with statements concerning it by the Church with which they may otherwise profoundly identify.

Before considering how to address such a troubling phenomenon, it is important to understand it more fully. In particular, consideration must be given to the historical forces that have given rise to current attitudes. What are the roots of this alienation among contemporary Catholics?

II. Sex: The American Ethos

In a recent book Peter Gardella traces some of the key social and intellectual forces that have shaped the American understanding of sexuality through the early 1980s.[8] The modern American ethos of sexuality, according to Gardella, has been shaped by influences as diverse as Roman Catholic moral theology, evangelical Protestantism, medical science, Romanticism, the Virgin Mary, the ideology of the birth control movement, and modern psychology.

While it is undoubtedly true that the "puritanism" of the early Puritans has been exaggerated, it is equally true that early American preachers and theologians said little about sex, even that between husband and wife.[9] This reticence created something of a vacuum regarding reliable

---

(Oct. 31, 1992): 318–23. Cf. Greeley's *Faithful Attraction: Discovering Intimacy, Love and Fidelity in American Marriage* (New York: Tor Books, 1991). Unfortunately, Greeley creates a somewhat superficial contrast between "popular tradition" and practice and a more oppressive "high tradition."

8. Peter Gardella, *Innocent Ecstasy: How Christianity Gave America an Ethic of Sexual Pleasure* (New York: Oxford University Press, 1985). I will be following Gardella's treatment in much of this section.

9. Gardella traces this reticence to convictions concerning the basically natural and secular (as opposed to biblical) character of marriage and sex as well as to Puritan fears about the corruption of sex by sin. See *Innocent Ecstasy*, 39–40.

public information about sex—a vacuum filled by the persons and writings of a primarily Protestant medical profession. This silence also explains some of the shock of a primarily Protestant United States to the influx of Catholic immigrants and ideas in the mid-nineteenth century. For the moral manuals used in Catholic seminaries to train priests contained very detailed treatments of the place of sex and love within marriage.[10] In time, this linking of sex and love within marriage would help to form a more personal concept of marriage different from its European predecessors. More immediately, however, it fed into the powerful anti-Catholic reaction that characterized the nineteenth-century United States and the lasting cultural association of Catholics and sexual immorality.[11]

If early medical treatments and Catholic moral theology presented sex in fairly straightforward and positive terms, this warm assessment cooled considerably in the Victorian period. Theological, scientific, and social views coalesced to produce a "medical Christianity" that closely identified sex with original sin. The essence of this sin was seen as disordered passion, which produced the physical lust that in turn was at the root of a whole host of personal and social evils. This perception caused both doctors and theologians to prescribe a kind of medical salvation in which passion could be restrained (and hence the ills of society cured) through a resolutely bland diet, strictly moderated sexual practice, proper sleep and exercise, and, in some cases, surgery.[12] Such medically inspired fears created a kind of consensus of sexual repres-

10. Gardella gives the example of the 1843 *Theologiae Moralis* of Francis Patrick Kenrick (then bishop of Philadelphia) which prescribed orgasm for women, even arguing, among other things, that women had the right to stimulate themselves to orgasm should their husbands fail to do so during intercourse. See Gardella, *Innocent Ecstasy*, 9–10, 14–24.

11. Gardella observes that many of the accusations that sparked riots against Catholics were sexually charged. Likewise, many anti-Catholic tracts and polemics through the present day have offered sensational accounts of Catholic immorality, so shaping American consciousness that the theme can also be found in mainstream American literature. See Gardella, *Innocent Ecstasy*, 25–38.

12. Gardella notes that among the theologians who lent their weight to this effort one can find liberals such as Horace Bushnell, evangelicals such as Charles Finney, and founders of wholly new groups such as Mary Baker Eddy and the Christian Science movement. Among scientists he notes the presence of John Harvey Kellogg and Sylvester Graham who offered their respective inventions—corn flakes and graham crackers—in the service of the eradication of vice through diet. See Gardella, *Innocent Ecstasy*, 44–54.

sion between Protestants and Catholics and a perfectionist optimism that society could indeed be transformed. It also conferred a new authority over the whole of human life on the medical profession, thereby contributing to the continuing medicalization of sexuality.

At the beginning of the twentieth century the attitudes of some doctors began to change, resulting in a new emphasis on the acceptance of sex and its concomitant pleasure as integral to physical and spiritual health. Such doctors counseled a more frank and open discussion of sex to banish its associations with sin and urged couples toward a "total yielding" to their sexual impulses in marriage. This notion resonated deeply in a culture influenced by the revivalist ideal of "total yielding" to Christ forged in the Great Awakenings and carried forward by various evangelical groups.[13] In this climate women came to be regarded as uniquely capable of the ecstasy that accompanied this self-abandonment. This development too was aided by religious perceptions such as accounts of sanctification by Methodist women, descriptions of receiving the Holy Spirit by female Pentecostal leaders, and Catholic appreciation for female visionaries such as Bernadette.[14] Such an impression was reinforced by the Romantic appreciation of Mary (by Protestants as well as Catholics) as the ideal woman, depicted as youthful, innocent, beautiful, and ecstatic.

But as the twentieth century progressed, two other forces emerged to purge this vision of salvific sexuality, "total yielding," and female ecstasy of their religious trappings. These forces were the ideology of the birth control movement and the rise of modern psychology.

Margaret Sanger, the U.S. apostle of contraception, effectively drew on all of these elements in her campaign to change legal prescriptions and social attitudes.[15] Sanger depicted sex as quasi-sacramental, that is,

13. Indeed, some of these very doctors who prescribed such views of sex were themselves fervent believers who had undergone conversion experiences. See Gardella, *Innocent Ecstasy*, 68–74. On the impact of the Great Awakenings on American culture and consciousness, see Sydney Ahlstrom, *A Religious History of the American People* (New Haven, Conn.: Yale University Press, 1972), 280–94, 415–54.

14. Gardella mentions Phoebe Palmer, an influential Methodist teacher, and Aimée Semple McPherson, a Pentecostal radio evangelist, as examples. See *Innocent Ecstasy*, 80–94.

15. Gardella's treatment of Sanger produces mixed results. On the one hand, he does a

as a kind of communion in mutual ecstasy. However, she carefully gendered her account of sexual roles, highlighting the activity of the male (who becomes almost godlike in sexual foreplay) and the active passivity of the woman who abandons herself to passion. But ideally, for Sanger, the couple would achieve the ecstasy of mutual orgasm together. Such sexual skill, she argued, would require practice and hence contraception—so that women could develop their "love nature" apart from their "maternal nature." This in turn would redeem motherhood and indeed all humanity, eliminating abortion, infanticide, child neglect, and abandonment. The utopia created by only "wanted" pregnancies would transform the world. Thus Sanger offered the nation her own form of secular perfectionism.

Another secularizing influence on twentieth-century American views of sexuality was provided by modern psychology, particularly the thought of Sigmund Freud. As influential as it was in Europe, Freud's thought had an even greater impact on U.S. culture. While some of his darker ideas concerning the death instinct and religion as an illusion were not widely received on American shores, his pansexualism proved enormously popular. In the hands of his popularizers, this view was wedded to the emerging views of sex as the highest of human experiences, orgasm as a form of spiritual ecstasy, and redemption as an aspect of sexual experience—apart from any connection to Christianity.[16]

The resulting cultural view of sex Gardella terms "innocent ecstasy," sex understood as bearing the promise of ecstatic release, personal fulfillment, and salvific power, yet completely freed from a religious frame-

---

good job of highlighting her political shrewdness in matters such as changing the terminology from "contraception" to the more innocuous "birth control," her harnessing of anti-Catholic sentiment in courting Protestant churches, and her use of Romantic and evangelical motifs in her descriptions of women. On the other hand, he downplays her socialist background, minimizes her affair with Havelock Ellis (himself a sexual psychologist and participant in radical politics), and simply ignores her racism and her open admiration for Nazi eugenics programs. See Gardella, Innocent Ecstasy, 130–40. For more critical examinations of Sanger, see George Grant, Grand Illusions: The Legacy of Planned Parenthood (Brentwood, Tenn.: Wolgemuth & Hyatt, 1988), 41–61; and Robert Marshall and Charles Donovan, Blessed Are the Barren: The Social Policy of Planned Parenthood (San Francisco: Ignatius Press, 1991), 5–33.

16. Gardella focuses on the work of American psychologist G. Stanley Hall. See Innocent Ecstasy, 140–49.

work or any association with original sin.[17] This ethos is not without certain advantages—Gardella points to increased sexual skills and sensitivity, and perhaps greater sexual pleasure. However, these advantages are bought at a high price. Gardella opines that the new focus on the "quality" of sex has led to increased divorce due to unrealistic expectations and has created added pressure to engage in sex before marriage in order to gauge one's own level of "performance." It has also created new burdens resented by both sexes: women must simultaneously embody innocence and certify sexual success, while men must satisfy women through their performance. Finally, Gardella notes that the "pursuit of orgasm as the equivalent of religious ecstasy quickly became an ascetic practice best performed by those who have disciplined their bodies to be clean, thin, and odorless."[18] Sex thus perceived becomes a utopian illusion that cannot deliver what it promises.

While Gardella's sketch covers a good deal of ground and brings into focus many of the diverse forces that have shaped current U.S. attitudes toward sex, there are a few factors that should be added to this portrait. First, one should not underestimate the importance of contraceptives, particularly the birth control pill, in launching the massive shift of cultural attitudes and practices known as the "sexual revolution."[19] Both modern contraceptives and the new sexual behaviors that they enabled can be correlated with some of the phenomena Gardella mentions, such as the growing incidence of extramarital sex and divorce.[20]

Second, another factor that made possible the sexual revolution of the 1960s and 1970s was the burgeoning consumer culture created by postwar prosperity.[21] It is not surprising that this same culture managed to repackage sex itself into a product in the enormous success of glossy magazines such as *Playboy* and its more explicit imitators, which transformed pornography from an underground traffic to a very public, multibillion-dollar industry. The crude debasement of sex into a com-

17. See ibid., 3–4.

18. Ibid., 7.

19. Cf. Carolyn J. Dean, *Sexuality and Modern Culture* (New York: Twayne, 1996), 66.

20. See Robert T. Michael, "Why Did the U.S. Divorce Rate Double within a Decade?," *Research in Population* 11 (1988): 361–99.

21. See Dean, *Sexuality*, 66.

modity for pleasure and profit became the dark underside of the modern pursuit of fulfillment in sexual release. Darker still is the widespread recourse to abortion in the name of sexual freedom which is itself enabled by a lucrative industry.[22]

Third, integral to the growth of consumerism has been the expansion of technology in an industrial and now increasingly informational society. One of the effects of this growing technology is the disconnection of people from one another. Traditionally, it was human contact in the home, workplace, and public life that fostered friendships and social relations. Technology has served to undercut much of this contact—whether solitary factory workers who put in long shifts tending massive machines, office workers huddled in cubicles whose only human contact in a workday is an e-mail, or the family whose meals are spent in silence huddled around a television. The result is a new search for intimacy to fill the void created by technology—a search that often gravitates toward sex.[23] This too has behavioral results as it drives some to seek intimacy in casual sex outside of marriage. It also heightens the strain on marriages as a couple's sexual relationship is expected to meet a host of interpersonal needs for which it is not equipped.[24]

Fourth, Gardella's portrait is somewhat dated in light of many of the fears created by new public awareness of sexually transmitted diseases, particularly the HIV/AIDS epidemic. There are indications that these concerns have somewhat dampened the fires lit by the sexual revolution, modifying indiscriminate sexual behavior by both homosexual and heterosexual persons.[25] While many may still hold to some variant

22. See Grant, *Grand Illusions*.

23. Marva J. Dawn makes this point, building on the work of Jacques Ellul. See her *Sexual Character: Beyond Technique to Intimacy* (Grand Rapids, Mich.: William B. Eerdmans, 1993); cf. her "The Concept of 'The Principalities and Powers' in the Work of Jacques Ellul" (Ph.D. diss., University of Notre Dame, 1992).

24. Those involved in marriage counseling or preparation rightly insist on distinguishing sex from the broader forms of intimacy that sustain and give it meaning. See, e.g., Scott Stanley, Daniel Trathen, Savanna McCain, and Milt Bryan, *A Lasting Promise: A Christian Guide to Fighting for Your Marriage* (San Francisco: Jossey-Bass, 1998), 248–55, 261–71.

25. See Edward O. Laumann, John H. Gagnon, Robert T. Michael, and Stuart Michaels, *The Social Organization of Sexuality: Sexual Practices in the United States* (Chicago: University of Chicago Press, 1994), 432–37; Michael Rust, "Sex and Salvation," *Washington Times*, December 15, 1997, 8–11; and Linda Ellerbee, "The Sexual Revolution: Well It

of a secularized concept of sex as integral to personal fulfillment, new fears of disease have reawakened an awareness of its dangers which its association with original sin supplied in previous generations.

Finally, while Gardella hints at the importance of the issue of contraception, particularly for Catholics, more should be said about the importance of this issue for shaping present attitudes and framing current debates in moral theology. It is to this issue that this study now turns.

III. *Humanae vitae:* Flashpoint of Controversy

The uneasy consensus between Catholics and Protestants forged by Victorian repression was split apart by the birth control movement. For not only did its proponents, such as Margaret Sanger, effectively play on religious antagonisms between these traditions, but also, for a variety of reasons, Protestant churches proved to be far more receptive to the message of the movement. In 1930 the Anglican bishops gathered at the Lambeth Conference reversed the condemnations of two previous conferences (1908 and 1920) and gave approval to the use of contraceptives.[26] Even though the Catholic Church strongly reiterated the condemnation of contraception in Pius XI's encyclical *Casti connubii,* other Protestant churches were swift to follow the Anglican lead. Catholics thus found themselves estranged from other Christians on a key issue of sexual behavior and ethics.

In addition to such religious factors, there were numerous other social and intellectual currents that coalesced to force further scrutiny of the issue of birth regulation within Catholicism. Some of these came from within the tradition itself, such as the increasing attention given within theology to the place of love within marriage and sexuality. This empha-

---

Seemed like a Good Idea at the Time . . . ," *New Choices: Living Even Better after 50* 38, no. 3 (1998): 8.

26. In so doing, William H. Shannon observes, they "gave their approval to the birth control movement." See *The Lively Debate: Response to "Humanae Vitae"* (New York: Sheed & Ward, 1970), 8. John T. Noonan sees the bishops as simply adjusting to the fact of widespread use of contraceptives by the people of Western Europe since the end of the nineteenth century. See Noonan, *Contraception: A History of Its Treatment by the Catholic Theologians and Canonists,* rev. ed. (Cambridge, Mass.: Harvard University Press, 1986), 409.

sis especially flowered in the treatments of personalist authors such as Dietrich von Hildebrand and Herbert Doms.[27] Other currents caused by changing social factors were effectively harnessed by the proponents of birth control: the new roles of women in postwar society, rising educational costs, and growing concerns about world population.[28]

Science also added to the growing pressure to reevaluate the Church's teaching concerning contraception. Modern psychology was not merely a secularizing force in shaping attitudes about sex, it also served to challenge the focus of previous moral teaching on individual sexual acts. For the findings of the discipline suggested that sex was something that pervaded and shaped the whole of one's personality; therefore individual acts could be seen as less important to one's moral growth or to the moral quality of one's marriage.[29] Biology also had an impact as key discoveries such as the existence of the female ovum (1827) and the union of ovum and sperm (1875) were made with the aid of microscopic technology.[30] These discoveries did more than discredit biological theories such as Aristotle's which denied that women contributed "seed" in procreation. They also made possible the development of far more reliable forms of birth control—both artificial and natural.

Utilizing new biological findings, doctors were able to demonstrate empirically what previous generations had already suspected: the presence of a cyclical pattern of fertility and infertility in women. These findings made possible the development of the so-called rhythm method of family planning. This method proved enormously popular, even if not wholly reliable, among Catholics.[31] In time, it won approval

27. For an analysis of the impact of Von Hildebrand and Doms on this issue, see Shannon, *Lively Debate*, 17–30; and Noonan, *Contraception*, 494–500. For a consideration of important differences between Von Hildebrand and Doms and their influence on subsequent reflection, see John S. Grabowski, "Person or Nature: Rival Personalisms in 20th Century Catholic Sexual Ethics," *Studia Moralia* 35 (1997): 283–312.

28. See Noonan, *Contraception*, 476–80.

29. Ibid., 481.

30. Ibid., 480–81.

31. It should be noted that the unreliability of the rhythm method has been exaggerated, winning for it unfortunate appellations such as "Vatican roulette." In its own day rhythm was a fairly reliable method of birth regulation that was approximately 80 percent user effective (or about the same as contemporary latex condoms) for those properly trained. It is also true that rhythm had definite limitations for women with less

by Catholic theologians and the magisterium.[32] This served to focus the disagreement between Catholics and Protestants insofar as both accepted the principle of family planning, but Catholic teaching drew a sharp distinction between *natural* and *artificial* means in the pursuit of this objective.

The same biological discoveries made possible the development of more effective artificial contraceptives. Of all the innovations in contraceptive technology in the twentieth century, the one with the greatest social and religious impact was undoubtedly the birth control pill. As noted above, the pill was a key ingredient in the widespread shift in sexual attitudes and behaviors known as the sexual revolution. It also proved to be the flashpoint for the birth control controversy within Catholicism.

When the progesterone pill was developed, it was perceived by many to elude traditional arguments against contraception. While *Casti connubii* condemned contraception as "an act against nature," the pill was not so easily stymied. Its proponents argued that it did not interrupt an act of intercourse (as in the case of withdrawal) or interrupt its natural finality (as in the case of barrier methods). Rather, it merely used progesterone—a hormone naturally produced by a woman's body—to suppress ovulation. Hence, some concluded, the pill was fully "natural," allowing human reason to control nature as technology and medicine had increasingly been doing for centuries. These perceptions were articulated with increasing volume by doctors, theologians, and even bishops.[33]

---

than regular menstrual cycles—limitations that have been largely overcome in contemporary forms of natural family planning. On the effectiveness of calendar rhythm, see R. Kambic and V. Lamprecht, "Calendar Method Efficacy: A Review," *Advances in Contraception* 12, no. 2 (1996): 123–28. I am indebted to Dr. Richard Fehring of Marquette University for this information and this reference.

32. On the evolution of the approval given to rhythm, see Shannon, *Lively Debate*, 24–30; and Noonan, *Contraception*, 438–47.

33. This argument was first put forward by John Rock, a Catholic physician and professor emeritus at Harvard University, who helped develop the progesterone pill. See his *The Time Has Come* (New York: Alfred A. Knopf, 1963). It was echoed by Louis Janssens, a moral theologian at the Catholic University of Leuven (Louvain), in his article "Morale conjugale et progestgènes," *Ephemerides Theologicae Lovanienses* 39 (1963): 787–826, esp. 820–24. On reactions to these arguments, see Shannon, *Lively Debate*, 46–50, 52–54; and Noonan, *Contraception*, 469–71.

Compounding the momentum of these arguments were two further developments—one religious, another social. Pope John XXIII, elected as a compromise interim pope, took the unexpected step of calling an ecumenical council. Even though it proposed no new doctrine, the teachings and reforms of the Second Vatican Council unleashed on the Church a host of changes in its language, prayer, and practice. To many Catholics it appeared that the entire Church was changing. Further, these sweeping religious changes were received in the cultural ethos of change and protest that were characteristic of the 1960s.

The convergence of all of these factors can begin to explain why there was such strong expectation in many quarters of the Church that the teaching on contraception would be changed. This climate of expectation was in turn fostered by the news that a majority of the Pontifical Study Commission on Family Population and Birth Problems, appointed by John XXIII and expanded by Paul VI, recommended a revision of the teaching. Even the minority of the commission was forced to conclude that the traditional natural law arguments against contraception were no longer convincing.[34] It was further fueled by Paul VI's apparent hesitation after news of this recommendation was leaked to the public.

All of this sheds some light on the explosion ignited by the appearance of the encyclical Humanae vitae some two years later. Many of the laity, having been told that birth control was a matter to be decided by individual conscience, were dismayed by what they perceived to be an attempt to reimpose an outdated teaching. Theologians complained that the encyclical's conclusions were unsupported by the natural law arguments to which it appealed, leaving papal authority as their only real foundation. Such complaints were not limited to academic venues but were increasingly offered in publicly organized ways, giving rise to the relatively new phenomenon of widespread public "dissent" within the Church.[35] Even some bishops' conferences subtly undermined the docu-

34. On the commission's work and aftermath, see Shannon, Lively Debate, 76–101. It is important to note that commission member Cardinal Karol Wojtyla, who had developed a new philosophical framework for the traditional teaching in Love and Responsibility, was prevented by the communist authorities in Poland from attending the decisive final meetings of the commission.

35. The most notable example was the "Washington statement" spearheaded by

ment, suggesting that considerations of conscience might outweigh the teaching.[36]

Of course, the encyclical also had vocal public defenders among the laity, theologians, and bishops. The conflux of these arguments, pro and con, amplified by the media, created a unique climate of heated public debate and argument within the Church.[37] Within moral theology, the polarization effected by debate over the encyclical quickly spread to other questions of sexual ethics as revisionist and traditionalist theologians argued over the morality of extramarital sex, masturbation, and homogenital activity in the light of questions raised by the controversy.

The force and explosiveness of these arguments before and particularly after the appearance of the encyclical is difficult to explain simply on the basis of recent intellectual and social developments. These were, undoubtedly, proximate causes each of which added to the substance and intensity of the debate. However, these were but the dry tinder that had collected around a far larger and older powder keg: the pervasive focus on law and authority in modern Catholic moral thinking.

IV. The Legal Powder Keg

Historical analysis has highlighted the fact that much of the modern Catholic moral tradition, embodied in the post-Tridentine moral manuals, was infected with a heavily voluntarist strain. That is, it conceived of morality primarily in terms of obedience to laws that were sufficiently known and authoritative to command it. Among the most incisive accounts of this voluntarism and its sources is that provided by Servais Pinckaers, O.P.[38]

Charles Curran of The Catholic University of America which was presented at a press conference at a Washington, D.C., hotel the day after the promulgation of the encyclical. See Shannon, *Lively Debate*, 148–50. For the text of the statement, see "Statement by Catholic Theologians Washington, D.C., July 30, 1968," in *Readings in Moral Theology*, No. 8: *Dialogue about Catholic Sexual Teaching*, ed. Charles Curran and Richard McCormick (New York: Paulist Press, 1993), 135–37.

36. This was most evident in the statements of the Dutch, German, and Belgian bishops. See Shannon, *Lively Debate*, 118–22.

37. On reaction to the document by various groups, see Shannon, *Lively Debate*, 117–91.

38. See Pinckaers, *Sources of Christian Ethics*.

According to Pinckaers, the leitmotif of early Christian moral teaching was its focus on beatitude. The key moral question was not "What is the law and must I obey it?," but rather "What must I do to be happy?"[39] Obviously, this reflects a basic continuity with some forms of ancient moral teaching, particularly that of Aristotle. However, it is recast in the context of Christian discipleship by Jesus' teaching in the Sermon on the Mount. For early Christian thinkers, such as Augustine, this sermon with the Beatitudes at its heart was the magna carta of Christian moral living.[40]

This focus was sustained in medieval thought, particularly in Aquinas's powerful synthesis of Augustinian theology and Aristotelian philosophy. Indeed, Pinckaers compares the three parts of his *Summa Theologiae* (hereafter *ST*) to the three naves of a gothic cathedral, all of which converge on the single choir of beatitude.[41] In Thomas's presentation, moral theology is integrated into theology and salvation history with all things coming from God the Creator and returning to God through Christ. The beginning and end of all reality is thus the blessedness that is God himself.

While the whole of the *Summa* is thus relevant to Christian moral living, its moral teaching is concentrated in its second part. Much can be learned about this teaching simply from its structure.[42] The overarching theme of the whole treatment is sounded by the treatise on beatitude that opens the first half of this part (the *Prima Secundae*).[43] Equally important is that the treatment of human freedom that follows is seen as *ordered* to the inclinations of human nature and *fully expressed* in the virtues and gifts of grace that perfect this nature. The same focus is maintained in the subsequent treatment of moral action. Among the interior principles of human action, Thomas treats not only the soul's

39. Ibid., 6, 17–22, 160, 208, 230.

40. See Pinckaers's analysis of Augustine's commentary on the Sermon and its impact on the subsequent theological tradition in *Sources of Christian Ethics*, 140–59. Cf. Benedict Ashley, O.P., *Living the Truth in Love: A Biblical Introduction to Moral Theology* (New York: Alba House, 1996), 32–33.

41. See, e.g., Pinckaers, *Sources of Christian Ethics*, 220, 229.

42. For an overview of the *secunda pars*, see Pinckaers, *Sources of Christian Ethics*, 221–29.

43. On the centrality of beatitude for human flourishing and virtue, see Cessario, *Introduction to Moral Theology*, 31–35, 183–91.

faculties, but its modification through acquired and infused virtue and its further perfection in the gifts and fruits of the Holy Spirit. While law in its various forms is considered an external principle of human action, it is balanced with a treatise on grace. Furthermore, the whole of the second half of this part (the *Secunda Secundae*) is entirely dedicated to treatments of individual virtues, their corresponding gifts, and the vices that oppose them. In short, Thomas's account of morality is focused on beatitude, virtues, and gifts—not on obligation and sin.[44]

Thomas's approach to the moral life that contextualized human nature and law within a grace-powered approach to virtue was challenged in the following century by the explosion of nominalist thought.[45] Denying the possibility of the knowledge of essences or natures, nominalism held that the only universal moral laws were those known to be commanded by God. In this view, God was arbitrary and omnipotent—a sovereign will unbounded by nature. For Ockham and others of the nominalist school, this meant that freedom was also the defining characteristic of humanity. And this freedom is utterly undirected—it is the power to choose between contraries such as good and evil. Nature is dissolved or reduced to sheer biological facticity. The passions and even virtue are seen as constraints upon freedom. Moral action becomes radically disconnected and singular. Mediating between this undirected human freedom and the freedom of an omnipotent God are God's commands. Obligation, not beatitude, becomes the beginning and end of the moral life.[46]

This voluntarist account of morality proved enormously influential on Catholic thought over the next five centuries, for it was widely disseminated in a new climate and through a new genre. In the face of the challenge posed by the Protestant Reformation, the Catholic Church assumed a kind of battle posture, emphasizing uniformity in teaching

---

44. Cf. Cessario, *Introduction to Moral Theology*, 17–19.

45. For the following overview of nominalist thought and its impact, see Pinckaers, *Sources of Christian Ethics*, 241–53; cf. 330–53.

46. A somewhat more nuanced and sympathetic portrait of Ockham's moral teaching is provided by Marilyn McCord Adams, "The Structure of Ockham's Moral Theory," in *The Context of Casuistry*, ed. James Kennan and Thomas Shannon (Washington, D.C.: Georgetown University Press, 1995), 25–52. However, Pinckaer's assessment of the impact of nominalist thought is largely accurate.

and establishing seminaries to provide a minimum of education for priests. In order to better prepare priests for their role as confessors within these seminaries, for the first time moral topics were studied in isolation from other issues of theology and spirituality.[47] In this newly isolated field of morality, a new genre of moral teaching arose: the manuals of moral theology.[48]

While many of these manuals claimed a Thomistic pedigree, Pinck-aers argues that their reading of Aquinas and the Fathers was colored by nominalist lenses. Hence, while they covered many of the same topics as Thomas—human acts, law, sin, and virtue—numerous manuals made telling changes as well.[49] Most notably, they dropped the treatises on beatitude and the gifts of the Holy Spirit that for Thomas were the beginning and end of the moral life. Likewise the treatise on grace was dismissed from moral teaching as a topic that belonged exclusively to systematic theology. Virtue was no longer conceived as a real change within the being of the person that bestowed a power to act excellently (*habitus*), but a mere psychological propensity (i.e., a habit) that actually constrained freedom.[50] The very possibility of speaking of a *telos* for human action was undercut, leaving human acts isolated and unrelated to one another. The genre was given a further juridical and penal cast by its aim to serve priests in the tribunal of the confessional.[51]

The net result of these sweeping changes, according to Pinckaers, was the creation of a new moral system far different from its predeces-

47. On the Council of Trent's focus on the establishment of seminaries and sacraments, particularly penance, see Mahoney, *Making of Moral Theology*, 22–27. On the separation of moral theology from theology proper in the wake of Trent's reforms, see Timothy E. O'Connell, *Principles for a Catholic Morality*, rev. ed. (San Francisco: Harper, 1990), 18–19.

48. For a detailed historical study of the emergence and contents of the manuals, see John Gallagher, *Time Past, Time Future: An Historical Study of Catholic Moral Theology* (New York: Paulist Press, 1990).

49. On the reconfiguration of Aquinas's thought within the manuals, see Pinckaers, *Sources of Christian Ethics*, 229–33, 260–73.

50. For an excellent overview of the Thomistic understanding of *habitus*, see Romanus Cessario, O.P., *The Moral Virtues and Theological Ethics* (South Bend, Ind.: University of Notre Dame Press, 1991), 34–44.

51. See ibid., 273. On the preoccupation with sin and law engendered by the manuals confessional context, see Mahoney, *Making of Moral Theology*, 27–36.

sors. The focus of this "morality of obligation" was no longer beatitude, but obligation. The moral life was depicted as a constant struggle
between an indeterminate freedom that was not ordered to any specific
goods and law that constrained it. Each moral choice, unrelated to
those that preceded it, was focused on the question "Am I free to do
whatever I want, or am I bound to obey a law?" This dialectic was
played out interiorly in the sphere of conscience and exteriorly in the
arena of human acts.[52]

This fundamental shift in moral reasoning had multiple effects.[53]
First, it gave new prominence to conscience as the interior place where
the clash between freedom and law played itself out.[54] This shift was is
in keeping with the new focus on individual interiority that the Reformation bequeathed to modern Western thought.[55] Second, it provided
the context for the rise of *casuistry*, moral theory centered around the
study of individual cases of conscience. It is little wonder that Catholic
moral thinking in the sixteenth through the eighteenth centuries witnessed the growth of competing moral systems, each of which attempted to mediate between the claims of freedom and the claims of law on

52. See Pinckaers, *Sources of Christian Ethics*, 268–72, 350.

53. It should be noted that these critical observations are not intended as a wholesale
repudiation of the manuals or of casuistry. Many of the manuals, even if limited by
their presuppositions, did have the salutary effect of encouraging a certain pastoral sensitivity and balance in attempting to avoid both overly rigorist and laxist opinions; see
O'Connell, *Principles for a Catholic Morality*, 20. This balance is perhaps most evident in the
work of Alphonsus Liguori; see Pinckaers, *Sources of Christian Ethics*, 276–77. Likewise, it
has been observed that casuistry arose in response to specific and complex historical situations and in this setting offered real contributions in the resolution of difficult cases.
See Mahoney, *Making of Moral Theology*, 135; and the essays by various scholars collected in
Kennan and Shannon's *Context of Casuistry*.

54. While Aquinas did treat conscience, much of the function ascribed to it by the
manualists he located in the workings of the virtue of prudence. See Cessario, *Moral
Virtues*, 79–93.

55. In this regard James Keenan, S.J., and Thomas Shannon observe that "[t]he reformers' claim of *sola fide* prompted them to replace the confessional with the conscience
as the locus for encountering the redemptive love of God"; see "Introduction" to *Context
of Casuistry*, xvii. On the idea of individual interiority as a hallmark of modern Western
consciousness, see Charles Taylor, *Sources of the Self: The Making of Modern Identity* (Cambridge, Mass.: Harvard University Press, 1989), 111–207. Taylor traces the roots of such a
view as far back as Augustine.

the basis of probability provided by expert opinions.[56] Third, in the area of sexuality, by reducing the inclinations of human nature to biological function, the manuals produced a heavily physicalist account of natural law.[57] It was precisely this reduction that made it impossible to formulate an effective argument against the pill in the debate prior to *Humanae vitae*.[58] Fourth, this approach to morality created generations of Catholics for whom the dominant moral category was law imposed as a restraint upon individual freedom. The resulting moral horizon was act-centered, individualistic, and often adversarial.

All of these developments shed some light on the explosion of bitter disagreement that followed *Humanae vitae*. Underlying the fuel provided by the convergence of social and intellectual factors in the twentieth century was the incendiary force provided by centuries of conceiving morality as a struggle between an undirected and privatized freedom and law imposed by external authority. In this case, it was the freedom of individual conscience to avail itself of new sexual opportunities afforded by twentieth-century attitudes and technology that were set against the pope's repetition of a seemingly discredited norm merely on the basis of his own authority. The encyclical provided the spark that would ignite both the tinder of new developments and the voluntarist powder keg that lay beneath it.

V. A Twofold Alienation

One unfortunate result of the massive explosion of public disagreement that followed *Humanae vitae* was the effect it had on many pastors and laypeople who found the controversy too much and simply "tuned out" of the discussion altogether. In many cases priests and religious educators ceased preaching or teaching about sexuality because it was seen as too controversial, too likely to offend their hearers, or because

56. On these moral systems and the casuistry they produced, see Pinckaers, *Sources of Christian Ethics*, 273–77; Mahoney, *Making of Moral Theology*, 135–43; and Cessario, *Introduction to Moral Theology*, 229–42.

57. See Pinckaers, *Sources of Christian Ethics*, 245, 437–38; and Brian V. Johnstone, C.Ss.R., "From Physicalism to Personalism," *Studia Moralia* 30 (1992): 71–96.

58. See Grabowski, "Person or Nature," 292–93.

they were unsure which side of the debate should be followed.[59] Some laypeople concluded that a Church so torn by disagreement could have little to say to them about sex and hence turned elsewhere for perspective.

From a pastoral perspective, the timing of these developments could not have been worse. Just as the sexual revolution was unleashed around them, Catholics found themselves in a Church that seemed paralyzed by argument and, at least on the local level, seemed to lapse into an uneasy silence about sex. For young people growing up in such an environment, the dominant voices that shaped their understanding of sexuality were those of the culture that prized individual autonomy, pleasure, and personal fulfillment through ecstatic release—or worse, reduced sex to a commodity for consumption. The Church to which they belonged seemed to be able to offer little by way of effective preaching or catechesis to challenge such viewpoints. When sex was mentioned in connection with the Church, it was often in reference to cases of sexual misconduct on the part of priests or religious, which were given disproportionate attention by the media, further undercutting the Church's credibility to speak on sexual matters. Hence, the alienation experienced by many younger Catholics flows from their experience of growing up in a Church that seemed to have lost its voice concerning sexual matters, while being part of culture that stridently proclaims its views through a host of symbols, attitudes, and practices.

The experience of older Catholics who lived through the changes unleashed by Vatican II and the controversy surrounding *Humanae vitae* was somewhat different. Raised in a morality of obligation, focused on the struggle between individual conscience and law, they saw this paradigm challenged by Vatican II and yet played out in the contentious debate surrounding the encyclical. To many, the document could be read as an attempt to reimpose a law (i.e., the prohibition of contraception) merely on the basis of the authority of the lawgiver (i.e., the pope). In a casuistic framework, the arguments of numerous reputable theologians in the face of a noninfallible teaching could surely raise enough doubt

59. For an incisive analysis of the impact of the storm of controversy that the encyclical ignited, see Avery Dulles, S.J., "*Humanae Vitae* and the Crisis of Dissent," delivered to the 12th U.S. Catholic Bishops Workshop in Dallas, Texas, on February 4, 1993.

about the binding force of the norm so as to leave individual conscience free to choose. Hence many older Catholics felt confident in setting aside the teaching on the grounds of conscience.

Yet such an effort is problematic in its very presuppositions. Rather than challenging the legalistic paradigm of post-Tridentine Catholic moral thinking, it remains entrapped within it. The deformation of morality in its reduction to the dialectic between freedom of conscience over against an external law is at the heart of such a reading of the encyclical and many of the debates that it produced. Yet it was precisely the narrow confines of a morality of obligation that Vatican II sought to challenge in its call for renewal. Much of the controversy following the encyclical is in fact a testimony to the continuing presence of a morality of obligation and the casuistry it breeds within Catholic moral thought.[60]

The alienation experienced by many older Catholics in regard to the Church and sexuality can be traced to the impact of a such a paradigm. Either they operate within this moral system, in which case the authority of the teaching can be doubted on the grounds of casuistry and conscience. Or, having rejected this paradigm to one degree or another, yet not being given a new way to think about morality, they simply find it difficult to relate their faith to moral teaching of any kind. Faith and morality are thus disconnected.[61]

How does one begin to address such a situation? Can these differing forms of alienation experienced by differing generations of Catholics each with complex historical roots be overcome? The preceding historical analysis can shed some light on the beginnings of an answer.

First, a more radical rethinking of moral reasoning about sex is re-

60. It is significant that both proponents and critics of contemporary moral methods such as proportionalism find parallels between it, early modern casuistry, and its Franciscan precursors. For examples of the former, see Keenan and Shannon, "Introduction," in *Context of Casuistry*, xvi–xvii; and Thomas Shannon, "Method in Ethics: A Scotistic Contribution," in ibid., 3–24 (see esp. 12). For an example of the latter, see Servais Pinckaers, O.P., "La question des actes intrinsèquement mauvais et le 'proportionalisme,'" *Revue thomiste* 82 (1982): 181–212.

61. This disjunction can also be found in classical Lutheran theology which tended to separate the faith necessary for salvation from conduct in the world (ethics). Such thinking also bears the marks of nominalist influence.

quired than one that simply represents or repackages the legalism of much of the manualist tradition. It is not enough to critique specific norms or formulations while remaining on the plane of a morality of obligation. Instead moral theology must be reenvisoned in the light of its most basic sources: Scripture, a treatment of the human person redeemed by Christ, and an account of how the person grows in moral excellence to achieve the happiness for which he or she was created.

Second, the controversy surrounding *Humanae vitae* makes it clear that it is not enough to propose norms on the basis of authority. Unless such norms are part of a larger vision of sexuality, they are unlikely to be found compelling by those who live in a culture that prizes individual autonomy and freedom. Such a vision must be compelling enough to offer a cogent alternative to dominant cultural visions of sex as merely ecstatic release, personal fulfillment, or a commodity of exchange. Further, this vision must be shaped and informed by the light of faith to allow people to begin to overcome the disconnect between their experience of sexuality and their lives of faith.

Third, this account of sexuality must face some of the critical questions that have been raised by a genuinely different intellectual and social context. The new appreciation of the values of love and intimacy within married sexuality, genuine concerns about rising population and limited environmental resources, the new social and political roles of women in Western society, changing attitudes and patterns of sexual behavior, and the difficulties faced by religious educators and parents in passing on their faith to children in a materialistic and increasingly secular culture all raise important questions that must be engaged in the light of faith. While no one treatment can fully resolve such issues, some attention must be given to them both on the level of theory and on the level of concrete moral praxis.

Addressing some of these critical questions will be the concern of the last three chapters of this book. However, before that effort can be undertaken, further attention must be given to the sources that are foundational to a more thorough renewal of moral theology—namely, Scripture and an account of the person's growth in moral excellence or virtue insofar as these can illumine an understanding of sexuality.

CHAPTER 2

Covenant and Sacrament

The task of addressing the disconnect experienced by many contemporary Catholics between their faith and their understanding of sexuality is a difficult one.[1] Recent debates in moral theology have often focused on specific moral norms and the authority that proposes them.[2] However, when such debates are heard within the framework of a morality of obligation, they are easily colored by the adversarial clash between individual freedom and laws imposed by an external authority. In order to resolve the tension, an emphasis is either placed on the binding force of the norms and the submission they require, or on a casuistic search for loopholes that give greater play to personal freedom. Neither approach addresses the deeper problems of an overly juridical moral framework. And neither offers a compelling alternative to current conceptions of sexuality prevalent in the wider culture.

A better way to address the alienation experienced by many in the Church is to attempt to offer a more compelling vision of sexuality in the light of faith. Such a vision must be formed by the basic sources of Christian faith: Scripture, the Church's tradition in which the understanding of the biblical text has deepened over time, and the concrete praxis of the Church, especially in its liturgical worship. This vision can provide an alternative to dominant cultural ideologies that reduce sex to mere personal fulfillment through ecstatic release or to a commodity for consumption. Furthermore, it can do so without reducing morality to

---

1. Portions of this chapter appeared previously as John S. Grabowski, "Covenantal Sexuality," *Église et Théologie* 27 (1996): 229–52.

2. See, e.g., the essays collected in *Readings in Moral Theology, No. 1: Moral Norms and Catholic Tradition*, ed. Charles Curran and Richard McCormick, S.J. (New York: Paulist Press, 1979); and those in *Readings in Moral Theology, No. 3: The Magisterium and Morality*, ed. Charles Curran and Richard McCormick, S.J. (New York: Paulist Press, 1982).

laws imposed as constraints upon personal freedom by an alien authority. This vision can then serve as a guide and stimulus to moral growth in sexual attitudes and practices that promote human flourishing.[3]

The following chapters will consider biblical, historical, liturgical, and contemporary sources that can aid in the development of a contemporary vision of sexuality in the light of faith. Specifically, the biblical theology of covenant, the Church's sacramental and liturgical tradition, the New Testament call to discipleship as a response to Jesus' announcement of the inbreaking of the Kingdom of God, the Beatitudes and beatitude, New Testament accounts of Christian character, and perspectives on the virtue of chastity drawn from patristic, medieval, and modern settings will be used to frame this vision. Of course, there are other sources within Scripture and the Church's tradition that could be consulted. However, the primary focus of this treatment will be on the sources mentioned above because of their importance and mutual coherence.

The present chapter will lay a foundation for this vision by focusing on the biblical understanding of covenant that frames much biblical teaching on sexuality. Specifically, it will argue that an understanding of sex drawn from key biblical traditions and the subsequent liturgical practice of the Church presents it as a gesture that recalls and enacts a couple's covenant pledge to one another. It will trace this view from the opening chapters of Genesis through subsequent Old Testament teachings to its transposition by the author of Ephesians. It will also consider the role of this paradigm in the developing sacramental theology and practice of the Church, as well as some theological and pastoral implications that flow from this.

I. Biblical Interpretation

There is widespread agreement among both moral theologians and biblical scholars that a more thorough integration of biblical teaching is

---

3. Gilbert Meilaender notes that the tradition of virtue that flows from Plato emphasizes the importance of vision in shaping moral imagination, action, and character. See *The Theory and Practice of Virtue* (South Bend, Ind.: University of Notre Dame Press, 1984), 45–62.

essential for the renewal of moral theology. This agreement reflects the directive of the Second Vatican Council that moral theology be "more thoroughly nourished by scriptural teaching."[4] It also reflects the result of historical research that has uncovered a sharp contrast between the immersion of patristic moral teaching in biblical thought and the proof-texting found in many modern moral manuals.[5]

However, there is less agreement on the specific form that this integration should take. Much of the postconciliar discussion has been sidetracked by debates over whether Scripture poses any concrete norms that could not be known by the natural light of human reason (i.e., the natural law).[6] The reduction of morality to law presupposed by these disagreements reveals the enduring influence of a morality of obligation. Further problems arise from the growing specialization found within the discrete areas of biblical studies that threaten to make it inaccessible to both theologians and laypersons. This is an especially acute problem for the moralist who in attempting to ascertain the relevance of biblical teaching for contemporary issues is confronted by a dizzying array of methods and conclusions about specific texts.[7]

How, then, can Scripture inform and eventually transform contemporary moral theology? Obviously, a complete answer to this question exceeds the scope of this study. However, certain parameters should be identified at the outset. At the very least, some unhelpful approaches

4. *Optatum totius*, no. 16. The citation is from *Documents of Vatican II*, 452.

5. Thus Pinckaers writes: "In the patristic period a dominant characteristic of Christian thought, which could even be called a first principle, was the acceptance of Scripture as the main, direct source of sacred science in all its forms.... For them [i.e., the Fathers], all of Scripture possessed a moral dimension and significance"; see *Sources of Christian Ethics*, 199. On the neglect of Scripture within the manuals, see Vincent MacNamara, *Faith and Ethics: Recent Roman Catholicism* (Washington, D.C.: Georgetown University Press, 1985), 14–16.

6. For an overview, see MacNamara, *Faith and Ethics*, passim. For examples see the essays collected in *Readings in Moral Theology, No. 2: The Distinctiveness of Christian Ethics*, ed. Charles Curran and Richard McCormick, S.J. (New York: Paulist Press, 1980).

7. Thus John R. Donahue, S.J., cautions that contemporary biblical studies is in danger of becoming a collection of "specialty fields" with the result that "moral theologians who turn to exegesis often find little help in determining what the bible says on a particular issue"; see "The Challenge of Biblical Renewal to Moral Theology," in *Riding Time Like a River: The Catholic Moral Tradition since Vatican II*, ed. William J. O'Brien (Washington, D.C.: Georgetown University Press, 1993), 59–80, quotation at 63–64.

can be ruled out and some basic principles for approaching biblical texts can be adduced.

One unhelpful approach widespread among some contemporary Christians is to engage in a fundamentalist reading of the biblical text. Unfortunately, a naive literal reading of Scripture that fails to attend to its historical setting, linguistic nuances, and literary forms often results in *eisegesis*, reading one's own ideas and presuppositions into the text.[8] In the moral realm this often entails using the Bible as a textbook for current questions and attempting to literally invoke isolated texts as answers. The results of this effort are often highly problematic.[9]

The other extreme is to view the Scriptures as a collection of archaic myths that have been rendered obsolete by modern sensibilities. Such a perception may be created by certain forms of scientific inquiry or simply a conviction concerning the superiority of present viewponts as more "enlightened" than those of primitive (i.e., biblical) times.

There are also more subtle variations of these extremes. The prooftexting of many manuals of moral theology bears some resemblance to the pitfalls of a fundamentalist reading of Scripture. And, on the other hand, some extreme variants of historical-critical exegesis see the Bible as a purely historical document that should be subjected to scientific study like any other ancient text. But historical-critical methodology alone is insufficient to allow Scripture a normative function in ethics.[10] When used by itself, such an approach can dissolve the unity of the biblical text and thus the intelligibility of Christian faith and practice.

Given such pitfalls, how should Scripture be used in augmenting the renewal of moral theology? First, it is crucial that adequate attention be paid to the literary form, historical context, and original language in or-

8. For a balanced assessment of fundamentalist readings of the text, see The Pontifical Biblical Commission, *The Interpretation of the Bible in the Church* (Vatican City: Liberia Editrice Vaticana, 1993), 18–19.

9. David Bohr sagely notes the problems posed by counsel of Old Testament texts that advise parents of a rebellious son to have him stoned (Dt 21:18–21); direct the people of Israel to exterminate even the women and children of their enemies; portray Lot's "hospitality" in offering his daughters to spare his angelic visitors from rape (Gn 19:7–8); or condone concubinage or divorce. See *Catholic Moral Tradition: In Christ, a New Creation*, rev. ed. (Huntington, Ind.: Our Sunday Visitor Press, 1999), 42–43.

10. See the remarks of Lisa Sowle Cahill (echoing Sandra Schneiders) in *Between the Sexes*, 49.

der to facilitate genuine exegesis and avoid reading one's own presuppositions into the text. Historical-critical study is indispensable in determining what Scripture meant in its original setting and in thus determining the "literal sense" of the text.[11]

Second, also important to the effort to separate one's own presuppositions and understanding and that of the biblical text is hermeneutical study that discerns the interplay between these horizons of meaning.[12] This effort can help us understand the relevance of biblical teaching for a very different historical age confronted by very different questions.

Third, it is also necessary to consider the Scriptures as a whole—not simply as discrete pericopes isolated from one another and their larger context. So-called synchronic methods of exegesis such as literary, narrative, and canonical criticism constitute attempts to maintain the unity of Scripture in a contemporary context.[13] These efforts serve as a reminder that, for all of its diverse genres and variety of historical settings, the collection of books that constitute the Bible form a larger unity and should be read as such.

Fourth, the Bible is not only a canonical and literary whole, but Christian faith also regards it as the Word of God. Because of this the Scriptures must be read in faith, and attention must be paid to senses beyond the literal. Premodern Christianity acknowledged not only the literal sense, but "spiritual senses" such as the moral, the allegorical, and the mystical as well. There is an effort today to recover this vital awareness through current studies of the "spiritual sense" of the text or efforts to read the text "in the same Spirit in which it was written."[14] Equally important, is the growing practice of prayerful reading of the

11. Cf. Constitution of Divine Revelation, *Dei verbum*, no. 12. For an overview of such methods, see Pontifical Biblical Commission, *Interpretation of the Bible*, 5–7.

12. See Raymond Brown, S.S., and Sandra Schneiders, I.H.M., "Hermeneutics," in *New Jerome Biblical Commentary*, ed. Raymond E. Brown, S.S., Joseph A. Fitzmyer, S.J., and Roland E. Murphy, O. Carm. (Englewood Cliffs, N.J.: Prentice-Hall, 1990), 1146–65.

13. For an overview, see Pontifical Biblical Commission, *The Interpretation of the Bible*, 7–12.

14. See, e.g., Ignace de la Potterie, "'Reading Scripture in the Holy Spirit': Is the Patristic Way of Reading the Bible Still Possible Today?," *Comunio* 4 (1986): 308–25; and "The Spiritual Sense of Scripture," *Communio* 23 (1996): 738–56; and also see Francis Martin, "St. Matthew's Spiritual Understanding of the Healing of the Centurion's Boy," *Communio* 25 (1998): 160–77.

biblical text among the faithful which is essential not only to the renewal of moral theology, but to the renewal of the Church as a whole.[15]

Fifth, biblical interpretation cannot take place in a vacuum. Insofar
as the Scriptures are the story of God's actions in the history of his
people, they must be read within that community and its history. Apostolic Tradition and the Church's teaching office provide a baseline for
authentic readings of the biblical text. Even in the formation of the
biblical canon this held true. For it was conformity to the rule of faith
along with the decisions of bishops as to which books would be read
during liturgical worship (along with considerations of apostolicity)
that provided the grounds for the inclusion or exclusion of individual
books.[16] So it is in the continuing life of the Church that Scripture, sacred tradition, and the Church's teaching office continue to form "one
sacred deposit of the word of God."[17]

Sixth, and finally, there must be a realization that the understanding
of the biblical text can develop and deepen over time. At times, this development can impact the reading of the literal sense of the text
through a deeper grasp of the ethos of the gospel message or through a
changed social situation.[18] Thus, while individual biblical texts seemingly accept the practice of slavery in the ancient world or countenance the
subordination of women, a literal reading of these passages can be challenged on the basis of a clearer understanding of the dignity of the human person redeemed in Christ which reflection on the New Testament
has provided.[19]

These somewhat abstract observations will be further concretized in
the examination of specific biblical themes and the texts from which
they emerge. Among the most important of these themes for an understanding of sexuality is that of covenant.

---

15. Cf. Pinckaers, *Sources of Christian Ethics*, 318–23.

16. For an excellent overview of the formation of the canon and the role of the
Church within it, see Joseph T. Lienhard, S.J., *The Bible, the Church, and Authority: The Canon of
the Christian Bible in History and Theology* (Collegeville, Minn.: Liturgical Press, 1995).

17. See *Dei Verbum*, no. 10. The citation is from *The Documents of Vatican II*, 117.

18. See John T. Noonan, "Development in Moral Doctrine," *Theological Studies* 54
(1993): 662–77.

19. Cf. Pope John Paul II, Apostolic Letter, *Mulieris dignitatem*, no. 24.

II. The Nature of Covenant

The importance of the covenant in structuring Israel's relationship to Yahweh has long been evident to even casual readers of the Old Testament. However, modern scholarship has uncovered an extensive and multifaceted use of this category in biblical materials to describe many relationships. This section will highlight certain features of the biblical theology of covenant *(běrît)* that are necessary to understand its application to the marriage relationship and sexual intimacy within it.

From the perspective of biblical thought, there is a fundamental difference between the legal category of contract and the more personal category of covenant.[20] A *contract* is an economic or legal agreement between two parties made before witnesses that involves a pledge of one's property.[21] If one of the parties breaks the contract, that party forfeits the property pledged. A *covenant*, on the other hand, is an agreement or oath of fidelity between parties made with or before God in which one promises one's very self to another. This is illustrated in dramatic fashion in the account of Abram's covenant with Yahweh in Genesis 15. Yahweh "cuts a covenant" *(kārat běrît;* Gn 15:18) with Abram by having him split in two a heifer, a goat, and a ram. Generally, in such covenant ceremonies, both parties would walk between the animal halves, indicating that if they ever broke the agreement, their own lives would be forfeit. The promise entailed in a covenant thus demands an unconditional and more personal form of fidelity even though it can be violated or even broken.

It is precisely because of the total claim that it makes on a person that a covenant creates a new relationship between its parties. These agreements can take numerous forms. One can find "secular" variations such as an unequal treaty between a powerful party who promises protection to the weak in exchange for service (cf. Jgs 9:11–15; 1 Sm 11:1; 2

---

20. On the biblical basis of this distinction, see Gene M. Tucker, "Covenant Forms and Contract Forms," *Vetus Testamentum* 15 (1965): 487–503; and Paul F. Palmer, S.J., "Christian Marriage: Contract or Covenant?," *Theological Studies* 33 (1972): 617–65, esp. 617–19, 639–40.

21. Extrabiblical examples of contract forms and biblical evidence for their use in Israel are considered by Tucker, "Covenant Forms," 497–500.

Sm 3:12ff.),[22] peace treaties (cf. Gn 14:13ff., 26:28, 31:43ff.), or agreements
between friends (cf. 1 Sm 23:18).[23] There are also the more "religious"
presentations of the covenant between Yahweh and Israel.[24] The new relationship created by such agreements is often described in familial
terms.[25] If one of the parties is the more powerful of the two, he becomes a "father" to the other (cf. Jer 35:18; Is 9:5) with obligations to
protect and care for him.[26] In other cases, parties are said to be made
"brothers" by such a pact (cf. 2 Sm 1:26; 1 Kgs 20:32–33). In every case,
covenant declaration formulae serve to "extend the bond of blood beyond the kinship sphere, or, in other words, to make the partner one's
own flesh and blood."[27]

Integral to most covenants is an oath. In fact, the two are so closely
related as to be virtually interchangeable.[28] Such oaths often invoke God

22. Walther Eichrodt holds that even in cases of covenants between those who are not
equal, there is still a certain mutuality of obligation. See *Theology of the Old Testament*, trans.
J. A. Baker (Philadelphia: Westminster Press, 1961), 1: 37.

23. For an extensive study of the declaration formulae of various "secular" covenants
found in the Old Testament, see Paul Kalluveettil, C.M.I., *Declaration and Covenant: A Comprehensive Review of Covenant Formulae from the Old Testament and the Ancient New East*, Analecta
Biblica 88 (Rome: Pontifical Biblical Institute Press, 1982).

24. There is some overlap between these various kinds of covenant. The covenant between God and Israel at Mt. Horeb, for example, is described by some biblical traditions
in terms that are redolent of Ancient Near Eastern suzerainty treaties. See Dennis J. Mc-
Carthy, *Old Testament Covenant: A Survey of Current Opinions* (Richmond, Va.: John Knox,
1972), and *Treaty and Covenant*, 2nd ed., Analecta Biblica 21A (Rome: Pontifical Biblical Institute Press, 1978).

25. The seminal work in this area was Johannes Pedersen's study on the familial nature
of covenant among the semitic Bedouin tribes of the Arabian Peninsula. Because Semites
tend to base all rights and duties on relationship, the covenant utilizes a juridical fiction
to make the parties into blood relatives. See *Der Eid bei den Semiten, in seinem Verhältnis zu verwandten Erscheinungen sowie die Stellung des Eides im Islam*, Studien zur Geschichte und Kultur
des islamischen Orients 3 (Strassburg: Trübner, 1914), 31.

26. On the use of such language in covenant forms, see Dennis J. McCarthy, "Notes
on the Love of God in Deuteronomy and the Father-Son Relationship between Yahweh
and Israel," *Catholic Biblical Quarterly* 27 (1965): 144–47; and Frank Charles Fensham, "Father and Son as Terminology for Treaty and Covenant," in *Near Eastern Studies in Honor of
William Foxwell Albright*, ed. H. Goedicke (Baltimore: Johns Hopkins University Press,
1971), 121–35.

27. Kalluveettil, *Declaration and Covenant*, 212. Cf. Gottfried Quell, "*diathēkē*," in *Theological
Dictionary of the New Testament*, ed. Gerhard Kittel, Gerhard Friedrich, and Geoffrey W.
Bromiley (Grand Rapids, Mich.: William B. Eerdmans, 1964), 2:114.

28. Numerous texts parallel the making of a covenant with the swearing of an oath

as a witness to the terms of the covenant (cf. Gn 21:23–24, 31:39–50). A similar notion is present in descriptions of covenants made in the sight of Yahweh (cf. 1 Sm 23:18; 2 Sm 5:3; 2 Kgs 23:3). Because God is witness to these pacts, he is understood to punish those who break them. Hence many covenant oaths take the form of a curse (ʾālāh), often self-imprecating in character, pronounced on those who fail to keep their word (e.g., Ru 1:17b; 1 Sm 3:17, 14:44, 25:22; 2 Sm 3:9–11, 3:35ff.; 1 Kgs 2:23, 19:2, 20:10; 2 Kgs 6:31).[29]

Also essential to covenant ceremonies is some act that seals or enacts the agreement. Thus, following Yahweh's revelation of himself and his laws to the Israelites at Sinai, the people three times express their consent to the words of the Lord (Ex 19:8, 24:3, 7) and then are sprinkled with the blood of their peace offerings. In this case, the blood symbolizes the bond between God and his people and their sharing of a common life. It should be remembered that the Israelites held blood to be sacred precisely because it was understood to contain the very life of the creature (cf. Lv 17:11, 14; Dt 12:23). Given this belief, one can begin to discern the role of blood in covenant ritual. The blood indicates not only the community of life among the covenant parties, but also the sanctification or being set apart of the object or person whom it marks (cf. Ex 12:12–23, 29:20–21). Such being made holy through sacrificial blood also recalls the demands made on those party to a covenant. The life of the creature forfeited in the sacrifice or offering bespeaks the totality of the claim made upon the faithful Israelite in his covenant with Yahweh.

There are still other ways of sealing or ratifying a covenant which, though not utilizing the symbolism of blood, bespeak a similar consecration or offering of self. These gestures that signify a similar familial

---

(cf. Gn 21:22–24, 21:31–32, 26:28, 31; Jos 9:15–20; 2 Kgs 11:4b; Ezek 17:13, 16, 18–19). On this point, see Petersen, Der Eid, 21–51; Norbert Lohfink, Die Landverheissung als Eid: Eine Studie zu Gn. 15, Stuttgarter Bibel-Studien 28 (Stuttgart: Verlag Katholisches Bibelwerk, 1967), 101–13; Tucker, "Covenant Forms," 488–90; and Gordon Paul Hugenberger, Marriage as a Covenant: A Study of Biblical Law and Ethics Developed from the Perspective of Malachi, Supplements to Vetus Testamentum 52 (Leiden: Brill, 1994), 182–84, 193–205.

29. On these conditional self-curses, see Pedersen, Der Eid, 103ff.; and Friederich Horst, "Der Eid im Alten Testament," in Gottes Recht: Gesammelte Studien zum Recht im Alten Testament, ed. Hans Walter Wolff (München: Chr. Kaiser, 1961), 301–14. On the variety of forms of covenant oaths, see Tucker, "Covenant Forms," 491–97.

intimacy include the giving of a hand, a kiss, or a gift (cf. Gn 21:27; Hos 12:2), the sharing of a meal (cf. Gn 26:30, 31:46; Jos 9:14–15; 2 Sm 3:20), or the bestowal of a garment (cf. 1 Sm 18:3–4; Ezek 16:8).[30] As will be seen below, in the case of marriage it is sexual intimacy that serves as the gesture that seals or symbolizes a couple's covenant oath.

III. Sex as Covenantal: Genesis 2

The fact that some of the Prophets, beginning with Hosea, used marriage as a symbol for Yahweh's covenant with his people is well known. Influenced by this symbolism, later biblical writings also use the term *běrît* for the relationship of marriage itself (cf. Mal 2:14; Prv 2:17). This has led some scholars to conclude that the idea of covenant and its application to marriage was a relatively late and rather inconsequential development within Israelite thought.[31] Such a conclusion overlooks the way in which the second creation account in Genesis, which dates from approximately the tenth century B.C., lays a foundation for these developments in its rich use of covenant language and imagery to describe the creation of woman and her subsequent union with man.

After describing the creation of the man (*ʾādām*) and his placement in Eden as its caretaker, the second creation account sounds a strikingly discordant note: "It is not good for the man to be alone" (Gn 2:18b).[32] The tension in the narrative builds as the search for an *ʿēzer* (suitable partner) remains unresolved in the creation of the animals (2:18–20).[33] The stage is set for the climax of this part of the narrative in the account of the creation of woman (2:21ff.).

30. Cf. Hugenberger (*Marriage as a Covenant*, 193–96, 199–200) who notes that many of these gestures can themselves be considered "oath-signs" and that some do suggest a self-maledictory character.

31. See, e.g., Lothar Perlitt, *Bundestheologie im Alten Testament*, WMANT 36 (Neukirchen-Vluyn: Neukirchener Verlag, 1969); and Ernest W. Nicholson, *God and His People: Covenant and Theology in the Old Testament* (Oxford, U.K.: Clarendon Press, 1986), 68–82.

32. English citations throughout this work are from the NAB unless otherwise noted. The discordant character of this statement is seen especially when juxtaposed against the affirmation of the goodness of all that God made in Genesis 1:31. The author of the first creation account, who did the final redaction of this material, presumably allowed the dissonance created by this statement to remain precisely because of the importance of what it introduces.

33. The basic equality indicated by the term *ʿēzer* will be considered in Chapter 5.

Of particular interest is the wealth of covenant language contained in this section of the Genesis narrative. Verse 21 describes Yahweh as casting a *tardēmah* (deep sleep) on the man. As used in the Old Testament, this term sometimes indicates God's activity in providing protection (cf. 1 Sm 26:12) or bringing judgment (cf. Is 29:10). It also denotes the slumber that precedes divine revelation whether in word or vision (cf. Jb 4:13, 33:15). But perhaps the closest use to this present one is that found in the narrative of Genesis 15. In Genesis 15:12 a *tardēmah* falls upon Abram prior to his vision of Yahweh in the culmination of their covenant ceremony. Thus the term, while usually associated with divine action or communication, also has the particular connotation of the state that precedes a covenant. It is this connotation that is suggested by the state of *(ʾādām)* in Genesis 2:21 before Yahweh creates the woman.

The man's poetic cry of joy upon meeting the mate given him by God is also redolent of covenant imagery, but injects it into a distinctively nuptial context.[34] *ʾĀdām* exclaims "this one, at last, is bone of my bone and flesh of my flesh" (Gn 2:23). As used in the Old Testament, the phrase "bone of my bone and flesh of my flesh" can indicate kinship (cf. Gn 29:14) or a covenant oath that expresses a claim or promise of allegiance. For example, when the northern tribes of Israel came to David in Hebron and wanted to express a claim on him as to why he should be their king, they said: "Here we are, your bone and your flesh" (2 Sm 5:1b–c; cf. Jgs 9:2; 2 Sm 19:13–14; 1 Chr 11:1).[35] In the present case, the exclamation indicates both the close relationship of the man *(ʾîš)* and the woman *(ʾiššâ)* created to be his suitable partner and the oath that unites them.[36] While the oath is not self-imprecating in its formulation, it nevertheless is made before God (since the woman is not ad-

34. Gerhard Von Rad describes the scene in this way: "God himself, like a father of the bride, leads the woman to the man"; see *Genesis: A Commentary*, trans. John H. Marks (Philadelphia: Westminster Press, 1961), 82.

35. Claus Westermann, following W. Reiser, describes the phrase as "the formula of relationship"; see *Genesis 1–11: A Commentary*, trans. John J. Scullion, S.J. (Minneapolis, Minn.: Augsburg, 1984), 232. For an analysis of these texts as covenant formulae, see Walter Brueggemann, "Of the Same Flesh and Bone," *Catholic Biblical Quarterly* 32 (1970): 535–38.

36. Brueggemann ("The Same Flesh and Bone," 533–35, 539) too sees Genesis 2:23 as a covenant oath and makes the further observation that both terms in the pair have a double meaning. Thus understood, "flesh-weakness" and "bone-power" describe the whole range of possibilities that might occur and test the fidelity of a couple's oath to one

dressed in the exclamation) and indicates a promise of allegiance or loyalty that now binds the pair together.[37] As noted in the preceding section, such an oath is in fact constitutive of a covenant.

The covenantal motif continues in the succeeding verse (2:24) with the statement of the narrator that "that is why a man leaves his father and mother and clings to his wife, and the two of them become one body."[38] Both the verb 'āzab (to leave, to forsake) and the verb dābaq (to cling) are often found in covenant formulations.

The first of these terms, 'āzab, is common in the Hebrew of the Old Testament. What is noteworthy is the variety of its uses in covenantal contexts. It is used in declarations of God's faithfulness (cf. Gn 24:27; Neh 9:17c, 19, 31; 1 Chr 28:20b; Ps 37:25, 28, 94:14; Ezek 9:9), God's promises of fidelity (cf. Gn 28:15; Jos 1:5; 1 Kgs 6:13), exhortations based on this fidelity (cf. Dt 31:6, 8), or promises of restoration (cf. Is 41:17, 42:16c, 54:7, 60:15, 62:12b). This verb can also be found in warnings against "forsaking" the covenant with Yahweh (cf. Dt 28:20; Jos 24:20; 2 Chr 7:19ff.), predictions of covenant apostasy and its consequences (see Dt 31:16–17), descriptions of actual covenant infidelity (cf. Jgs 2:12–13, 10:6; 1 Sm 12:10; 1 Kgs 19:10, 14; 2 Kgs 17:16; 2 Chr 21:10), or pronouncements that reprove the infidelity of the people to the covenant (cf. Jer 22:9; Ezek 20:8).[39] The term also figures in prayers of repentance (cf. Jgs 10:10; 1 Sm 12:10) or those that beg the Lord for his continued fideli-

---

another (similar to the "in sickness and in health, in plenty and in want" of more recent wedding vows).

37. Cf. Hugenberger, *Marriage as a Covenant,* 164–65. Hugenberger also gathers a wealth of ancient Near Eastern and biblical examples of oaths or gestures that are not self-maledictions but are in fact solemn declarations made before God, or *verba solemnia,* many of which are used in the context of sex and marriage (see 185–279).

38. The text can also be translated "one flesh" since the Hebrew word *bāśār* has both meanings. In fact, "flesh" is the more typical Old Testament usage. See John A. T. Robinson, *The Body: A Study in Pauline Theology* (Philadelphia: Westminster Press, 1952), 17–19. The verse as a whole is curious given the etiological character of the second creation account, since the legal situation of woman in the rather patriarchal Israelite society was just the opposite—it was she who left her family to become part of the *bêt* ('house') of her husband. Cf. Cahill, *Between the Sexes,* 55.

39. One finds numerous uses of the term in the context of condemnations of infidelity of the people to the Lord or the law of the Lord, some of which may have covenant connotations (cf. Jgs 10:13; 1 Kgs 11:33, 18:18; 2 Kgs 22:17; 2 Chr 12:5, 24:20, 34:25; Is 1:4, 58:2b; Jer 1:16, 2:13, 2:17, 5:19, 16:11, 19:4).

ty (cf. 1 Kgs 8:57; Ps 27:9, 71:9, 71:18, 119:8). It is also used in covenant oaths where the people swear fidelity to Yahweh (see Jos 24:16). Or it can indicate an oath in which one person binds himself or herself to another (cf. Ru 1:16, 2:11; 2 Kgs 2:2, 2:4, 2:6, 4:30).

The common denominator in these varied uses is the idea of the covenant. God's faithfulness to his people demands that they leave or forsake all that deflects them from their covenant relationship to himself. It is particuarly noteworthy that *ʿāzab*, is sometimes used in conjunction with covenant marital symbolism either to reprove those who refuse to forsake evil (see Ezek 23:8), or those who have forsaken the Lord (see Hos 4:10) or their spouse (see Prv 2:17), or to promise restoration (cf. Is 54:6, 62:4). In this way, the reciprocal hermeneutic of covenant imagery becomes apparent as the exclusivity of Israel's relationship with Yahweh inscribed at the head of the Decalogue (i.e., "You shall have no other gods besides me"; Ex 20:3) begins to color its later understanding of the marriage covenant with growing expectations of fidelity.[40] The marital symbol will in turn impart an undercurrent of love and intimacy to Israel's relationship with Yahweh.

The second of the two verbs, *dābaq* (to cling), also has covenantal connotations. Specifically, it is found in admonitions to "hold fast" or "cleave" to Yahweh in faithful obedience (cf. Dt 10:20, 11:22, 13:18, 30:20; Jos 22:5, 23:8), in declarations of real or intended fidelity (cf. 2 Kgs 18:6; Ps 101:3, 119:31; Jer 13:11), or even in self-imprecating oaths (cf. Jb 31:7–8;

---

40. One can discern a gradual evolution in Old Testament traditions in this regard. While monogamy was regarded as a theological and practical ideal, the value of fecundity and desire for a powerful family led, in some cases, to the practice of polygamy. Hence the Genesis narratives describe rather straightforwardly the fact that some of the Patriarchs (e.g., Abraham, Jacob) had more than one wife. This reality is reflected in laws that prevent the children of the favorite wife from inheriting an unjust share (cf. Dt 21:15–17). But even here, there is growing awareness of the pitfalls of such a practice. This is highlighted through a kind of genealogical editorializing in some traditions: the Patriarchs of Seth's line are monogamous (e.g., Noah; Gn 7:7), while Cain's descendants (esp. Lamech; Gn 4:19) are polygamous. The point is underscored by the descriptions of Esau's marriage to foreign women (Gn 26:34, 28:9, 36:1–5). Later Old Testament traditions reveal monogamy to be increasingly normative in Israelite society. The books of Samuel and Kings, for example, do not record one instance of bigamy among commoners (with the exception of Elkanah; see 1 Sm 1–2). Likewise, the Wisdom literature presupposes monogamy in its teaching on the joys and difficulties of faithful monogamous marriage.

Ps 137:6). It also designates the curses for disobedience that will "cling" to those unfaithful to God (cf. Dt 28:21, 60; Jer 42:16). In at least one instance, *dābaq* is used to indicate the bonds of friendship (see Prv 18:24). This term, too, can have specifically marital connotations indicating affection (cf. Gn 34:3; 1 Kgs 11:3a) or intermarriage with other nations (cf. Jos 23:12; 1 Kgs 11:2–3; Dn 2:43).

As used together in Genesis 2:24, the two terms build upon the covenant oath that precedes them by indicating respectively the termination of one loyalty and the espousal of a new one in the marriage relationship.[41] Hence when the narrative is read within the linguistic horizon of the Old Testament, it becomes clear that the singular devotion and fidelity required by Yahweh is also to characterize the commitment of spouses to one another.

Thus, the net effect of this wealth of covenant terminology used by the second creation account is to describe the relationship of male and female as covenantal in character.[42] Emerging from his covenant sleep, the man binds himself to the woman by an oath. This oath is then used as an explanation for the man's leaving his family and clinging to his wife so that together they form a new entity: "one flesh." This term denotes the new familial communion that the oath creates between male and female—a communion that includes and is expressed by sexual intimacy.[43]

The relationship of the following verse to that which precedes it is

41. Cf. Brueggemann, "The Same Flesh and Bone," 540; and Hugenberger, *Marriage as a Covenant*, 159–60.

42. It is noteworthy that the marriage prayer of Tobiah and Sarah (Tb 8:5–9) draws not on prophetic theology but on the account in Genesis 2. See Palmer, "Christian Marriage," 623. In the New Testament, Jesus will appeal to the same text to ground his teaching concerning marital indissolubility (see Mk 10:2–12 and par.).

43. While the particular expression "familial communion" is my own, it is basically a synthesis of two related positions. The first is that of Maurice Gilbert, S.J., whose excellent study of the term in Genesis and subsequent biblical traditions concludes that "one flesh" is to be understood in the sense of bondedness that results from and is expressed by sexual union; See "'Une seule chair' (Gn 2, 24)," *Nouvelle Revue Théologique* 100 (1978): 66–89. The second is that of Hugenberger (*Marriage as Covenant*, 162–63), who adds the nuance of a "familial" bondedness. This, as he points out, creates a balance between the family of parents that is "left" in 2:24 and the new one created by marriage. He also points out that *bāśār* is used in other Old Testament texts with the connotation of family or kin (cf. Gn 29:14, 37:27; Lv 18:6, 25:49; 2 Sm 5:1; and Is 58:7).

less clear. The text says that "the man and his wife were both naked, yet they felt no shame" (2:25). The interpretation of the couple's "naked-ness" is difficult for a number of reasons. First, the reference is obvious-ly a transition verse to the next part of the narrative.[44] Second, there is a wealth of patristic interpretation, undoubtedly colored by various forms of dualistic thinking, that associates sex in some way with sin and thus refuses to consider the possibility of prelapsarian sex.[45] Third, in many cultures, including that of the Old Testament, nudity can have multiple associations or meanings attached to it.[46] Thus the Israelite reader might well see here an allusion to the lack of deceit (symbolized by the absence of veils) or to the openness that characterized the com-munication and community of the pair.[47]

However, in spite of this ambiguity, the "nakedness" of the couple, for both the Israelite and the modern reader, is also a circumlocution that bespeaks sexual intimacy. This is especially evident when the text is considered in the context of the passage as a whole and of the preced-ing verse in particular.[48] Sex serves to both express and foster the "one flesh" unity of the couple. In terms of the depiction of the covenantal nature of the male-female relationship, sexual intimacy seals or enacts

44. This is indicated both by the wordplay of *rărûmmîm* (naked) in 2:25 with ʿ *ārûm* (cunning) in 3:1 and by the contrast this verse offers to the association of shame with nakedness after the interposition of sin (3:7). Cf. Hugenberger, *Marriage as a Covenant*, 152 n. 113. However, this observation causes Hugenberger to regard 2:25 as merely transitional and therefore to overlook its meaning.

45. On the prevalence of such ideas among various groups and thinkers of the early Christian era, see Peter Brown, *The Body and Society: Men, Women and Sexual Renunciation in Ear-ly Christianity* (New York: Columbia University Press, 1988), 86, 93–96, 175, 186, 268, 294–98.

46. For an overview of nudity and its associations in various cultures, including that of the Old Testament, see Mario Perniola, "Between Clothing and Nudity," in *Fragments for a History of the Human Body*, pt. 2, ed. Michel Feher with Ramona Naddaff and Nadia Tazi (New York: Zone, 1989), 237–65.

47. Hence André-Marie Dubarle, O.P., sees it as an indication of "mutual trust and esteem"; see "Original Sin in Genesis," trans. John Higgens, *Downside Review* 76 (1958): 242. This sense of nakedness is obviously at work in Genesis 3:10 where the inability to remain naked in God's presence follow's the couple's sin, thus indicating the breakdown of open communication between humanity and God.

48. Indeed, von Rad argues that "the Jahwist's story of creation practically issues in this aetiological explanation of the power of *eros* as one of the urges implanted in man by the Creator himself (v. 24f.), and so gives the relationship between man and woman

the covenant oath that binds them.[49] It is the embodied gesture that expresses the new relationship which their covenant creates between them. Sex, therefore, as a recollection and enactment of the covenant oath, takes on a liturgical function within the marriage relationship akin to other covenant-making gestures (e.g., the sprinkling with blood, table fellowship) described above. Indeed, one of the primary functions of liturgy in biblical thought is to remember in a way that makes present the event commemorated.[50] Sexual union is thus understood as a kind of anamnesis that recalls precisely the totality of a couple's gift to one another expressed in their oath.

IV. Covenantal Sexuality Fallen and Redeemed

The very positive presentation of the equality of man and woman and the sexual union as a ratification of the marriage covenant found in Genesis 2 is sharply qualified by the account of the couple's sin in Genesis 3. At the instigation of the serpent, the woman and the man misuse their freedom by trying to "be like gods who know what is good and what is bad" (Gn 3:5c). This act of rebellion produces dramatic consequences. No longer will they be able to be naked in one another's presence without shame (cf. Gn 3:7, 10), a condition indicating both the entrance of deceit into human communication and the disordering of

---

the dignity of being the greatest miracle and mystery of creation"; see *Old Testament Theology*, trans. David M. G. Stalker (New York: Harper, 1965), 1:150.

49. This is also the view of Hugenberger (*Marriage as a Covenant*, 216–79) though he bases it upon Old Testament traditions other than Genesis 2. His argument stands upon the convergence of a number of strands of evidence: the consensus in current scholarship against the notion of "marriage by purchase" (which views the marriage as primarily a transaction between a man and his father-in-law vs. covenant between a man and a woman); the fact that there is both biblical and extrabiblical evidence for the idea that intercourse consummates a marriage; that a number of texts (e.g., Gn 34; Ex 22:15–16; Dt 22:28–29; 2 Sm 13) all evidence a view that a marriage should be formalized after sexual union (in some cases even after forced sex); the fact that even marriages based on deception (e.g., that between Jacob and Leah in Gn 29) appear to have been regarded as irrevocable once ratified in intercourse; and the apparent connection between oath taking and genitalia evident in practices such as circumcision or placing one's hand under another's thigh (cf. Gn 24:2, 24:9, 47:29).

50. See, e.g., the injunctions concerning the celebration of the Passover in Exodus 12:1–28.

sexuality. Shame thus marks the boundary of the experience of postlapsarian sexuality, signaling the body's vulnerability to exploitation alongside its capacity for self-donation.[51] Instead of relationships founded on honest mutual attraction and lived in covenantal unity, relationships between men and women will be marked by the poles of domination and subservience in a continuing struggle for power (see Gn 3:16d–e).[52] Sexuality, while still understood in covenantal terms, will henceforth be lived within a markedly diminished existence.

Numerous Old Testament traditions highlight this diminishment of historical sexuality yet also offer a trajectory of hope for its ultimate healing. One example of this can be found in the developing understanding of adultery. In what has usually been regarded as the older version of the Decalogue (Ex 20), the prohibition regarding adultery (20:14) is modified by that concerning coveting (20:17). This latter injunction begins with the basic precept that "you shall not covet your neighbor's house" and then goes on to specify the contents of this house: wife, slaves, property. Thus, the prohibition focuses on the (property) rights of the husband. A man could presumably have sex with unmarried women or prostitutes without violating the commandment. The later Deuteronomic formulation of the Decalogue (Dt 5) expands this one law into two by separating the woman (5:21a) from the neighbor's house and property (5:21b–e).[53] This development has the effect of suggesting that married Israelite women are not mere posses-

---

51. On shame as a boundary between prelapsarian and historical experience of the body and sexuality, see John Paul II's weekly general audiences of April 30, May 14, and May 28, 1980, in *The Theology of the Body: Human Love in the Divine Plan*, trans. L'Osservatore Romano, English edition (Boston: Pauline Books and Media, 1997), 108–17. Cf. Karol Wojtyla, *Love and Responsibility*, trans. H. T. Willets (New York: Farrar, Straus and Giroux, 1981; rpt., San Francisco: Ignatius Press, 1993), 186–93.

52. On domination over the other, and particularly male domination of women as the effect of sin, see John Paul's weekly general audiences of June 18 and 25, 1980, in *Theology of the Body*, 120–25, and Apostolic Letter, *Mulieris dignitatem*, 10. This issue will be considered more fully in Chapter 5.

53. It should be noted that some scholars have argued the Deuteronomic version of the Decalogue is in fact older than the material found in Exodus. See, e.g., Frank-Lothar Hossfeld, *Der Dekalog: Seine späten Fassungen, die originale Komposition und seine Vorstufen*, Orbis Biblicus Orientalis 45 (Freiburg, Schweiz: Universitätsverlag, 1982); and Reinhard Gregor Kratz, "Der Dekalog im Exodusbuch," *Vetus Testamentum* 44 (1994): 205–38. However, this is still not the view of most scholars.

sions within the household. Later biblical traditions will more clearly exclude extramarital sex for men (cf. 2 Sm 12; Jb 31:1, 9–12; Prv 5:15–23; Sir 9:5–9, 41:22ff.).[54]

Another example of the promise of a restored sexuality in the midst of its historical diminution can be found in the Old Testament insistence on the holiness of sex. Over against the cosmologies and ritual practices of many of its neighbors, Israel steadfastly refused to deify sex by crudely projecting it onto God and equating it with worship. Yet this did not prevent sexuality from being seen as something holy—the de-mythologization of sex did not necessarily entail its desacralization.[55] This is evident both in the view of it as quasi-liturgical activity within marriage (described above) and the injunctions against specific kinds of sexual activity found in the legal traditions of the Pentateuch such as those embedded in the Holiness Code (Lv 17–26) in Leviticus 18. Not only do such norms show significant development as outlined above, but they themselves serve as stimuli for deeper theological reflection. One can find adultery referred to as "the great sin" (ḥăṭā 'ā gĕdolā) in various traditions (e.g., Gn 20:9, 39:9). The same term is used elsewhere to describe idolatry (cf. the account of the Golden Calf in Ex 32:21, 30, 31, and its application to Jeroboam's calves in 2 Kgs 17:21).[56] Such texts suggest a parallel between adultery and idolatry. Historically this association undoubtedly is in reaction to the fertility rituals and child sacrifice found in the idolatrous worship of many of Israel's neighbors.[57] Theo-

54. On this development, see Wilhelm Ernst, "Marriage as an Institution and the Contemporary Challenge to It," in *Contemporary Perspectives on Christian Marriage* (Chicago: Loyola University Press, 1984), 39–90, esp. 42–46, 51.

55. On the difference between Israelite and Canaanite religion on this point, see Von Rad, *Genesis*, 58–59, and *Old Testament Theology*, 1, 28, 146. Von Rad unfortunately uses the terms "demythologize" and "desacrilize" interchangeably, thereby obscuring an important nuance in Old Testament thought.

56. The usage has other ancient Near Eastern parallels. See Jacob J. Rabinowitz, "The 'Great Sin' in Ancient Egyptian Marriage Contracts," *Journal of Near Eastern Studies* 18 (1959): 73; and William L. Moran, "The Scandal of the 'Great Sin' at Ugarit," *Journal of Near Eastern Studies* 18 (1959): 280–81.

57. On the prevalence of "sacralized unchastity" and child sacrifice in the cultures surrounding ancient Israel and its parallel to our own culture's pursuit of sexual license and frequent recourse to abortion, see Patrick Riley, *Civilising Sex: On Chastity and the Common Good* (Edinburgh, U.K.: T. & T. Clark, 2000), 100–113.

logically, however, it indicates a judgment that adultery and idolatry are both, at root, forms of covenant infidelity.

This points to yet another example of the Old Testament's promise of a restoration of sexuality—the very idea of covenant. The analogy between the marriage covenant and the people's covenant with Yahweh found in the Pentateuch and historical books is reflected and developed further in prophetic theology. This teaching works on different levels. First, one can find condemnations of actual adultery (cf. Jer 7:9–10; Hos 4:1–2) where it is classified with other sins such as treachery (see Jer 9:2), misuse of God's name (see Jer 29:23), and oppression of widows (see Mal 3:5). Second, adultery is also used as a symbol to condemn the people's infidelity to God. In its worship of false gods, Israel has played the harlot or adulterated her covenant with Yahweh (this imagery recurs throughout texts such as Jer 2–3, 30–31; Ezek 16; 23; Hos 1–4). Third, the positive expression of this marital understanding of the covenant is found in promises of restoration when Yahweh promises that he will again marry his people (cf. Is 54:1, 62:1–7; Zep 3:14–18).

In these various strands, one observes again the reciprocal hermeneutic between these covenant relationships that were central to Israel's life. Both the covenant with Yahweh and the covenant of marriage demand a faithful and exclusive promise of self. To give oneself to a stranger in worshiping a false god or to have sex with someone other than one's spouse falsifies this covenant oath. The gesture is authentic only in relation to the oath that it recalls and enacts. Here one can begin to discern an analogy between sex and worship as activities that ratify or seal the covenant oath.[58] Both parallel other liturgical gestures that seal or ratify a covenant.

A related theology can be found in the New Testament, transposed by the author of Ephesians to the relationship between Christ and the Church.[59] The text (Eph 5:21–33) appears to utilize the literary form of a *Haustafel* (household code) and builds upon Pauline new creation the-

---

58. In this same vein, one can also consider the increasing tendency toward allegorical interpretation of the postexilic love poetry found in the Song of Songs. While it seems remarkable to apply sexual imagery to divine/human love, it is perhaps understandable in light of the theology of covenant and the implicit parallel between sex and worship.

59. One can see the connection with some of the Old Testament texts considered above (especially Gn 2) even though the author does not use the term *diathēkē* (covenant).

ology.[60] Here the human and divine spheres of relationship are even more tightly interwoven with the thread of marital symbolism as the passage moves back and forth between the two levels. The mutual self-giving love of husband and wife images the union of Christ and the Church. The head-body relationship of Christ and the Church illumines the "one flesh" unity of husband and wife (cf. 5:23, 31).[61] The seal of this marital relation in the case of Christ and the Church is the sacrificial love demonstrated in Christ "handing himself over" for the Church "to sanctify her, cleansing her by the bath of water and the word" (5:25c, 26). The baptismal imagery here is an allusion to Jesus' self-giving love on the cross.[62] This in turn demands an equally selfless love on the part of Christian spouses who are joined as *mia sarx* (one flesh; 5:31). The place of sex within this vision is largely left unstated except perhaps in the allusion to the "one flesh" of Genesis 2:24 and an implied contrast between the holiness demanded by new life in Christ and pagan sexual excess (see Eph 4:19–20).

The preceding overview of select biblical traditions discloses a connection between God's covenant relationship to his people (in the New Testament identified as the relationship of Christ and the Church), the covenant between man and woman in marriage, and sexual intimacy, which serves to seal or enact the nuptial oath. The analogous character of the covenant relations allows a flexible application of marital imagery: idolatry is tantamount to adultery, adultery is reductive idolatry.

60. See Stephen F. Miletic, *"One Flesh": Ephesians 5:22–24, 5:31. Marriage and the New Creation*, Analecta Biblica 115 (Rome: Pontifical Biblical Institute Press, 1988). Some have raised questions as to whether this text (and its New Testament counterparts) should be considered examples of this broader literary form. See, e.g., Francis Martin, "Family Values in the First Century," in *A Vision for Humanity: Marriage and Family in the Letter to Ephesians* (unpublished paper).

61. The language of "headship" in the passage need not indicate an inferior standing on the part of wives. The context of the passage is explicitly one of mutual submission (5:21); the duties enjoined on spouses are reciprocal (unlike those in Hellenistic versions of the *Hastaufeln*); and the exhortation, while using language reflective of the culture of the time, calls both spouses to unselfish love, service, and respect. See John Paul II, Apostolic Letter, *Mulieris dignitatem*, no. 24. These issues will be considered more fully in Chapter 5.

62. The verb *paredōken* is often used in the New Testament as a technical term for the Passion. Likewise one can note the close association of baptism with the death and Resurrection of Christ in Pauline theology (see Rom 6:1–11).

The intensity and exclusivity of covenant relationships require a complete and faithful offering of self in worship and sexual self-donation, respectively. In this association of covenant, marriage, and sex, one finds the foundations for a theology of sexuality. It is to the historical and theological implications of this view that this chapter now turns.

V. Intercourse as Anamnesis: Theological Developments

It is fairly clear that the early Church did not have a developed theology of marriage as a sacrament. While it is true that texts such as Ephesians 5:21–33 laid a foundation for the beginning of theological reflection on the meaning of this relationship "in the Lord,"[63] nevertheless marriage was basically a long-standing social institution that, in spite of typically religious associations in differing cultures, was usually administered by the family and perhaps regulated by the state.[64] Thus it is not surprising to find in Christian theology and practice differing understandings of marriage.

63. This can be seen through the fact that the term *mystērion* used by the Letter to the Ephesians to indicate the relationship of husband and wife is translated by various ante-Nicene authors into Latin as *sacramentum*. In Roman society, this term had the meaning of a sacred oath (made by a soldier to the emperor); see Émile de Backer, "Tertullien," in *Pour l'histoire du mot "Sacramentum,"* ed. Joseph de Ghellinck et al. (Paris: É. Champion, 1924), 66–71. This, along with the fact that the Romans too tended to see marriage as sacred and, indeed, covenantal provided an atmosphere in which the assimilation of biblical theology was possible in spite of some linguistic and cultural differences; see Palmer, "Christian Marriage," 618–19, 625–30. Cf. Pheme Perkins, "Marriage in the New Testament and Its World," in *Commitment to Partnership: Explorations in the Theology of Marriage,* ed. William P. Roberts (New York: Paulist Press, 1987), 26.

64. However, the view of Edward Schillebeeckx that marriage was a basically secular institution later sacralized by "clerical intervention" is overstated; see his *Marriage: Human Reality and Saving Mystery,* trans. N. D. Smith, 2 vols. (New York: Sheed & Ward, 1965), 2:245; cf. 1:194. This view is problematic on at least two counts. First, it overlooks a wealth of evidence from Roman, patristic, and liturgical sources that marriage was seen and celebrated as a religious—specifically covenantal—reality in the first millennium A.D. Cf. Palmer, "Christian Marriage," 625–35. Second, it fails to observe that it was precisely a kind of secularization that enabled medieval theology to delimit marriage and the other six sacraments from the other rites in the Church's possession—a distinction rendered difficult in an earlier worldview that considered reality as indistinguishably sacral. See Walter Kasper, *Theology of Christian Marriage,* trans. David Smith (New York: Seabury Press, 1980), 31–32.

One very ancient tradition with New Testament roots saw the essence of marriage in the marriage "debt" (see 1 Cor 7:3–5)—that is, in the sexual intercourse that husband and wife owe one another.[65] Marriage thus grants spouses particular rights to one another's bodies—a rather revolutionary assertion, given the prevailing view of women as the possessions of men and the double standard regarding sexual morality common in the Hellenistic culture that surrounded the nascent Church.[66]

A somewhat different view, flowing from Roman law and introduced by St. Ambrose and St. Augustine, saw marriage rooted in the consent of the couple and existing even in the absence of intercourse.[67] Such a position served to underscore the freedom of the couple and aided the later emancipation of marriage from family control. It also coincided with the growing embrace of virginal or spiritual marriage on the part of the Church leaders and theologians inspired by the monastic ideal and somewhat wary of the body and sexuality.

The controversy between proponents of these two traditions came to a head in Western theology in the theological renewal of the High Middle Ages.[68] In the thirteenth century, for example, the canon law faculty of the University of Bologna held to the "debt-oriented"

65. This view was defended by authorities such as Jerome, the Emperor Zeno, and later Gratian. See P. Lyndon Reynolds, "Marriage, Sacramental and Indissoluble: Sources of the Catholic Doctrine," *Downside Review* 109, no. 375 (1991): 131.

66. Peter Brown, in *Body in Society*, 21–24, notes that, while Christian portrayals of the debauchery of the Roman world are sometimes overstated, it is nevertheless true that female infidelity was harshly punished by law, but male adultery earned no such stricture. Indeed, the "chastity" expected of the male was often thought to be limited to the walls of his house, leaving upper-class men free to seek sexual outlets in the bodies of their female (and male) servants.

67. See Ambrose, *De institutione virginis* 6 (41), *PL* 16, 331A; Augustine, *De nuptiis et concupiscentia* I.11, *CSEL* 42, 224; *De consensu evagelistarum* 2.1.2, *CSEL* 43, 82. For the Roman understanding of marriage as based on consent versus consummation, see Karl Ritzer, *Le mariage dans les églises chrétiennes du Ier au XIe siècle* (Paris: Les Éditions du Cerf, 1970), 218–9; and Christopher N. L. Brooke, *The Medieval Idea of Marriage* (Oxford, U.K.: Clarendon Press, 1989), 128–29.

68. For the history of this controversy during the medieval period, see Brooke, *Medieval Idea of Marriage*, 129–33, 137–41; and Art Cosgrove, "Consent, Consummation and Indissolubility: Some Evidence from Ecclesiastical Medieval Courts," *Downside Review* 109 (1991): 94–104.

view, while the theology faculty at Paris championed the consensual po-sition.[69] The outcome of the debate was basically a victory for the the-ologians in that consent came to be seen as that which effects the sacra-ment.[70]

But this is not the end of the story. The Pauline emphasis on the sex-ual and bodily basis of the marriage relationship has been accommo-dated within past and present canon law through the insistence that it is consummation that renders a sacramental union indissoluble.[71] This seems an odd notion given that it has existed alongside a high sacra-mental theology that holds to the *ex opere operato* efficacy of the sacra-ments and the indissolubility of marriage. How can a sacrament be caused by the consent of the couple and yet remain dissoluble until consummation?

An answer emerges when one considers the biblical theology of covenant that provided the soil from which later theological reflection and legislation grew. The oath or promise that one makes in a covenant is indeed its central component, but the covenant is not completed until it is sealed or ratified. In the case of marriage, it is the mutual consent of the couple expressed in their promise to one another in their vows that causes the sacrament, but this consent remains incomplete until en-acted sexually. In coition a couple seals their covenant with one another by an embodied enactment of their complete self-giving. The uncondi-tional and exclusive character of their mutual promise is enfleshed in the giving of their bodies completely and exclusively to one another. Sex is thus the embodied symbol of a couple's love and communion in way

69. However, one can find canonists as well as theologians who defended the consen-sual view before and during this same period; see James A. Brundage, *Law, Sex, and Chris-tian Society in Medieval Europe* (Chicago: University of Chicago Press, 1987), 348–55, 414–15, 433–39.

70. Hence even though consummation is considered typical, intercourse is not seen to belong to the essence of marriage; see Bonaventure, *Breviloquium* 6.13. This also solves the problem that the Pauline view creates in regard to the tradition concerning Mary's perpetual virginity. If one sees intercourse as the essence of marriage, doubt is cast upon Mary and Joseph's union. Cf. Aquinas, *In Sententiarum (Commentary on the Sentences)* 4.30.2.1–3; Bonaventure, *In Sententiarum (Commentary on the Sentences)* 4.27.2.1.

71. Thus the present code continues to maintain that for a Christian marriage to be valid and indissoluble, it must be *ratum et consummatum* (ratified and consummated; can. 1061).

similar to that in which liturgy symbolizes and enacts the communion between God and his people through gesture and ritual. Though in some sense a very private act, as liturgical, sexual intimacy also completes and signifies the relation of the couple as "one flesh" and is an enactment and recollection of their public commitment within the community of faith.[72]

Pope John Paul II has aptly described this total self-donation and fidelity communicated by sexual intimacy within the marriage covenant as a "language of the body."[73] Just as one can communicate through bodily gestures as well as through words, in sexual union a married couple "speak" a language on the basis of their masculinity and femininity. That which is communicated in this somatic dialogue is both a word of fidelity and of total self-giving. Fidelity because a couple gives themselves to one another in this way and to no other. Total self-donation because intercourse enacts in bodily form the unconditional promise and acceptance articulated by the couple in their wedding vows.

In this sense marital sex is genuinely sacramental—that is, it is integral to the sacrament itself as the completion and recollection of the consent that causes it. This is true not only of the first time a marriage is consummated—as a narrow reading of canon law might suggest—but of all of the conjugal acts that make up the sexual communion of a couple. These too recall and in fact make present the grace that a couple's consent conferred on them. They thus participate in the marriage bond that unites a man and woman as "one flesh" over the whole of their lives.

Such observations suggest a fundamental analogy between the offering of self to God in the act of worship and the sexual self-giving of spouses to one another. Both are liturgical actions that recall and symbolize a covenant relation through a bodily gesture of self-donation. They are embodied gestures meant to symbolize and deepen commun-

72. It is in this sense that we can understand the public and juridical standing of a marriage that is *ratum et consummatum*. Cf. Karl Lehmann, "The Sacramentality of Christian Marriage: The Bond between Baptism, Faith and Marriage," in *Contemporary Perspectives*, 91–115, esp. 112–13; and, in the same volume, Gustav Martelet, "Sixteen Christological Theses on the Sacrament of Marriage," 275–83, esp. 281–82.

73. See his weekly general audiences of January 5, 12, 19, and 26, 1983, in *Theology of the Body*, 354–65.

ion. Both are encounters of love that are basic to establishing the I-Thou relation that underlies community—whether this be the community between God and humanity in the covenant or that between male and female in marriage. An awareness of this parallel can be discerned within some of the prayers found in the Church's liturgical tradition, such as the ancient formula for the blessing of the nuptial chamber that names it as the place of the "worthy celebration" of marriage.[74] It is equally evident in the late medieval formula for the bridegroom's gift of the ring to his bride: "With this ring I thee wed and this gold and silver I thee give; and with my body I thee worship, and with all my worldly chattel I thee honor."[75]

The Second Vatican Council's Pastoral Constitution on the Church *Gaudium et spes* has been widely hailed for its recovery of the biblical language of covenant to describe marriage. According to the Second Vatican Council, marriage is "an intimate partnership of . . . life and love . . . rooted in the conjugal covenant of irrevocable personal consent" which comes into being through "that human act whereby spouses mutually bestow and accept one another."[76] One important result of this recovery is the opportunity it affords to once again situate not only marriage but sexuality within a biblical framework.

This chapter has argued that, in light of both the biblical witness and aspects of the Church's liturgical and sacramental tradition, sex can be understood as an activity that seals the covenant relationship between man and woman in marriage. As such, it has an anamnetic quality

74. The citation is from the Spanish, *Liber ordinum,* in Mark Searle and Kenneth W. Stevenson, eds., *Documents of the Marriage Liturgy* (Collegeville, Minn.: Liturgical Press, 1992), 122.

75. *The Sarum Missal,* in Searle and Stevenson, *Documents,* 167. The text here is somewhat modernized from the Old English spelling. The Sarum rite originated in the diocese of Salisbury in the thirteenth century. From there it spread to other English dioceses and became the preferred rite of the English churches both before and after the Reformation, finding its way into both English versions of the Roman rite and the Book of Common Prayer. On the rather tumultuous history of this particular form in the Anglican communion, see Paul Elmen, "On Worshipping the Bride," *Anglican Theological Review* 68 (1986): 241–49. For a contemporary Catholic consideration of this view, see German Martinez, "Marriage as Worship: A Theological Analogy," *Worship* 62 (1988): 332–53.

76. *GS,* 48. The citation is from *The Documents of Vatican II,* 250. On the significance of this language, see Theodore Mackin, *The Marital Sacrament: Marriage in the Catholic Church* (New York: Paulist Press, 1989), 539–44.

in that it is a recollection and enactment of what the couple promise in their vows to one another. There is a fruitful convergence here between the biblical insistence on the covenant as a personal oath and contemporary personalist descriptions of sex as embodied self-giving. This convergence brings into view the analogy between worship and sex as parallel forms of self-donation that seal a covenant relationship.

That such analogous relations exist is unsurprising given the relational quality of the human person. To be in relation to God and to be in relation to other human beings is fundamental to human existence. The witness of the biblical tradition suggests that the primordial form of human relationality is the partnership of women and men in marriage. It is for this reason that the intimacy at the heart of this relation can symbolize and even mediate something of the love of God made available to humanity in the death and resurrection of Christ. It is this same self-giving love that husband and wife both promise and enact bodily in their sexual relationship.

This understanding of sex as a covenantal and indeed sacramental reality can serve as a foundation for the development of a more cogent and compelling vision of sexuality for contemporary Christians. Yet the preceding treatment also raises further questions. What kind of moral qualities does this vision require persons to have or acquire in order to live it? What other important ideas from Scripture and the Church's theological tradition can be used to further refine and concretize this account of sex as covenantal? What specific personal and cultural practices are necessary to foster genuine excellence in realizing this vision? Such questions will be taken up in succeeding chapters.

CHAPTER 3

Kingdom, Discipleship, Character

While the idea of covenant is integral to the development of a vision of sexuality grounded in the teaching of Scripture and the Church's liturgical tradition, there are other important biblical themes that should also be consulted in this effort. This chapter will focus on some of the most important of these: Jesus' preaching of the Kingdom of God, the invitation to discipleship, the teaching of the Sermon on the Mount, particularly the Beatitudes, and New Testament descriptions of Christian character. Some implications of the interplay of these various themes will then be considered in the form of a contemporary sketch of a spirituality of sexuality within marriage.

Even though they do not afford a systematic account of morality or a comprehensive sexual ethic, these varied strands of New Testament teaching can supplement and concretize the paradigm traced in the previous chapter. It should be noted that there are other texts and themes which could be added to this picture, some of which will be noted in passing.[1] But to attempt to offer a comprehensive account of biblical teaching about sexuality in both its diversity and its unity is beyond the scope of this work.

I. Conversion and Discipleship

On one level the bulk of the New Testament does little to alter the covenantal pattern for understanding marriage and sexuality seen in the Old Testament. Both St. Paul and the Evangelists offer little explicit teaching on these subjects, and when they do, they often simply affirm Old Testament teaching (e.g., the exclusions of certain kinds of con-

---

1. Still others will be treated in upcoming chapters.

duct such as fornication or adultery). In this way, it is apparent that the Old Testament teaching creates a framework that is largely presupposed.[2]

Yet, on another level, everything is changed by the announcement of the arrival of the Kingdom of God present in the person of Jesus: "This is the time of fulfillment. The Kingdom of God is at hand. Repent and believe in the gospel" (Mk 1:15). This summary statement of Jesus' early preaching brings with it radical moral demands—even in the area of sexuality.[3] The call to repentance (*metanoia*) is a call to change both one's thinking and one's behavior and is thus aimed at the whole person.[4] Ironically, it was those whose behavior excluded them from the mainstream of society and religion in Jesus' day—tax collectors, prostitutes, and other public "sinners"—who were the most responsive to this call. This is in keeping with Jesus' novel inclusion of others marginalized by their gender (i.e., women), socioeconomic status (i.e., the poor), or ethnic background (e.g., Samaritans) in his ministry of teaching and healing.[5]

The call for radical moral change becomes even more intense in the call to follow Jesus as a disciple. "To be a disciple" in biblical thought meant more than entering into a teacher-student relationship. It was even more encompassing than the relationship between a master and an apprentice in a craft, which would involve a long process of study, imi-

2. On the continuity between Old Testament and New Testament teaching regarding family, see John W. Miller, *Biblical Faith and Fathering: Why We Call God Father* (New York: Paulist Press, 1989), 88–100. Cf. Raymond Collins, *Christian Morality: Biblical Foundations* (South Bend, Ind.: University of Notre Dame Press, 1986), 183.

3. See Ronald Lawler, O.F.M., Cap., Joseph Boyle, and William E. May, *Catholic Sexual Ethics: A Summary Explanation and Defense. Updated* (Huntington, Ind.: Our Sunday Visitor Press, 1996), 24.

4. On the meaning of *metanoia* as a summons to the whole person in biblical tradition, see Wolfgang Schrage, *The Ethics of the New Testament*, trans. David E. Green (Philadelphia: Fortress Press, 1988), 40–46. On this idea in Scripture and the Church's tradition, see David Bohr, *Catholic Moral Tradition*, 104–20. For an analysis of the meaning of "the whole person" from the perspective of Bernard Lonergan's theology and developmental psychology, see Bohr, *Catholic Moral Tradition*, 101–9; and Walter Conn, *Christian Conversion: A Developmental Interpretation of Autonomy and Surrender* (Mahwah, N.J.: Paulist Press, 1986).

5. On this "praxis of inclusion" in the New Testament, see Lisa Sowle Cahill, *Sex, Gender, and Christian Ethics*, 124–26, 150–52.

tation, emulation, and ultimately the acquisition of excellence on the part of the apprentice.[6] Discipleship was more demanding in that it involved existential commitment of oneself to the authority of another as a teacher of truth or God's word.

In the Old Testament, discipleship usually involved the commitment of oneself to a particular sage or prophet.[7] This could be a one-to-one relationship as in the case of Elisha and Elijah (see 1 Kgs 19:19ff.). Or it could involve a circle or group who had attached themselves to one specific figure as in the case of the circle that surrounded Isaiah (see Is 8:16). In either case, the commitment of the disciple was based on his or her conviction that the prophet had a revelation or word from God.

In the New Testament, the concept of discipleship is focused on those who acknowledge Jesus as master and Lord. Originally, the term primarily described the twelve (see Mt 10:1). Later, it was also applied to the seventy(-two) sent out by Jesus to further his mission (see Lk 10:1) and ultimately it was used to designate all believers (cf. Acts 6:1, 9:10–26). Taken together, the portraits offered by the New Testament Evangelists present Christian discipleship as having certain characteristics. First, a disciple is one who is personally called by Jesus (e.g., Mk 1:17–20; Jn 1:38–50) and ultimately by the Father who gives disciples to his Son (cf. Jn 6:39, 10:29, 17:6, 12). Especially as presented by Mark, this call is not based on aptitude or ability.[8] Second, a disciple is one who is personally and unconditionally attached to Jesus. A disciple must sever all ties with his or her old life in order to imitate him in his conduct, and listen to and accept his word (cf. Mk 8:34ff., 10:21; Jn 12:26).[9] Third, disciples are those who share in Jesus' suffering (see Mk 8:34 and par.)

6. This, of course, was Aristotle's model for the acquisition of virtue.

7. The following overview of discipleship in the Old and New Testaments is indebted to the fine treatment of André Feuillet, P.S.S., "Disciple," in *Dictionary of Biblical Theology*, 2nd ed., ed. Xavier Léon-Dufour (New York: Seabury Press, 1973), 125–26. See also the overview provided by Schrage, *Ethics of the New Testament*, 46–52.

8. On this point, see Luke Timothy Johnson, *The Writings of the New Testament: An Interpretation* (Philadelphia: Fortress Press, 1986), 155–58, 161–64; and Richard Hays, *The Moral Vision of the New Testament: A Contemporary Introduction to New Testament Ethics* (San Francisco: Harper San Francisco, 1996), 75–77.

9. Feuillet ("Discipline," 126) observes that unlike other Jewish teachers, Jesus' disciples could not break away and teach on their own because attachment was not simply to the teaching, but to the person of Jesus. Cf. Schrage, *Ethics of the New Testament*, 48.

in order to share in his glory (cf. Mt 19:28ff.; Lk 22:28ff.; Jn 14:3). Even in the absence of persecution there is always a cost to be paid for genuine discipleship.[10]

What are the moral implications of this announcement of the inbreaking of God's Kingdom and the invitation to discipleship in the area of sexuality and marriage? On the one hand, Jesus' message brings with it a radicalization of certain Old Testament teachings. Thus, the Old Testament prohibition of adultery or coveting the spouse of another, enshrined in the Decalogue, is made a matter not simply of external behavior but of the dispositions and attitudes of one's heart.[11] The permanence of monogamous marriage implied in the covenantal paradigm of the Old Testament is emphatically stated in Jesus' radical assertion of the unbreakable character of marriage. Multiple New Testament traditions give a consistent, if complicated, picture of Jesus' repudiation of the permission to divorce in Deuteronomy (cf. 1 Cor 7:10–11; Mk 10:1–12 ; Mt 5:32, 19:1–12; Lk 16:18).[12]

Yet there are still more radical demands imposed upon the followers of Jesus. Even family ties, which in the Old Testament were understood to be critical to one's socioeconomic well-being as well as to be religiously significant because covenantal, are contextualized by Jesus' call to follow him. It is impossible to prefer parents, siblings, or spouse to Jesus and still be his follower (cf. Lk 9:59–62, 14:26–27; Mt 8:21–22). Indeed, Jesus' followers are themselves a kind of spiritual family that transcends mere blood relationships (cf. Mk 3:13–35; Lk 8:19–21). The meaning of such sayings becomes more clear when it is understood that they were recorded in a context when being a Christian might well mean repudiation by one's family and one's people (see Jn 9:22). This teaching makes clear the priority of God's covenant with humanity reestablished in Jesus over all human covenants, however sacred—even that of marriage.

The radical nature of Jesus' summons is made even more clear in the

10. Richard Gula, S.S., observes that this suffering can take the form of renunciation of wordly power for the power of love; see *Reason Informed by Faith*, 191–96.

11. Some examples will be considered below.

12. For an overview of these texts and some of the literature that surrounds them, see Hays, *Moral Vision of the New Testament*, 347–61; and Raymond Collins, *Divorce in the New Testament*, Good News Studies 38 (Collegeville, Minn.: Liturgical Press, 1992).

call given to some to renounce sex and marriage altogether in order to follow him more closely. Diverse New Testament traditions make it clear that this practice, modeled on the witness of John the Baptist and Jesus himself, was highly regarded in early Christian communities (cf. Mt 19:12; 1 Cor 7:7–9, 32–35). In a world dominated by concern to reproduce offspring for one's city or nation, the practice of sexual renunciation was itself a dramatic proclamation of the gospel message. To deliberately step outside the seemingly endless cycle of reproduction, birth, growth, sickness, decay, and death was an announcement writ in bodies and behavior that in Jesus, time as it had been previously known had come to an end and a new era of immortality had broken into human existence.[13]

II. Kingdom, Covenant, Beatitude

If the announcement of the arrival of the "Kingdom of God" in his own person was a central theme in Jesus' preaching, this raises the question "What does this term mean?" As used in the synoptic Gospels, "the Kingdom of God" denotes the time of the fulfillment of God's promises to his people. This mysterious reality, announced by Jesus' miracles and exorcisms, demands a decision to be converted and live as a disciple. It is this decision and the gift of faith that accompanies it that makes it possible to understand the paradoxical nature of the Kingdom and its growth in the world.[14]

Key among God's promises to his people realized in Jesus is the promise of a new covenant. According to prophetic teaching, this covenant would be different from the multiple covenants between God and humanity recorded in the Old Testament that were continually broken by human sin. This new covenant would be far more interior than its predecessors. It would be written on the very hearts of the people, giving them a direct and immediate knowledge of God (see Jer 31:31–34)

13. On the early Christian practice of sexual renunciation as a form of proclamation, see the generally excellent treatment provided by Brown, *Body and Society*.

14. On Mark's understanding of the Kingdom of God, see Hayes, *Moral Vision of the New Testament*, 85, 87–89. For an overview of the Kingdom in New Testament thought, see Raymond Deville, P.S.S., and Pierre Grelot, "Kingdom," in *Dictionary of Biblical Theology*, 292–95.

or creating an entirely new heart and spirit within them, forgiving their sins and rendering them capable of obedience (see Ezek 36:25–32).[15]

It is the concern of a number of New Testament authors and traditions to show that this promise of a new covenant is fulfilled in Jesus. Paul argues strongly that the cross itself is the enactment of a covenant oath in Jesus' being "cursed" (see Gal 3:13) or even "becoming sin" (see 2 Cor 5:21) for us. In this he fulfills God's unilateral promise of faithfulness intimated in his use of self-imprecating covenant symbols in the Old Testament—whether the "bow" of God's wrath aimed heavenward rather than toward the earth following the flood (see Gn 9: 13–17) or his symbolic passage between the bodies of the slain animals in his pact with Abram (cf. Gn 15:9–10, 17). The sign that recalls and makes present Jesus' offering of himself on the cross is the new covenant meal of the Eucharist. In Matthew's account of the Last Supper, Jesus calls the eucharistic cup "the blood of the covenant" (Mt 26:28a). In Luke's version, he is more explicit, stating "this cup *is* the new covenant in my blood which will be shed for you" (Lk 22:20c–d).[16] The Eucharist is an anamnesis of the new covenant oath made in the cross. As such, it is analogous to the role of a couple's sexual communion in recalling and making present their covenant oath to one another described in the previous chapter.

The new covenant established in Jesus thus builds upon and deepens the nuptial character of the covenant between Yahweh and his people in the Old Testament. It is therefore not surprising to find nuptial imagery throughout the New Testament. Thus, in a number of texts Jesus refers to himself as the "bridegroom"—whether in controversies with his opponents (see Mk 2:18–22 and par.) or in parables concerning the need for preparedness for his final return (see Mt 25:1–13). The same image is applied to Jesus by John the Baptist who describes himself as the "best man" whose role must decrease (see Jn 3:29–30). Other New Testament texts use the image of a wedding banquet in order to envision the fulfillment of the Kingdom of God in the eschaton (cf. Mt 22:1–14; Lk 12:35–38) or the wedding feast of the Lamb (cf. Rev 19:7, 19:9, 21:9).

15. This focus on the heart is characteristic of New Testament and patristic moral teaching, including the area of sexuality.

16. Emphasis added.

Such imagery transfers to Jesus the role of Yahweh as bridegroom in God's covenant relation with his people, pointing to the divine origin of his redemptive mission.[17]

The New Testament uses still other covenant imagery to present Jesus as the fulfillment of what was promised and foreshadowed in the Old Testament. While the first creation account presents God creating through his word, various New Testament traditions proclaim Christ to be the Word through whom the Father created all things (cf. Jn 1:1–4; Col 1:15; Heb 1:1–4). Because he is the one who overcomes humanity's bondage to sin and the forces of evil, Jesus is the gō'el (kinsman redeemer) par excellence (cf. Rom 3:24; Eph 1:7; Col 1:14; Ti 2:14; Heb 9:12, 9:15; 1 Pt 2:18; Rev 14:3–4). As firstborn Son of God, Jesus shares his divine inheritance with us by making us sons and daughters of God (cf. Jn 1:12; Rom 8:14–17; Gal 4:5; Heb 2:10; 1 Jn 3:1–2). He founds a new Israel by reconstituting the Twelve Tribes through his Apostles and a new Sanhedrin in his seventy Disciples sent out to proclaim the Kingdom.[18] This new covenant people formed out of many nations (cf. Gn 12:3) is also his bride, the Church, for whom he gave his life (see Eph 5:21–33).

Among these many images that present Jesus as the fulfillment of God's covenant promises to his people in the Old Testament is that of Jesus as a prophet like Moses or as the new Moses who reveals and makes possible the radical demands of God's will. While reflected in a numerous New Testament traditions,[19] this parallelism between Jesus and Moses is perhaps most prominent in Matthew.[20] The Evangelist weaves some of this imagery into the masterpiece of his moral teaching:

17. On the significance of this biblical theme for a theology of the Incarnation, see Peter J. Elliott, *What God Has Joined: The Sacramentality of Marriage* (New York: Alba House, 1990), 16–38.

18. While this imagery of the Church as the New Israel is found in many places in the New Testament, it is especially emphasized in Luke and Acts. See William Kurz, S.J., *The Acts of the Apostles*, Collegeville Bible Commentary 5 (Collegeville, Minn.: Liturgical Press, 1983); cf. Johnson, *Writings of the New Testament*, 217–19, 223–27.

19. On the use of this symbolism in Luke and Acts, see Johnson, *Writings of the New Testament*, 208–10. For an overview of this parallelism throughout the New Testament, see René Motte, O.M.I., and Michel Join-Lambert, "Moses," in *Dictionary of Biblical Theology*, 368–70.

20. Johnson argues that for Matthew, Jesus is not merely presented in Mosaic terms,

the Sermon on the Mount. As Moses received God's revelation of himself in the Decalogue on a mountain, so Jesus offers his own restatement of some of this same teaching on a mountain (see Mt 5:1a).[21]

But the Sermon on the Mount does far more than restate and deepen the teaching of the Decalogue. The sermon is addressed to Jesus' disciples (see Mt 5:1b–2), inserting its teaching into the larger New Testament motif of discipleship.[22] Furthermore, the preamble and touchstone of the Sermon is not found in laws, but in the Beatitudes (Mt 5:3–12). These statements are not commands given in the imperative mood, but descriptive statements offered in the indicative. As such, they describe the qualities of Jesus himself, offering a kind of "self-portrait" of him and hence of those called to be conformed to him in discipleship.[23] These qualities themselves constitute the blessedness or happiness that is the wellspring and heart of Christian morality.

When Jesus' teaching in the Sermon does turn to specific laws in a series of antitheses (Mt 5:21–48), these laws are radicalized and, in some cases, overturned. Thus Jesus abrogates the teaching of Deuteronomy 24:1–4 which allowed divorce—except in cases of *porneia*—going so far as to describe remarriage as adultery (Mt 5:31–32).[24] Later in the Gospel, this same teaching is repeated in an appeal to God's original intention for marriage disclosed in Genesis which had been obscured by hard-heartedness (see Mt 19:3–12).[25] Other antitheses make it even more

---

but is depicted as the teacher who fulfills and personifies the Torah; see *Writings of the New Testament*, 185–90.

21. On the Mosaic parallels in the Sermon, see Raymond Brown, S.S., *An Introduction to the New Testament* (New York: Doubleday, 1997), 178–79.

22. On the idea of the Sermon as teaching addressed to disciples, see Hays, *Moral Vision of the New Testament*, 321.

23. On the Beatitudes as descriptive of the content of discipleship, see Raymond Collins, "The Beatitudes: The Heart of Jesus' Preaching," *The Living Light* 33, no. 1 (1996): 70–81; and I. Chareire, "Les Béatitudes, espace de la vie théologale," *Lumen Vitae* 47, no. 234 (1997): 85–92. On the Beatitudes as a self-portrait of Jesus, see John Paul II, Encyclical Letter, *Veritatis splendor*, no. 16.

24. Wolfgang Shrage notes that the conflict that this creates between the norms of the Torah and the Decalogue would have been unthinkable to most of Jesus' Jewish audience; see *Ethics of the New Testament*, 96. On some of the possible renderings of *porneia*, see Hays, *Moral Vision of the New Testament*, 354–55; and Collins, *Divorce in the New Testament*, 199–205.

25. Jesus' appeal "to the beginning" to answer a fundamental question about marriage

clear that for Jesus morality is a matter of the heart. This is evident in the teaching on the Sixth Commandment: "You have heard that it was said, 'You shall not commit adultery.' But I say to you, everyone who looks at a woman with lust has already committed adultery with her in his heart" (Mt 5:27–28).[26] This location of morality in the heart is paralleled elsewhere in this section in the teaching on anger (Mt 5:21–26) and love of enemies (Mt 5:43–48) and in other New Testament texts that root specific vices, including sexual practices, in the heart as the cause of impurity (cf. Mk 7:21; Mt 15:19).

The Sermon thus offers a new basis for morality—related to, yet qualitatively different from, that of both the Old Testament and the ancient world. The Old Testament focus on law, even while located within the interpersonal context of the covenant between God and his people, often was colored by legalism and formalism as it was understood and lived in various historical settings. In Jesus' teaching in the Sermon, "he lays the foundations of a new morality, in fact re-lays anew the foundations of ethics as such, by making the moral value of an act depend only on the inner disposition of the heart."[27] This new primacy of the heart recalls the prophetic promises fulfilled in Jesus' establishment of the new covenant. The new heart and the Spirit (see Ezek 36:26) conferred by Jesus' death and Resurrection is the fulfillment of what Old Testament morality pointed toward in the Law, but was unable to deliver because of sin.

Likewise, while the notion of beatitude or happiness figured prominently in some ancient systems of ethics such as Aristotle's, this notion

---

and human sexuality serves as the warrant for John Paul II's catechesis on the opening chapters of Genesis in weekly general audiences given from Sept. 5, 1979, to March 26, 1980; see *Theology of the Body*, 25–102.

26. John Meier calls Jesus' teaching on the Sixth Commandment "a radicalizing which is interiorizing"; see *The Vision of Matthew: Christ, Church and Morality in the First Gospel*, Theological Inquiries (New York: Paulist Press, 1979), 246. Pope John Paul II uses this text as a springboard for a consideration of the struggle between the impulse to view others as things for one's own domination, enjoyment, and consumption (i.e., lust) and the choice to see others as persons with inalienable dignity who are worthy of respect and self-donation (i.e., love). See his general audiences of April 16, 1980, to December 10, 1980, in *Theology of the Body*, 103–88.

27. Rudolph Schnackenburg, *The Moral Teaching of the New Testament*, trans. J. Holland-Smith and W. J. O'Hara (New York: Seabury Press, 1979), 63.

was often understood as an abstract and intellectual contemplation of an impersonal good. The Sermon recasts this blessedness as characteristic of those who follow Christ as disciples and like him live in concrete historical situations of poverty, sorrow, and persecution. This beatitude is an interior wellspring that accompanies and sustains discipleship in such conditions as well as an eschatological promise of complete blessedness.[28]

Does the Sermon have practical import for actual moral life and praxis? It is true, as Servais Pinckaers notes, that the tendency of various groups over the last few centuries has been to dismiss it as a form of works righteousness, an unattainable ideal, or special counsels given only to a heroic few.[29] However, the Fathers of the Church and the great Scholastic doctors of the Middle Ages saw it as the distinctive text of the New Law over against the Ten Commandments and the Old Law.[30] St. Augustine, echoed by St. Thomas Aquinas, called it "the total formation of the Christian life."[31] As such, the Sermon was understood to be eminently practicable. The same might be said for Matthew himself, who saw it as a teaching that would enable the members of his community to live a kind of "righteousness [which] surpasses that of the scribes and Pharisees" (Mt 5:20b).

It is equally clear that the Evangelist saw this teaching to be relevant for an understanding of sexuality, as the inclusion of the sayings concerning adultery and divorce make clear. Therefore, sexuality too is addressed by Jesus' call to conversion and discipleship and potentially transformed by the new covenant established on the cross. The presence of the Bridegroom and his nuptial offering of himself makes it possible for his followers to have new hearts capable of love instead of lust and capable of behavior that reflects lifelong covenant fidelity.

---

28. On the role of beatitude in the eschaton, see Cessario, *Introduction to Moral Theology,* 34–35.

29. These are the views of Luther, modern commentators influenced by idealism, and post-Tridentine Catholics, respectively; see Pinckaers, *Sources of Christian Ethics,* 136–39.

30. See ibid., 134–35.

31. See Augustine, *Sermon on the Mount,* PL 34, 1231; Aquinas, *Summa Theologiae,* III, q. 108, a. 3. The translation is that of Ashley, *Living the Truth,* 32.

III. The Character of a Disciple

Like the Old Testament, the New Testament does not offer a systematic account of moral character. In fact, it hardly uses the term virtue (*aretē*) at all with the exception of a few isolated texts (e.g., Phil 4:8; 2 Pt 1:3, 5). Therefore, it seems an unlikely place to turn to find resources to develop an account of the moral excellences entailed in living as a disciple of Christ. Yet a closer examination of New Testament traditions reveals that in fact they offer numerous considerations that are directly relevant to such an account. These considerations are given in a variety of sources, images, and literary forms.

It should be noted at the outset that, unlike much modern thought, both Catholic and Protestant, biblical authors did not make a sharp distinction between faith and morality. Hence the very presuppositions and basic convictions of Christian faith would have enormous relevance for the behavior of believers. Benjamin Farley lists some of these in a recent book: the fundamental Christian conviction that God has become incarnate in Christ (most explicit in John; see Jn 1:1–3, 14); the unmerited gift of Christ's reconciliation of the world to God; the establishment of a new creation in Christ (see 2 Cor 5:17–18); the concomitant belief that human life is ordered to and belongs to the God who created and redeemed it (see 1 Cor 6:19–20); Christ's conquest of death, which frees believers to live for eternity in the present; and the fact that Christian life is lived within the community of the Church.[32]

These foundational Christian beliefs that structure the gospel message are perceived and lived through powers (virtues) given by God which are rooted in the very being of the believer as a new creation.[33] The first of these "theological virtues" is faith, which both gives the light to perceive the realities of Christian faith and the power to believe in and live them.[34] For Paul, it is faith that both justifies the sinner and characterizes his or her subsequent life as a child of God in this world.

32. See Benjamin Farley, *In Praise of Virtue: An Exploration of the Biblical Virtues in a Christian Context* (Grand Rapids, Mich.: William B. Eerdmans, 1995), 96–101.

33. For a biblical and theological overview of the theological virtues as the content of Christian discipleship, see Bohr, *Catholic Moral Tradition*, 121–36.

34. For an overview of faith in biblical thought, see Ashley, *Living the Truth*, 44–51.

The second of these virtues is hope, which enlivens and directs faith toward its final realization. This power is crucial for those who live in a world still marred by evil and sin, while waiting for the final completion of Christ's victory over them.[35] The third and most important of these virtues is love. Love is both the beginning and the end of faith and hope. It is the "love of God . . . poured out in our hearts through the Holy Spirit that has been given to us" (Rom 5:5b) that awakens and empowers faith in God's love for sinful humanity embodied in the cross (cf. Rom 5:8; 1 Jn 4:10). Love is also the end of faith insofar as it will remain even when we "know as we are known" and the need for faith and hope have passed (see 1 Cor 13:12).[36]

But love is equally central to the life and behavior of a Christian in this world. This love takes two forms: to love God with one's whole being and to love one's neighbor as oneself (see Mk 12:28–34 and par.).[37] To love God and neighbor is the fulfillment of the whole of the Old Testament Law. It is thus the primary vocation of every disciple of Jesus. Insofar as it is the Holy Spirit who is "the love of God" poured into the heart of a believer, the call to love is realized by yielding to the Spirit's transforming work. Indeed, for Paul the whole of the Christian life can be described under the heading "life in the Spirit" (see Rom 8:2–4).

There are still other qualities or dispositions necessary to answer Jesus' call to follow him.[38] To love God with one's whole heart and being necessitates single-heartedness, and perseverance in prayer (see Lk 10:25–11:13). To heed the summons to repent and be converted calls for humility. Listening to Jesus' word in order to be formed as a disciple requires docility. To imitate Jesus in his mercy toward those broken by sin presupposes compassion. Breaking off all ties with one's past life and fol-

35. For a good summary of hope in biblical perspective, see Ashley, *Living the Truth*, 151–59.

36. For an overview of love in New Testament thought, see Ashley, *Living the Truth*, 435–43. Cf. Farley, *Praise of Virtue*, 130–32.

37. On the inseparability of these two aspects of the "great commandment" in the teaching of Jesus, see Schnackenburg, *Moral Teaching of the New Testament*, 90–109. While admitting that love is fundamental to moral living as described by numerous New Testament traditions, Hays cautions against using it as a unifying theme for New Testament ethics as a whole; see *Moral Vision of the New Testament*, 200–203.

38. For a more complete overview of the "virtues" described by the Gospels, see Farley, *Praise of Virtue*, 101–27.

lowing Jesus even in the face of persecution entails courage, endurance, and fidelity (see Mt 10:16–39). To wait for the full manifestation of the Kingdom in a world marred by evil calls for patience, diligence, and prudence, as numerous parables make clear (e.g., Mt 25:1–30). Living in the Body of Christ requires mutual forgiveness, patience, and, above all, love (cf. 1 Cor 12–14; Mt 18:15–35). While many of these virtues have parallels in the moral teaching of the ancient world, as Stanley Hauerwas and Charles Pinches observe, their insertion into the paradigm of Christian discipleship often invests them with new meaning.[39]

New Testament authors use a variety of other images to capture the challenge of growth as a follower of Jesus, many of which reflect the tension between good and evil that the later tradition will describe in terms of virtue and vice. Some texts draw on a motif common in the wisdom literature of the Old Testament in speaking of the "two ways," one that leads to life, the other to destruction (see Mt 7:13–14).[40] The practice of listing specific vices is used not only in the Gospels, as noted above, but also in the Pauline literature as a means of identifying sins that break down the Christian community and may exclude those who commit them from the Kingdom of God (cf. 1 Cor 6:9–10; Gal 5:19–21; Rom 1:24–32, 13:13; Col 3: 8–10). Included in such lists are sexual behaviors such as adultery, fornication, prostitution, and homosexual practices. In contrast to these lists of vices are lists that exemplify characteristics of life in Christ and are vital to life in community, including qualities such as compassion, kindness, humility, gentleness, patience, forgiveness, love, and gratitude (see Col 3:12–17). In keeping with his understanding of the Christian life as life in the Spirit, Paul will sometimes cast these opposed lists as "works of the flesh" versus the "fruits of the Spirit."[41] Thus in his Letter to the Galatians he writes:

39. In particular they offer insightful contrasts between pagan and Christian conceptions of prudence and courage. See their *Christians among the Virtues: Theological Conversations with Ancient and Modern Ethics* (South Bend, Ind.: University of Notre Dame Press, 1997), 89–109, 149–65.

40. For an overview of this motif in the Old Testament and New Testament, see André Darrieutort, "Way," in *Dictionary of Biblical Theology*, 647–48; and S. V. McCasland, "The Way," *Journal of Biblical Literature* 77 (1957): 220–30.

41. On this use of the the term "flesh" (*sarx*) as the ethical opposite of living in the Spirit in Paul, see Frank Matera, *New Testament Ethics: The Legacies of Jesus and Paul* (Louisville, Ky.: Westminster John Knox Press, 1996), 170–72.

Now the works of the flesh are obvious: immorality, impurity, licentiousness, idolatry, sorcery, hatreds, rivalry, jealousy, outbursts of fury, acts of selfishness, dissensions, factions, occasions of envy, drinking bouts, orgies, and the like. I warn you, as I warned you before, that those who do such things will not inherit the kingdom of God. In contrast, the fruit of the Spirit is love, joy, peace, patience, kindness, generosity, faithfulness, gentleness, self-control. Against such there is no law. Now those who belong to Christ have crucified their flesh with its passions and desires. If we live in the Spirit let us also follow the Spirit. (Gal 5:19–25)

Biblical traditions will also speak directly of what classical Greek thought designated the cardinal (hinge) virtues of prudence, justice, temperance, and fortitude (cf. Wis 8:7; 2 Pt 1:5–7).[42]

These varied motifs indicate that, although the New Testament does not offer a fully developed virtue ethic, it is profoundly concerned with both the transformation of the believer's interior desires, values, and attitudes and the exterior behavior that flows from this change. In short, its teaching engages the character of the Christian disciple, and this concern embraces every area of life and conduct. As baptized, Christians are called to put off the attitudes and practices characteristic of their old lives of sin and "put on Christ" (cf. Gal 3:27; Eph 4:24; Col 3:12f) and to have their minds renewed (cf. Rom 12:2; Eph 4:17–24). This outworking of baptism is not limited to, but certainly includes, the often vexing area of sexuality.

IV. Sex and Character

The varied New Testament themes surveyed above form a kind of mosaic in which to locate a Christian understanding of sexuality that supplements and concretizes the covenantal paradigm considered in the previous chapter.

Jesus' teaching in the Sermon on the Mount, echoed in Gospel vice lists, make it clear that for a disciple morality is first a matter of the heart. The fidelity demanded by the new covenant entails far more than avoiding behaviors such as adultery or fornication; it requires a heart free from the lust that is at the root of such acts. Yet to so remake a sin-

---

42. For an overview of this usage in biblical thought, see Ashley, *Living the Truth*, 35–38.

ful human heart is beyond the ability of the most disciplined ethical program. Such a transformation is rather the gift of the new covenant established in the cross, which confers a "new heart and spirit" on the followers of the crucified one.[43]

But as Gilbert Meilaender notes, the justification of humanity by Christ is not only a gift, but also a task. Grace is not only pardon for sin, it is also the power to live differently.[44] The task of the disciple is to make the gift of redemption real and efficacious in attitudes, consciously chosen moral values, and behavior. Set free from the drives of self-assertion and self-preservation, the Christian is able to begin to live in gratitude to God and service to others. Empowered by the indwelling Holy Spirit, the believer can embark on his or her true vocation, which is love. Self-donation rather than domination can be the aim of his or her relationships. Yet it takes time, training, and concrete praxis to learn how to love well, how to desire things that are genuinely excellent. This training is the role of moral education—to channel the transformation begun in the heart into praxis, which in turn reinforces and deepens this change. Such education takes place within the practices and life of the Christian community.

Love requires concretization. At least in the horizon of biblical teaching, it is impossible to love someone in the abstract or to love a mere ideal. And the means by which we love one another, or indeed carry on any relationship, is through the body.[45] The Old Testament repudiates dualism in upholding the dignity of the body and its creation by God. For New Testament authors, the body redeemed by Christ belongs to God in a unique way and has an eternal destiny in the resurrection (see 1 Cor 15). The body is therefore the locus for the disciple's vocation to love God and neighbor.

The fact that the body belongs to God and is the place where love is enfleshed in deeds has immediate relevance for sexuality. For example, in 1 Corinthians 6:12–20, Paul deals with the issue of members of the com-

43. On the presence of lust within the human heart as an invitation to the redemption given by Christ, see Pope John Paul II's weekly general audiences of October 22 and 29, 1980, in *Theology of the Body*, 162–68.

44. See Gilbert Meilaender, *Faith and Faithfulness: Basic Themes in Christian Ethics* (South Bend, Ind.: University of Notre Dame Press, 1991), 74–84.

45. See Xavier Léon-Dufour, "Body," in *Dictionary of Biblical Theology*, 53–55.

munity visiting prostitutes.[46] Against those who would excuse such behavior, perhaps on the basis of his own teaching on freedom from law,
Paul argues against this practice on the basis of the body's eternal destiny (6:14), the bodily basis of incorporation into the Church (6:15), the
holiness of sex as a covenant ratifying gesture (6:16—citing Gn 2:24),
and the body's dignity as a temple of the Holy Spirit (6:19). Sexual behavior is a key component of the moral life and growth of the Christian. And, as Raymond Collins observes, sexual sin is uniquely detri-
mental to this life insofar as it offends the bodily basis of incorporation
into the body of Christ and the indwelling presence of the Holy Spirit.[47] Life in the Spirit is enfleshed in the body and indeed in sexuality.

Christian celibacy is perhaps the most direct witness of the fact that
the body and sexuality belong directly to God. It is also a unique expression of the vocation to love. The celibate is most able to devote
him- or herself directly to God in both body and spirit (see 1 Cor
7:32–35). As such, it is a nuptial sign of the eschatological intimacy that
all of the redeemed will enjoy with God when there is "neither marry-
ing nor giving in marriage" (see Lk 20:27–39).

Yet the same reality is true of Christians who marry "in the Lord"
(see 1 Cor 7:39)—their bodies, including sexuality, belong first to God.
Yet the bodies of married Christians also belong to one another as Paul
teaches in 1 Corinthians 7:3–5, pointing toward a unique equality between men and women in the ancient world—at least in the area of
sex.[48] Further, the unconditional nature of the marriage oath cannot be
broken or dissolved—except perhaps in the case of an incestuous marriage (Mt 5:32c, 19:9c) or a marriage between a Christian and an unbe-
liever who is unwilling to live peacefully with the believing spouse (see 1
Cor 7:12–15). Such a lifelong commitment demands patience, fidelity,
forgiveness, and, above all, love.

The relationship between spouses who give themselves faithfully and
exclusively to one another is also an image of the union of love between

46. Raymond Collins, however, argues that there is no indication in the text that
members of the community were engaged in this practice. He sees it as a standard topic
for sexual morality drawn from Hellenistic literature; see *Sexual Ethics and the New Testament:
Behavior and Belief* (New York: Crossroad, 2000), 113–14.

47. See Collins, *Christian Morality*, 198; cf. Collins, *Sexual Ethics and the New Testament*, 118.

48. Cf. Collins, *Sexual Ethics and the New Testament*, 186–87.

Christ and his body and bride the Church. Yet it is more than a reflection, it is also a sharing in this love—a *mystērion* (see Eph 5:32). It is Christ who joins spouses in the covenant of marriage and enables them to live faithfully for one another in body and heart. Likewise, it is Christ who calls and sustains some within the Church to devote themselves unreservedly to him in the practice of celibacy.

Marriage and consecrated virginity are two uniquely intense concretizations of the twofold commandment of love. They are two vocations where the transformation of the heart effected in baptism and sustained in the sacramental worship of the Church works itself out in the bodily gift of self.[49] For the Christian, the practices of both sexual expression and sexual renunciation are part of a pattern of life conformed to Christ. Yet imitation—following—is also an anticipatory participation in Christ's own beatitude—the overflowing joy of his communion with the Father in the Holy Spirit. As such it is sustained in the nuptial meal of the Eucharist in which the Bridegroom gives himself bodily to his bridal Church—the ultimate analogue of the "one flesh" unity of spouses effected by their mutual self-donation in sexual intimacy.[50] These observations, coupled with those of the previous chapter, can serve as the basis for an outline of a spirituality of sexuality that is at once biblical, eucharistic, and trinitarian.

V. Toward a Spirituality of Christian Sexuality

Frederick Parrella, among others, has noted the lack of distinctive models of spirituality for the married within the tradition.[51] Following

49. On marriage and celibacy as complementary vocations involving a total nuptial gift of self, see John Paul II's weekly general audience of April 14 and 28, 1982, in *Theology of the Body*, 276–78, 281–84.

50. Cf. Hans Urs von Balthasar, *The Glory of the Lord*, Vol. 7: *Theology: The New Covenant*, trans. Brian McNeil, C.R.V. (Edinburgh, U.K.: T. & T. Clark, 1989), 470–84; and Donald J. Keefe, S.J., *Covenantal Theology: The Eucharistic Order of History*, 2 vols. (Lanham, Md.: University Press of America, 1991), esp. 1:123–25, 316–83, 389–92, 495–515, and 2:9–25, 160–69, 173–75, 268–78, 282–84, 304–15.

51. See Frederick J. Parrella, "Towards a Spirituality of the Family," *Communio* 9 (1982): 127–41. Cf. Ladislas Örsy, S.J., "Married People: God's Chosen People," in *Christian Marriage Today*, ed. Klaus Demmer and Aldegonde Brenninkmeijer-Werhahn (Washington, D.C.: The Catholic University of America Press, 1997), 38–54, esp. 48–50.

the emergence of various forms of monasticism and the religious life, lay Christians—particularly the married—were often relegated to a kind of second-class citizenship within the Church. In some cases, the married were merely encouraged to avoid breaking the commandments, but offered little hope of achieving genuine holiness.[52] In other cases, various forms of monastic spirituality were "watered down" so as to make them practicable for the married.

The heart of the problem has often been precisely that of sexuality. The demands of a relationship centered on "the flesh," even if faithful and procreative, were seen as incompatible with genuine excellence in the spiritual life.[53] While the Church has condemned the most overt cosmological forms of dualism, its spiritual theology and practice has continued to struggle against more subtle forms that elevate the interior life by denigrating the body and sexuality.

In spite of the presence of contrary witnesses in the tradition and the affirmation of *Lumen gentium* that "everyone belonging to the hierarchy, or being cared for by it, is called to holiness,"[54] the question remains as to how to articulate a spirituality for the married that can embrace their sexual relationship. It is outside the scope of this book to attempt a complete answer to this important question. However, insofar as some sense of this spirituality is integral to a vision of sexuality formed by Christian faith and the practices necessary to implement it, the remainder of this section will sketch some ideas that could be used in this effort.

A place to begin in developing a spirituality for laypersons in general and the married in particular is in the incorporation into Christ and his offices effected by baptism. It is this baptismal reality that lays the foundation for a life of discipleship lived in faith, hope, and love over the

---

52. Cf. Mahoney, *Making of Moral Theology*, 29.

53. Cf. Parrella, "Spirituality of Family," 132.

54. Dogmatic Constitution on the Church, *Lumen gentium*, no. 39; the citation is from *The Documents of Vatican II*, 66. Regarding previous affirmations of the laity's call to holiness, Parrella mentions the teaching of the *Didache* and Clement of Alexandria (see "Spirituality of the Family," 131). Mention should also be made of many of the later homilies of John Chrysostom (see the excellent collection of excerpts in *On Marriage and Family Life*, ed. Catherine Roth [Crestwood, N.Y.: St. Vladimir's Seminary Press, 1986]) and the teaching of St. Francis de Sales in his *Introduction to the Devout Life*.

course of a Christian's life. In virtue of their baptism, Christian men and women share in the threefold office of Christ as priest, prophet, and king.[55] It is baptism that enables those who marry "in the Lord" (see 1 Cor 7) to confer the sacrament of marriage on one another in their mutual consent and thus found a family.[56] It is this same reality that establishes the couple and the family as "a specific revelation and realization of ecclesial communion" or a "domestic church."[57]

This teaching, as Parrella observes, means that families and their members are in a certain sense "sacraments" to one another by concretely embodying grace over the course of their lives and in very ordinary and day-to-day events.[58] The service that is Christian kingship is exercised not only in heroic acts performed by members of a family (e.g., a parent who gives his or her life to save a child) or even in significant sacrifices (e.g., a spouse who gives up his job for the other spouse's career), but also in the mundane daily tasks that make up the common life of a household: preparing food, washing dishes, caring for a sick child in the middle of the night, or carpooling. When these actions are done in love for others in the family, they constitute the "self-giving" that reflects and makes present Trinitarian love. The couple or family is made holy not just in hearing and speaking the word of God (the prophetic office) or in individual and communal prayer, but also in the "liturgy" of everyday life offered to God. This exercise of priesthood in every day life is symbolized in the very ordinariness of gifts offered in the Eucharist. The simple elements of bread and wine represent the day to day sustenance, joys, and sacrifices of life which are joined by the

55. Cf. Vatican II's Dogmatic Constitution on the Church, *Lumen gentium*, no. 10; and Pope John Paul II, Apostolic Exhortation, *Christifideles laici*, 49–51.

56. On the origin of the family in the consent of the couple, see Pope John Paul II, Letter to Families, *Gratissimam sane*, no. 7. For a more complete study of the meaning of "family" in recent Church teaching, see Donald Miller, O.F.M., "A Critical Evaluation and Application to Various Situations in the United States of the Official Roman Catholic Position on Family Life from Vatican II through *Christifideles laici*" (Ph.D. diss., The Catholic University of America, 1995).

57. Pope John Paul II, Apostolic Exhortation, *Familiaris consortio*, 21. The citation is from *The Role of the Christian Family in the Modern World*, trans. Vatican Polyglot Press (Boston: Daughters of St. Paul, 1981), 37. Cf. *Lumen gentium*, 11; *Catechism of the Catholic Church* (hereafter *CCC*), 2204.

58. See Parrella, "Spirituality of the Family," 139–41.

Holy Spirit to Christ's own offering of himself to the Father and returned as transformed into His body and blood.

Analogously, it might be said that while sexual union is but one small part of a couple's overall relationship, it "sacramentalizes" their self-gift lived out in a multitude of daily acts of service and love. It is a concretization and expression of the other forms of intimacy in their relationship: physical (but nongenital), emotional, relational, and spiritual. Furthermore, the couple's bodily union signifies and effects the union of their persons. They realize themselves precisely in the gift of themselves. They become more deeply an "I" in the bodily dialogue with the "Thou" who is their spouse. When this embodied dialogue results in the creation of new life—a third term whom the couple can address as a "We"—then the couple's communion presents a striking analogy of Trinitarian life.[59]

But this analogy can be taken even further. The previous chapter argued that both key biblical texts and the Church's sacramental and liturgical tradition support the idea that sex can be understood as a recollection and enactment of a couple's marriage promise to one another. As such, it can be said to be truly sacramental insofar as it mediates the grace of the marriage bond. It can also be understood to be analogous to the role of worship in being a bodily gesture of self-offering that is integral to a covenant relationship.

These observations provide the foundation for a much more complete and positive estimation of the role of sexual pleasure in conjugal communion than some aspects of the theological tradition have been willing to allow.[60] When sex is genuinely personal in the sense described above, the pleasure that accompanies it is a genuine perfection of this activity and a means to deepen the couple's communion with one another.[61] In this sense, it bears a certain analogous resemblance to the

---

59. See ibid., 137. Cf. John Paul II's weekly general audiences of March 5 and 12, 1980, in *Theology of the Body*, 77–83; his Apostolic Letter, *Mulieris dignitatem*, nos. 7–8; and his Letter to Families, *Gratissimam sane*, nos. 6–11.

60. On the sources of this pessimism concerning pleasure within the tradition, see Noonan, *Contraception*, 46–47, 53–54; and Gareth Moore, O.P., *The Body in Context: Sex and Catholicism* (London: SCM Press, 1992), 43–50.

61. The roots of this modern personalist approbation of pleasure lie in Aquinas's adaptation of the Aristotelian teleology of human action according to which pleasure is

role of mystical experience as an aid to the achievement of union with God. It should be added, however, that the mystical tradition as well as most wedding vows also show an awareness of the need for commitment and fidelity even in times of desolation when the "other" seems distant.

A common objection to such a view of sexual intimacy as a bodily self-gift that recalls a couple's wedding vows is that it creates an unrealistic and overly romantic view of sex far removed from the everyday experience of most couples. But to describe sex as liturgical and analogous to worship is not to suggest that every conjugal act will approximate mystical experience, any more than liturgical prayer always involves ecstasy. It simply means that spouses give themselves to each other as they are (joyful, anxious, tired, energetic, preoccupied, attentive, etc.) and in so doing symbolically enact their vows to one another. The "objective" meaning of the bodily language they speak may or may not be fully assimilated in the couple's "subjective" experience at any given moment.

Because both worship and conjugal love are forms of *personal* self-giving love, there is still a higher analogate to be considered. The self-emptying death of Christ reveals something of the love present from all eternity within the Godhead. It thus concretizes the New Testament teaching that God is *agapē* (see 1 Jn 4:8). Christian faith sees this love as uniquely actualized in the self-giving of the Divine Persons to one another within the communion of the Trinity. As noted above, the New Testament also uses the cross as the paradigm of love between Christian spouses who are "one flesh" (see Eph 5:21–33). Thus, the cross as an act of supreme self-gift illumines both Trinitarian and spousal self-donation. On the human level, this self-donation includes, and indeed is expressed in a special way by, sexual intimacy. On this basis it can be said

---

a natural accompaniment of all human action. Given this view, the pleasure of a good action can be considered morally good, while only the pleasure of evil actions is morally evil. See Aquinas, *In Sent.* 4.31.2.3; 4.49.3.4.3. It was this development that freed considerations of sexual pleasure from the long shadow cast upon it by the Augustinian doctrine of concupiscence and enabled an increasingly positive evaluation of it by later theology. On this development, see Noonan, *Contraception,* 292–95, 305–12, 321–30, 395, 491–504. See also Albert Plé, *Chastity and the Affective Life,* trans. Marie-Claude Thompson (New York: Herder & Herder, 1966), 76–111.

that, when fully personal, sexual communion in marriage serves as a created image of the transcendent and spiritual self-giving that is the basis of Trinitarian communion.[62]

Of course, such language is analogous. While one might find real analogies between worship and sex or human sexual communion and Trinitarian life, there is obvious discontinuity as well. The attempt to regard such language univocally could only produce a revivified fertility ritual in the case of the former or would crudely project human sexuality onto God, who transcends such distinctions, in the latter.

The consideration of the above New Testament themes and their implications serves to sharpen the understanding of sexual expression as a covenantal reality developed in the previous chapter. In particular, it brings into focus the centrality of the heart and the importance of character for the follower of Christ. Sexual morality in a Christian perspective, therefore, can never merely be comprised of a set of rules—it must flow from the very center of the person and shape his or her day-to-day conduct. Yet the gift of self lived in the ordinary fabric of bodily existence is ordered to the final communion of love, which is a sharing in the beatitude of Trinitarian life. Fostering this capacity for self-giving both in concrete historical practices and in the wedding feast of the eschaton is the aim of the virtue of chastity, the focus of the next chapter.

62. The Trinitarian character of marital community has long been recognized in Eastern theology. Here man and woman are understood to be icons of God, united as persons in mutual love in reflection of Trinitarian life. See Paul Evdokimov, *The Sacrament of Love*, trans. Anthony Gythiel and Victoria Steadman (New York: St. Vladimir's Seminary Press, 1985), 50–54; and Clifford Stevens, "The Trinitarian Roots of Nuptial Community," *St. Vladimir's Theological Quarterly* 35 (1991): 351–59.

CHAPTER 4

Sex and Chastity

Certainly one of the most maligned and misunderstood virtues in contemporary culture is chastity.[1] The word often evokes connotations of inhibition, prudery, dysfunction, and perhaps even neurosis. This is especially true in a culture that sees sexual expression and pleasure as integral to personal health, happiness, and fulfillment. If one has to be sexually active to realize oneself, then continence or celibacy can seem perverse and any form of sexual restraint suspect. If sexual expression is not necessary limited to monogamous covenantal relationships for it to be seen as good, then even the notion of fidelity can come to be seen as arbitrary and oppressive.

The recent resurgence of interest in the notion of virtue as the basis for the moral life in the wake of the groundbreaking work of Alasdair MacIntyre and others has not yet removed the negative associations that have surrounded this virtue.[2] One reason for this is that the renewal of virtue theory that the last two decades have witnessed has yet to engage the issue of sexuality in a systematic way. But it is also the case that the understanding of virtue found in various parts of the theological tradition is perceived as problematic because of its association with rigorist moral positions or negative views of sexuality. Further, it is not immediately evident how even the strengths of the classical understanding of chastity can be reconciled with developments in modern thought that

1. Portions of this chapter originally appeared as "Chastity: Toward a Renewed Understanding," in *The Living Light: Return to Virtue,* 32, no. 4 (Summer 1996). Copyright 1996 United States Catholic Conference, Inc., Washington, D.C. Used with permission. All rights reserved.

2. Alasdair MacIntyre, *After Virtue* (South Bend, Ind.: University of Notre Dame Press, 1981). For the names of others who have contributed to this renewal of virtue theory see Introduction, note 12, above.

focus on the person and his or her cognitive development and specific cultural location.

This chapter will undertake an examination of chastity both as it was understood in various historical epochs and in light of some crucial contemporary perspectives. It will consider some of the strengths and weaknesses of the way in which chastity was articulated in early Christianity and in medieval thought, focusing in the latter case on the understanding of St. Thomas Aquinas. The chapter will then examine the way in which this classical tradition can be enriched by modern developments such as modern personalism, aspects of modern psychology, and the awareness of the historical and cultural horizon of moral thought and praxis. In this way, a renewed understanding of this specific moral virtue can be used to complement the biblical motifs of the previous chapters in order to address issues of sexuality in a contemporary context.

I. Chastity and Early Christianity

Servais Pinkaers correctly points out that the moral teaching of early Christianity had certain distinctive characteristics and strengths that distinguish it from that of postmedieval modernity.[3] One such strength was the rootedness of patristic theology within Scripture. Indeed, most patristic moral teaching was presented in the form of homilies, commentaries, or treatises on specific biblical texts—not as freestanding theological or philosophical argument. So, for example, as Pinckaers observes, John Chrysostom gave almost sixty homilies on the Psalms, ninety homilies on the Gospel of Matthew, eighty-eight on the Gospel of John, and some two hundred and fifty on Paul's letters.[4] A good number of these homilies on Paul's writings dealt with issues of chastity and marriage.[5] Especially striking in many of these homilies is the very optimistic view Chrysostom in his mature oratory paints of the possibilities for growth in chastity and the attainment of genuine holi-

3. See Pinckaers, *Sources of Christian Ethics*, 195–206.
4. Ibid., 196.
5. See, e.g., Chrysostom's homilies collected in *On Marriage and Family Life*, ed. Catherine P. Roth (Crestwood, N.Y.: St. Vladimir's Seminary Press, 1986).

ness in marriage[6]—views that have echos elsewhere in patristic teaching.[7]

A second hallmark of early Christian moral reflection was the focus on beatitude (as opposed to law) as the starting point for the moral life. This explains why, as noted above, for St. Augustine, the Sermon on the Mount and particularly the Beatitudes could be appreciated as the very heart of Christian morality.[8] It also explains why the use of specific norms such as the Sixth or Ninth Commandments as catchalls for the Church's catechesis and theological reflection on sexuality was a relatively late development in the tradition.[9] While early Christian authors treat

6. In his *Epistolam ad Colossenses Homilia* 12 (*Homily 12 on Colossians* [on Col 4:18]), *PG* 62: 583, Chrysostom argues forcefully for the goodness of pleasure within marital intercourse. Elsewhere he makes the claim that intercourse can help a couple to become holy. See *In Illudi, Propter Fornicationes autem Unusquisque suam Uxorem Habet* (traditionally known as *Sermon 1 on Marriage*, on 1 Cor 7:2), *PG* 51: 213. In short, a married couple with an active sexual relationship can be as holy as any monk (cf. *In epistulam ad Ephesios Homilia* 20 [*Homily 20 on Ephesians*—on Eph 5:22–33], *PG* 62: 145–46).

These views are markedly different from those of his early monastic period. In an early treatise he described marriage as a postlapsarian concession to human weakness (cf. *De virginitate* [*On Virginity*] 15–19; *Sources Chrètiennes*, no. 125, 144–59) and the sex within it as an impediment to real spiritual progress (cf. *De virginitate* 41.2; *Sources Chrètiennes*, no. 125, 236–39). It seems that Chrysostom's later experience as a pastor in Antioch and Constantinople gave him a far more positive view of sex, marriage, and the possibilities for holiness in it. On this point, see Catherine P. Roth, "Introduction," in *On Marriage and Family Life*, 8.

7. One can find precursors to Chrysostom's positive treatment of marriage in the catechetical teaching of Clement of Alexandria. See, e.g., *Stromata* (*Stromateis*) 3, 12, *PG* 8: 1177–92; ibid., 7, 12, *PG* 9: 317–25. Similar views can also be found in the teaching of St. Gregory of Nazianzus; see the overview provided by Constantine N. Tsirpanlis, "Saint Gregory the Theologian on Marriage and Family," *Patristic and Byzantine Review* 4 (1985): 33–38.

8. Though echoing St. Paul, St. Augustine insists that the beatitude conferred by virtue is fully realized hereafter; see *De civitate dei* (*City of God*) 19, 4, *PL* 41: 627–32.

9. Historical studies have demonstrated that the use of the Ten Commandments as a catechetical basis for all moral instruction emerged only through a convergence of factors in the High Middle Ages (rather than in patristic thought, as has sometimes been held). Such developments were then codified in the *Roman Catechism* that was issued after the Council of Trent. See Joseph A. Slattery, "The Catechetical Use of the Decalogue from the End of the Catechumenate through the Later Medieval Period" (Ph.D. diss., The Catholic University of America, 1980). For a specific consideration of the Sixth Commandment, see John S. Grabowski, "Clerical Sexual Misconduct and Early Traditions Regarding the Sixth Commandment," *The Jurist* 55 (1995): 527–91.

of the Ten Commandments in addressing issues of sexual morality, they
will also use other biblical motifs or the language of virtue and vice to
communicate their teaching in a variety of settings and genres. At times
these treatments of virtue are found in an apologetic context, defending
the chastity of Christians against pagan charges of immorality,[10] or defending the chastity of marriage against Gnostic detractors.[11] In other
cases, these treatments take the form of exhortations to Christians
themselves to grow in chastity as befitting those who are temples of the
Holy Spirit[12] or to clergy to foster modesty as the accompaniment and
protector of chastity.[13]

Furthermore, as located within the teaching of Scripture and focused on beatitude, patristic moral thought was thoroughly integrated
with the basic mysteries of Christian faith: creation, the Incarnation,
the redemption won by Christ, the Trinity, the last things. So for some
Fathers, the image of God within the human person lay not merely in
the intellect of will, but also and especially in the acquisition of *aretē*.[14]
In the same vein, the Fathers could use the great Christological texts
and themes of the New Testament to teach the meaning and content of
virtue.[15] Or the divinity of the Holy Spirit could be understood to be

---

10. See, e.g., Athenagoras of Athens, *Legatio pro Christianus (Supplication for the Christians)*
32–34, PG 6: 964–68; Aristides of Athens, *Apologia (Apology)*, XV, XVII (cf. Johannes
Quasten, *Patrology* [Westminister, Md.: Newman Press, n.d.] 1:192–94); and Justin, *Apologia
I pro Christianus (First Apology)* 15, PG 6: 349–52. At times this could take the more aggres-
sive form of attacking the lack of chastity within Hellenistic mores. See, e.g., Theodoret
of Cyrrhus, *Graecarum affectionum curatio (On the Cure of Pagan Maladies)* 9, PG 83: 1034f; or,
more strongly, Tertullian, *Apologeticus (Apology)* 39, PL 1: 472–73.

11. Thus Clement of Alexandria defends the equal virtue of both women and men in
marriage (see *Pedagogus [The Teacher]* 1, 4, PG 8:259–62), and even goes so far as to suggest
that greater virtue is exercised by the married rather than the consecrated virgins (*Stromata [Stromateis]* 7, 12, 70, PG 9:495–96?).

12. See Tertullian, *De bono pudicitiae (On the Good of Modesty)* 2–3, PL 2: 983–84.

13. See St. Ambrose, *De Officiis Ministorum (On the Duties of the Clergy)* I, 18, PL 16: 43–47.

14. See St. Gregory of Nyssa, *De opificio hominis (On the Making of Man)* 5, 1, PG 44:137.
Cf. *Oratio Catechetica Magna (Catechetical Oration)* 5, PG 45:20–25. Others would see the image
of God as that naturally given to human beings, while the outworking of baptismal
grace in the acquisition of virtue would be equated with the "likeness of God" of Genesis 1:26c. See Diadochus of Photice, *Capita centum de perfectione spirituali (One Hundred Chapters on Spiritual Perfection)* 2–5, PG 65:1167–69.

15. Thus St. Gregory of Nyssa responded to a query from a monk named Olympius

the ground of his communication of graces to those in the Church, whether chastity, virginity, detachment from worldly goods,[16] or the charity that makes such gifts efficacious.[17]

Finally, the moral teaching of the Fathers was also inseparable from the spiritual experience generated by prayer, liturgy, and ascetic practice, and therefore not subject to the modern bifurcation of faith and morality. For this reason Gregory of Nyssa could allegorize Moses' ascent of Mount Sinai to receive the Ten Commandments as indicative of both progress in virtue and growth in knowledge of God.[18] Or, as he says simply elsewhere, "The goal of a virtuous life is to become like God."[19]

Nevertheless, at least in regard to its teaching regarding sexuality, patristic thought also faced unique challenges and had specific limitations. Confronted by an immoral society that trivialized human sexuality through the bawdy entertainment of the theater, the tolerance of prostitution and concubinage, and the acceptance of a double standard of sexual morality for men, early Christian preachers and writers often approached matters of sex rather narrowly and in largely negative terms.[20] To respond to the challenge of gnosticism that attacked procreation as

---

regarding the achievement of perfection and virtue by treating the Christological images of Paul's letters. The Christ who acts in the Christian soul is the power and wisdom of God, the High Priest, Pasch, source of redemption, image of the invisible God, head of the Church which is his body, firstborn, only begotten Son, and principle of being. See his treatise *De perfectione et qualem oporteat esse Christianum (On the Kind of Perfection Proper to Being Christian)*, PG 46:252–85. Or St. Augustine could treat Christ as the justice of God who makes possible the healing of the human will from vice and its redirection toward virtue; see *De trinitate (On the Trinity)* XIII, x, 17; CCL 50, 400.

16. Cf. Cyril of Jerusalem, *Catechetical Lecture* 22, PG 33:1097–1105.

17. Cf. St. Augustine, *De Trinitate (On the Trinity)* XV, xviii, 32, CCL 50, 508. Elsewhere Augustine argues that the efficacy of the moral virtues depends upon their being enlivened by faith; see *De civitate dei (The City of God)* 19, 4, PL 41: 627–31.

18. See *De vita Moysis (Life of Moses)* II, 152–69, SC 1, 202–16.

19. *De beatitudinibus (On the Beatitudes)* 1, PG 44, 1200D. The citation is from the *CCC*, par. 1803, trans. U.S.C.C. (Washington, D.C.: U.S.C.C., 1994), 443.

20. On the social milieu of patristic catechesis regarding sexuality, see Lawler, Boyle, and May, *Catholic Sexual Ethics*, 47–48. Cf. Frank Bottomley, *Attitudes to the Body in Western Christendom* (London: Lepus, 1979), 1–15, 157–8; and Brown, *The Body and Society*, esp. 31–32 and 432–42. On the acceptance of a double standard of sexual morality in the Greek and Roman worlds, see Aline Rousselle, "Personal Status and Sexual Practice in the Roman Empire," trans. Janet Lloyd, in *Fragments*, 301–33; and Judith Evans Grubbs, "'Marriage More Shameful than Adultery': Slave-Mistress Relationships, 'Mixed Marriages,' and

an evil, most patristic thinkers responded with a fairly univocal view of the purpose of sex as ordered to procreation.[21] The contrary view of St. John Chrysostom and Lactantius that it was legitimate for spouses to engage in intercourse to avoid immorality or to promote chastity was largely overridden in the West by St. Augustine's teaching.[22]

There were still other currents of thought that eddied through the ancient world that washed teachers within the bark of the Church in the first few centuries after Christ. Many early Christian writers were influenced in varying degrees by stoicism with its ideal of *apatheia,* the notion that the virtuous person was utterly unmoved by the passion that was the enemy of reason.[23] Others were affected by Neoplatonism which added to the stoic focus on reason an additional mistrust of the body and sexuality.[24] In the chill of such currents, chastity was often understood in rather stringent and narrow terms.

In a context such as this the possibilities for chastity on the part of married couples in many cases appeared to be limited indeed. Marriage was regarded as the "ordinary" way of life, which required a certain moderation. But complete continence or virginity was an "angelic" way of life that far surpassed it.[25] Chastity could be understood as a hierar-

---

Late Roman Law," *Phoenix* 47, no. 2 (1993): 125–54. It should be noted, of course, that the accusation of sexual immorality against groups whose ideas were considered strange or heterodox was commonplace in the ancient world and was employed by both Christians and their opponents. See Wolfgang Speyer, "Zu den Vorwürfen der Heiden gegen die Christen," *Jahrbuch für Antike und Christentum* 6 (1963): 129–35.

21. See, e.g., Justin Martyr, *Apologia I pro Christianus (First Apology)* 29, PG 6:373; Clement of Alexandria, *Stromata (Stromateis)* 3, 7, PG 8:1162; Athenagoras, *Legatio pro Christianus (Embassy on Behalf of Christians)* 33, PG 6:965; Augustine, *De bono coniugali (On the Good of Marriage)* 6, PL 40:377–78.

22. See John Chrysostom, *In Illudi (Sermon 1 on Marriage),* PG 51:213; Lactantius, *Divinarum Institutionnum (The Divine Institutes)* 6, 23, PL 6:715f.

23. For examples of Stoic influence on patristic and early monastic thought, see Noonan, *Contraception,* 75–77, 144. Cf. Colish Marcia, *The Stoic Tradition from Antiquity to the Early Middle Ages,* 2 vols. (Leiden: Brill, 1990). However, other scholars have argued that, in spite of convergences of language, early Christian sexual ethics owed little to Stoicism or other Greco-Roman sources but rather represented a unique development of New Testament themes. See Richard Price, "The Distinctiveness of Early Christian Sexual Ethics," *Heythrop Journal* 31 (1990): 257–76.

24. Cf. Mahoney, *Making of Moral Theology,* 37–38: and Bottomley, *Attitudes to the Body,* 44–97.

25. See Athanasius, *Epistula ad Amunem monachum (Letter to Amun),* PG 26:1169–79. Brown

chy with consecrated virginity being its highest expression, fidelity to one's spouse its lowest, and continence (refraining from sex after a certain point in one's life) the mean between them.[26] Some of the Fathers praised virginity so strongly that marriage could only appear as something to be left behind or shunned.[27] Tertullian, even in his Catholic period, went so far as to suggest that marriage be regarded as nothing but a kind of legitimized debauchery, inspired by lust.[28] Hence the married could either content themselves with a second-class exercise of virtue or foreswear sexual relations altogether.[29]

These rather chill currents were given a persuasive theological rationale by St. Augustine's doctrine of concupiscence. According to the bishop of Hippo, *concupiscentia* is the result of original sin and disorders all human desires—the more intense the desire, the greater the disorder. Because of its intensity, sexual desire is profoundly affected by concupiscence and casts down the human mind from the heights of rationality that it ought to occupy.[30] While sex for the purpose of procreation was morally blameless, it was still viewed with some suspicion and as a merely secondary good:

In marriage, intercourse for the purpose of generation has no fault attached to it, but for the purpose of satisfying concupiscence, provided with a spouse,

notes that the "chastity" expected of lay couples by many of the desert fathers was merely that they avoid adultery; see *Body and Society*, 256.

26. See Novation, *De bono pudicitiae (On the Good of Modesty)* 4, *CSEL* 33:16. Cf. Augustine, *De bono conjugali (On the Good of Marriage)* 6, *PL* 40:371–78.

27. See, e.g., Origen, *In Num. Hom. (Homilies on Numbers)* 24, 2, *PG* 12:759–61; Jerome, *Adversus Iovianum (Against Jovinian)*, *PL* 23:211–338.

28. See Tertullian, *De exhortatione castitas (Exhortation to Chastity)*, 9 *PL* 2:924–25. On the dating of this text, see Quasten, *Patrology*, 1:304. Such views are in some tension with his earlier treatise *Ad uxorem (To My Wife)*, *PL* 1:1275–1304), which had praised the blessings of a Christian marriage.

29. Such views undoubtedly contributed toward the impulse toward "spiritual marriage"—the practice of couples taking vows of continence at some point in their marriages, at times immediately following their vows—within later patristic and medieval thought. On this phenomenon, see Dyan Elliott, *Spiritual Marriage: Sexual Abstinence in Medieval Wedlock* (Princeton, N.J.: Princeton University Press, 1993).

30. Cf. Augustine, *Soliloquiroum (Soloquies)* 1, 10, *PL* 40:864–65; cf. *De Nuptiis et concupiscentia (On Marriage and Concupiscence)* 1. 6 *PL* 44:417–18, and *De Civitate dei (City of God)* 14, 16, *PL* 41:424–25. For an overview and analysis of Augustine's mistrust of pleasure, see Mahoney, *Making of Moral Theology*, 61–66.

because of the marriage fidelity, it is a venial sin; adultery or fornication, however, is a mortal sin. And so, continence from all intercourse is certainly better than marital intercourse which takes place for the begetting of children.[31]

While it is overstated to regard Augustine's views as a form of crypto-Manichaeanism, there is little room here for a positive estimate of sexual desire or pleasure.[32] One can find, however, echos of Augustine's early Neoplatonic phase in his focus on the impact of pleasure on rationality as well as in his identification of sex with the fall into materiality and diversity.[33] In this context, the renunciation of sexual desire and activity become a way to return to a primordial unity: "Indeed it is through chastity that we are gathered together and led back to the unity from which we were fragmented into multiplicity."[34]

II. Chastity in Aquinas

From the perspective of the classical Aristotelian Thomist tradition of virtue, chastity is a specification of the virtue of temperance related to matters of sex, enabling reason to control and moderate sexual impulses.[35] A virtue, for St. Thomas Aquinas, "denotes a certain perfec-

---

31. *De bono conjugali (On the Good of Marriage)* 6, PL 40:377–78. The citation is from *The Fathers of the Church* 15 (Washington, D.C.: The Catholic University of America Press, 1955), 17. Cf. *De Nuptiis et concupiscentia (On Marriage and Concupiscence)* 1, 15, 17, PL 44:423.

32. It is true that St. Augustine's strong doctrine of original sin, sharpened in the heat of his controversy with Pelagius and coupled with his understanding of *concupiscentia* as disordering all human desires, produced a fairly pessimistic view of sexual desire and pleasure. Such sensations could only be disordered and hence must be sublimated in the service of an acceptable good (i.e., procreation) or foresworn altogether in a life of continence. It is for this reason that some scholars speak of a "dark strain" within St. Augustine's thought. See Mahoney, *Making of Moral Theology*, 44–48.

33. However, St. Augustine never went so far as some of the more Neoplatonic Eastern thinkers such as St. Gregory of Nyssa, St. John Chrysostom, St. Theodoret, and St. John Damascene who saw sexual differences and reproduction as introduced by God only after human sin.

34. St. Augustine, *Confessionum libra tredecim (Confessions)* 10, 29, 40, CCSL, XXVII, 176. The citation is from the *CCC*, 2340.

35. See Thomas Aquinas, *ST* II–II, q. 151, a. 3. For a clear overview of the Thomist understanding of chastity, see Josef Pieper, *The Four Cardinal Virtues* (South Bend, Ind.: University of Notre Dame Press, 1966), 153–75. For a more complete treatment, see the very fine analysis of Plé, *Chastity*, esp. 115–84. For an overview of Aristotle's understanding of

tion of a power."[36] The specific power that virtue grants is that to act in a way that is morally excellent. The *habitus* of virtue is productive of good works.[37] Aquinas cites with approval St. Augustine's definition of virtue: *"Virtue is a good quality of the mind, by which we live righteously, of which no one can make bad use,"* noting that its final part *"which God works in us without us"* is specific to the infused virtues, while the first part is applicable to all virtues.[38]

The virtue of chastity is so named because it is that which "chastises" the concupiscence that comes from venereal pleasure.[39] As in the case of the other moral virtues, chastity does not eliminate one's appetites or passions, but moderates them, enabling them to be governed by practical reason informed by prudence and in this way ordered to the true good of the person.[40] Indeed, even pleasure can be good, according to Aquinas, since St. Thomas, like Aristotle, held that pleasure is a natural accompaniment and perfection of all human action. Hence, it is the goodness or badness of the act itself that determines the moral quality of the pleasure that it produces.[41] This is true of sexual pleasure as well.[42] This Aristotelian teleology of pleasure introduced by Aquinas would open the way for a more positive estimate of sexual pleasure in succeeding centuries.[43]

---

virtue, see Yves Simon, *The Definition of Moral Virtue,* ed. Vukan Kuic (New York: Fordham University Press, 1986), 91–123.

36. *ST* I–II, q. 55, a. 1. The citation is from the translation by the Fathers of the English Dominican Province (New York: Benziger, 1947), 1:819. Subsequent references will be to this edition. For an exposition of the Thomistic understanding of the nature and structure of virtuous action, see Cessario, *Introduction to Moral Theology,* 100–144. On the general definition of virtue, see ibid., 196–200.

37. Cf. *ST* I–II, q. 55, a. 3.

38. *ST* I–II, q. 55, a. 4. Emphasis in original. St. Thomas gleans this definition from Augustine's *De Libero Arbitrio* ii, 19.

39. See Aristotle, *Nichomachean Ethics* III, 12; Aquinas, *ST* II–II, q. 151, a. 1.

40. Cf. *ST* II–II, q. 152, a. 2: "In human acts, those are sinful which are against right reason." On the centrality of prudence in virtuous action, see Cessario, *Introduction to Moral Theology,* 128–44. On the role of the passions in Aquinas's account of virtue, see the insightful treatment offered by G. Simon Harak, *Virtuous Passions: The Formation of Christian Character* (New York: Paulist Press, 1993), 71–98.

41. See Aquinas, *In Sententiarum (Commentary on the Sentences)* 4.31.2.3 and 4.49.3.4.3.

42. See, e.g., *ST* I, q. 98, a. 2, ad. 3; II–II, q. 152, a. 2, ad. 2; q. 153, a. 2, ad. 2.

43. On this development, see Noonan, *Contraception,* 292–95, 305–12, 321–30, 395, 491–504.

As with the Fathers, St. Thomas regards virginity as the highest form of chastity, and in fact superior to its other expressions.[44] Like other medieval theologians, he does not see virginity in purely physical terms, arguing that virginity can lack its matter (i.e., physical integrity), but still possess or, though repentance, recover its form (i.e., the offering of one's body to God).[45] While virginity is objectively superior to marriage as a state, married persons may in fact be more virtuous than consecrated virgins in other respects or may even possess greater chastity.[46]

As virginity is higher than chastity, mere continence is lower. It is, in fact, a virtue only in a rather loose sense. According to Aquinas, the continent person has evil desires but resists or controls them, while the truly chaste person's appetites are integrated with and controlled by reason.[47]

The vice opposed to chastity is that of lust. Aquinas denies the rigorist position that all sex is somehow tainted by lust.[48] However, he retains St. Augustine's instrumental view of the goodness of sex as ordered to the good of the race.[49] Lust exceeds the order of reason which directs human beings to intelligently use their sexual powers in keeping with the inclinations of their nature—that is, primarily for the purpose of procreating and educating offspring.[50] This is not merely an argu-

---

44. See *ST* II–II, q. 152, a.3. However, Aquinas notes that there are virtues (such as the theological virtues of faith, hope, and love, or the virtue of religion) and states of life (such as martyrdom or monasticism) that are higher than virginity. See *ST* II–II, q. 152, a. 5.

45. See *ST* II–II, q. 152, a. 3, ad. 1 and ad. 3.

46. See *ST* II–II, q. 152, a. 4, ad. 2.

47. See *ST* II–II, q. 155, a. 1; A. 3.

48. See *ST* II–II, q. 153, a. 2. The rigorist opinion, found in some of the penitentials, may have been generated by a mistake. Bede's *Historia Ecclesiastica Gentis Anglorum* cited a letter supposedly from Gregory the Great to Augustine of Canterbury that drew a distinction between intercourse for the purpose of procreation and that which was undertaken because of "fleshly desire," after which one should avoid entering a church or receiving the Eucharist for a time. Later commentators often failed to distinguish between *voluptas* (pleasure) and *voluntas* (desire) and so arrived at the position that all marital intercourse could not take place without at least venial sin. See Francis Firth, "Catholic Sexual Morality in the Patristic and Medieval Periods," in *Human Sexuality and Personhood* (St. Louis: Pope John Center, 1981), 43–44. On the debate concerning the authenticity of this letter, see Noonan, *Contraception*, 150 n. 9.

49. See *ST* II–II, q. 153, a. 2.

50. Cf. *ST* II–II, q. 153, a. 3.

ment based on biological function, but one based on reason and its ability to grasp the goods that perfect and fulfill human beings and are therefore conducive to human flourishing. For St. Thomas, the worst forms of lust are those that violate the natural procreative purpose of sex: bestiality, homosexual sex, nonvaginal heterosexual sex, and masturbation. Less grave expressions of lust are those that violate our relations with others: rape, adultery, seduction, and fornication.[51] However, sexual sins are not the worst of sins for Aquinas; spiritual sins (those directed against God) or sins against the life of a person (e.g., murder) are far more grievous.[52]

Most modern readers would rightly raise questions regarding aspects of this hierarchical ordering of the parts of lust—particularly the view that masturbation is a worse violation of chastity than rape or adultery merely because it is *contra naturam*. Yet this deficiency is not necessarily the result of physicalist thinking, as some have claimed, but may well be the result of a failure to fully appreciate the import of the personal values at stake within sexual intimacy.[53] Aquinas's treatment, focused as it is on the demands of nature, requires the insights of modern personalism. Equally reflective of the limitations of Aquinas's historical vantage point and scientific information is his treatment of women as passive in the process of human procreation and hence as "misbegotten" mem-

---

51. See *ST* II–II, q. 154, a. 12.

52. See *ST* II–II, q. 154, a. 3.

53. Gula attributes this position of Aquinas to physicalist thinking; see *Reason Informed by Faith*, 225–28. However, it should be noted that Michael Nolan has argued that Aquinas's use of the term *raptus* is used in the sense that it was found in the canon law of the day—as denoting abduction rather than sexual assault per se. Further, Nolan notes that Aquinas is only comparing types of sin, not individual acts that need to be considered according to their circumstances. See "Aquinas and the Act of Love," *New Blackfriars* 77, no. 92 (1996):115–30, esp. 116–18. Lawler, Boyle, and May further observe that Aquinas is here speaking only of offenses against chastity and that in the order of justice rape or adultery are clearly more evil than masturbation; see *Catholic Sexual Ethics*, 58.

In spite of these welcome efforts to offer a more careful and contextual reading of Aquinas on this point, from a contemporary vantage it still appears that his treatment of sexuality is somewhat limited by its focus on human nature and its inclinations without sufficiently integrating these into an understanding of the person as the locus of moral value and action. Furthermore, it remains problematic that while St. Thomas decries violence between spouses as sinful, he denies that rape can occur within a marriage (cf. *ST* II–II, q. 154, a. 7, ad. 4).

bers of the human species,[54] and as generally less rational than their male counterparts (though capable of virtue and holiness).[55]

Yet in spite of these real limitations, Aquinas's treatment has much to recommend it. It successfully integrates an account of human nature and its inclinations into a larger framework of virtue.[56] Chastity enables the person's sexual powers to be exercised intelligently and freely in accord with goods of human nature—particularly the inclination to procreate, educate, and care for offspring. While human beings share this inclination (and that to preserve their own lives) with other animals, they can pursue them through the use of reason.[57] Furthermore, since sexual union can express the unique form of friendship that exists in marriage, the person's sexual powers are also ordered to the excellent and distinctively human inclinations—that is, to live in society and to seek after truth.[58] The chaste person is able to intelligently order his or her sexual appetites in a way that contributes to authentic human flourishing.

St. Thomas's teaching also presents chastity as a form of excellence

54. See ST I, q. 92, a. 1; cf. II–II, q. 154, a. 1. Based on his Aristotelian biology, Aquinas will note that women are "misbegotten" only from the standpoint of an individual human nature. Considered from the standpoint of human nature as a whole and God's plan for it, women are not misbegotten (ST I, q. 92, a. 1, ad. 1).

55. See ST II–II, q. 156, a. 1. For a balanced account of Aquinas's treatment of women and men in regard to natural and spiritual potential, see Prudence Allen, R.S.M., The Concept of Woman: The Aristotelian Revolution 750 B.C.–A.D. 1250 (Montreal: Eden Press, 1985), and "Two Medieval Views of Women's Identity: Hildegard of Bingen and Thomas Aquinas," Studies in Religion 16 (1987): 21–36.

56. On the complementarity of natural law and virtue in Aquinas's thought, see Jean Porter, "What the Wise Person Knows: Natural Law and Virtue in Aquinas' Summa Theologiae," Studies in Christian Ethics 12 (1999): 57–69; John Peterson, "Natural Law, End, and Virtue in Aquinas," Journal of Philosophical Research 24 (1999): 397–413; Maria Carl, "Law, Virtue, and Happiness in Aquinas' Moral Theory," The Thomist 61 (1997): 425–47; and Cessario, Introduction to Moral Theology, 94–95. For a helpful overview of Thomistic natural law theory in relation to other theological topics and contemporary debates, see ibid., 52–99.

57. On the unity of the inclinations and reason's grasp of them, see ST I–II, q. 94, a. 2, ad. 2. Cf. Cessario, Introduction to Moral Theology, 87–90; and Jean Porter, Moral Action and Christian Ethics, New Studies in Christian Ethics (New York: Cambridge University Press, 1995), 107–10.

58. See Pinckaers, Sources of Christian Ethics, 432–34, 442–47; and Plé, Chastity, 140–42.

acquired together with the other moral virtues, through human action empowered by grace. St. Thomas integrates his account of chastity into the Christian life, noting that, understood spiritually, the essence of chastity is found in charity and the other theological virtues.[59] Chastity represents not the elimination, but the reasonable integration, of the sexual appetites. Aquinas's account develops and in turn makes room for further developments in the articulation of a more balanced account of sexuality than that found in many of its patristic sources.

This is especially true in regard to its treatment of the purposes of intercourse within marriage and the place of pleasure within these. According to St. Thomas, sexual union between a husband and wife for the purpose of procreation or to preserve mutual fidelity are not just tolerable, but positively virtuous.[60] Indeed this union can be the reflection and expression of the spiritual friendship that unites the couple.[61] While other medieval theologians developed theologies of marital friendship that could encompass a couple's sexual union, in the case of Aquinas this friendship reflects something of the fabric of the moral life as a whole since the purpose of the virtues is precisely to make us capable of friendship with God.[62] Even the pleasure produced by sexual union can be understood as good if the acts that produce it are themselves good. The role of chastity is to moderate and control such pleas-

59. Cf. *ST* II–II, q. 151, a. 2. For a more complete analysis of Christian chastity in St. Thomas, see Plé, *Chastity*, 144–47.

60. St. Thomas holds that intercourse for the purpose of procreation actually has the goodness of virtue—since it belongs to the virtue of religion for couples to intend to have children whom they will raise to know and love God. See *ST*, Supplement, q. 41, a. 4; cf. *ST*, Supplement, q. 49, a. 4. Though constrained by St. Augustine's authority in holding that a spouse who requests intercourse to avoid fornication is guilty of venial sin, he also argues that the spouse who grants the request acts according to the virtue of justice since the married owe their bodies to one another. See *ST*, Supplement, q. 41, a. 4. For helpful overviews of Aquinas's teaching in this area, see Lawler, Boyle, and May, *Catholic Sexual Ethics*, 60–63; and Marie LeBlanc, O.S.B., "Amour et procréation dans la théologie de saint Thomas," *Revue Thomiste* 92 (1992): 433–59.

61. At times Aquinas will associate the intensity of marital love with a couple's "one flesh" union. See *ST* II–II, q. 26, a. 11. Cf. *Summa Contra Gentiles* 3, 123, 6; *In VIII Ethicorum* 488, 268–78.

62. On this point, see the fine study by Paul Wadell, C.P., *Friends of God: Virtues and Gifts in Aquinas*, American University Studies, Series 7, Vol. 76 (New York: Peter Lang, 1991).

ure so that it can be subject to reason's prudential grasp of the true good of the person.[63]

Chastity, as presented by St. Thomas, is the virtue that enables human beings to use their sexual powers wisely and well. In so doing they contribute not only to their own flourishing, but to a well-ordered society that reflects God's plan for human sexuality.[64]

III. The Eclipse of Chastity in Moral Teaching

The balance achieved by St. Thomas in his account of chastity was not always maintained in succeeding generations. In particular, many Catholic moralists after Aquinas struggled to balance law and virtue in their theory.[65] The cultural upheaval of the fourteenth century gave birth to philosophical currents such as nominalism. In its denial of the intelligibility of nature as a source for moral judgment and it emphasis on the sovereign will of God, nominalism opened the way for an account of the moral life conceived primarily in terms of law.[66] It is therefore not surprising that *The Roman Catechism*, issued after the Council of Trent, organized the whole of its teaching about sexual morality under the heading of the Sixth Commandment.[67] Many of the authors of the manualist tradition followed the *Catechism*'s lead in their treatments of sexual morality.[68]

63. See *ST* II–II, q. 151, a. 1; cf. I–II, q. 64, a. 1.

64. On the social implications of this concept of chastity considered from the perspective of Thomistic political philosophy, see Riley, *Civilising Sex*, passim.

65. It is interesting to note that while Aquinas suggests that all moral precepts can be located within the Decalogue (as first principles of the natural law), he does not treat chastity or lust under this heading. See *ST* I–II, q. 100, a. 1. It is equally instructive to compare the relative brevity of the treatise on natural law within the *ST* to the very extensive tract on the virtues.

66. For a more complete discussion of these developments, see Chapter 1.

67. See *The Roman Catechism*, III, 6, 3–5. It should be noted that in many respects the teaching of the *Catechism* regarding sexuality and marriage was quite balanced. As Michel Rouche observes, "For the first time in a conciliar text, the sacrament of marriage is seen in an optimistic light. The reasons for marriage are instinct, mutual support, children and sometimes, even passion. The human and divine dimensions [of marriage] are indistinguishable"; see "The Many Changes in the Concept of Christian Marriage and the Family throughout History," in *Christian Marriage Today*, 31.

68. On this topic, see John Touhey, "The Correct Interpretation of Canon 1395: The

When law becomes the dominant paradigm for the moral life, chastity takes on a rather different meaning. Chastity becomes that virtue that safeguards one from violations of the law concerning matters of sex whether inwardly or in external conduct. Rather than a dynamic principle enabling one to use one's sexual powers intelligently in the pursuit of human flourishing and happiness, chastity is seen as a form of conditioning that elicits adherence to extrinsic rules that restrain human freedom. The *habitus* of virtue is thus reduced to mere habit.[69]

Though by no means universal, it was this somewhat truncated view of virtue in general and chastity in particular that colored many presentations of Catholic sexual morality during the twentieth century. Such a pale approximation of virtue theory offered little counterweight to the dominant morality of obligation and its heavily physicalist reading of the natural law that fed the explosion of debate on birth control in the 1960s. Yet even prior to the Second Vatican Council, there were impulses stirring within the tradition that would make possible a renewed understanding of virtue and sexuality.

IV. Chastity and Personalism

The rise of personalist philosophy and ethics and its application to matters of sexuality by Catholic moralists in the 1920s and 1930s made possible the development of new and more experiential perspectives on sexuality and chastity.

Personalist approaches highlighted the fact that there is more to the experience of conjugal love than its orientation to procreation. For Dietrich von Hildebrand, even if procreation is the primary purpose of marital intercourse, love is its primary meaning.[70] Wedded love finds its privileged expression in this form of bodily self-donation. Herbert

---

Use of the Sixth Commandment in the Moral Tradition from Trent to the Present Day," *The Jurist* 55 (1995): 592–631, esp. 596–603.

69. Cf. Pinckaers, *Sources of Christian Ethics*, 336.

70. See Von Hildebrand, *Marriage: The Mystery of Faithful Love* (London: Longmans Green, and Co., 1942), 6–7, 19–27, and *In Defense of Purity* (Baltimore: Helicon Press, 1962), 10–12.

Doms, while echoing this formulation, went even further, arguing for the primacy of the "two-in-oneship" (*Zweieinigkeit*) that intercourse effects and seeing biological ends such as procreation as secondary.[71] Both of these thinkers would describe sex as a privileged form of self-giving between spouses that both expresses and fosters their communion of love.[72] The pleasure that accompanies sexual love is unique, then, and far different from the pleasure of other forms of human activity precisely because it serves to engage the full attention of the lovers in their mutual gift of self and because it effects their unity of consciousness.[73]

Building on these early analyses, Karol Wojtyla would see chastity as not merely the mastery of reason over the passions, nor still less a flight from all sexual activity, but rather a form of self-possession that makes sexual and other forms of self-donation possible. Chastity serves to integrate rather than repress or sublimate both sexual desire and the range of human affectivity in the service of love.[74] Indeed, chastity cannot be considered apart from the virtue of love.[75] The essence of chastity, for Wojtyla, lies in a "quickness to affirm the value of the person in every situation, and in raising to the personal level all reactions to the value of 'the body and sex.'"[76] Chastity thus enables others to be regarded as integral persons worthy of respect and love rather than as mere objects of use and enjoyment.[77] For Wojtyla, chastity has two principal parts: shame and continence. Shame is an inescapable feature of postlapsarian

71. Herbert Doms, *The Meaning of Marriage*, trans. George Sayer (London: Sheed & Ward, 1939), 67–69, 85–88, 93–94, 119. It was in part because of this position that Doms's work was ordered to be withdrawn from publication by the Congregation of the Holy Office in the early 1940s.

72. See, e.g., Von Hildebrand, *Marriage*, 19–20; Doms, *Meaning of Marriage*, 14–15, 23, 50.

73. See Doms, *Meaning of Marriage*, 187; cf. Von Hildebrand, *Purity*, 12. Von Hildebrand shows some ambivalence on this point, at times suggesting that the intensity of orgasm is where human corporeity most closely approaches the spiritual (see *Purity*, 61), while at other times arguing that its intensity threatens to swamp the human person "in the waves of animal life which at this moment break violently upon it" (*Purity*, 70).

74. See Wojtyla, *Love and Responsibility*, 170.

75. See ibid., 169.

76. Ibid., 171. Elsewhere he will describe chastity's effect as producing "a 'transparent' attitude to a person of the other sex" which is the precondition of love (p. 170).

77. See ibid., 171; cf. 21–44.

existence that occurs when the body or sex is sought independently of the value of the person.[78] Continence is another term for the self-mastery that makes the gift of self in love possible.[79] A person can only truly give as a gift that which they themselves first possess. This is particularly true in the case of the gift of self. To give oneself in the absence of this possession is to be compelled by various kinds of drives or impulses rather than to genuinely offer oneself in freedom.[80]

While having a different form depending upon the specific vocation in which it is lived, this personalist perspective makes it clear that chastity is needed equally by single, married, and celibate persons. Since the vocation of all believers is to love, chastity enables them to give themselves in love to others in a way specific to their own vocations. Chastity makes possible the integration of one's sexuality into the commitments that structure the person's life. In so doing, chastity makes it possible for persons to discover the communion for which they were created: "[M]an, who is the only creature on earth which God willed for itself, cannot fully find himself except through a sincere gift of self."[81]

Pope John Paul II, in his catechesis on the body, has observed the fundamental analogy between the married and the celibate vocations since both are ways of giving oneself in which the body expresses the person and his or her commitments.[82] It follows from this that one can refrain from sex out of very unchaste forms of repression and one can be quite chaste in the midst of a passionate sexual relationship.[83] The "objective superiority" of celibacy claimed by the Catholic tradition

78. See ibid., 174–79. See also John Paul II's weekly general audiences of May 28, 1980, and June 4, 1980, in *The Theology of the Body*, 114–19.

79. See Wojtyla, *Love and Responsibility*, 194–95. Other aspects of Wojtyla's treatment of continence will be considered in Chapter 6.

80. Von Hildebrand contrasts the free self-surrender of self-donation with the experience of throwing oneself away in sexual excess in the absence of chastity; see *Purity*, 21–26.

81. *Gaudium et spes*, no. 24. The citation is from *Documents of Vatican II*, 223.

82. See the pope's weekly general audience of April 28, 1982, in *Theology of the Body*, 281–84.

83. See William F. Kraft, *Sexual Dimensions of the Celibate Life* (Kansas City, Mo.: Andrews & McNeil, 1977), 130.

need not be understood as devaluing marriage, but rather can be seen to affirm it.[84] For celibacy itself signifies the nuptial union between the Church and Christ that is the eschatological destiny of all the redeemed.

The virtue of chastity takes three distinct forms.[85] Celibate chastity is ordered to the gift of one's body and sexuality in nongenital expressions of friendship, love, and service within the Church. In living chastely and refraining from genital activity celibates do not cease to be sexual or embodied persons.[86] Rather, their sexuality is given as a gift (in nongenital ways) in the service of God and members of the Christian community. Conjugal chastity is ordered to fidelity and the totality of the bodily gift of self within the marriage covenant—to the full articulation of the "language of the body" when it is spoken in the life of the couple. The chastity lived by unmarried or widowed persons resembles that of those vowed to celibacy in that it requires continence. However, in the case of unmarried Christians not vowed to celibacy, the practice of continence may not be permanent should they marry.[87] All three forms of the virtue involve renunciation and ascesis in developing the capacity to give oneself in love in ways appropriate to the person's state of life.[88] Those who marry renounce their allegiance to all others and give themselves only to their spouse. The single person devotes him- or herself to pursuing nongenital forms of friendship and the service of the Christian community. The celibate permanently renounces marriage and genital expression for the sake of the love of God.

84. See Pope John Paul II's weekly audiences of April 7, 14, 28, and May 5, 1982, in *The Theology of Body*, 273–78, 281–84, and 285–87.

85. Cf. *CCC*, 2349–50.

86. Cf. William F. Kraft, *Whole and Holy Sexuality: How to Find Human and Spiritual Integrity as a Sexual Person* (St. Meinrad, Ind.: Abbey Press, 1989), 55–58.

87. This is not to imply that unmarried Christians live in a kind of imperfect "half state" somewhere between marriage and celibacy. More theological and practical reflection needs to be devoted to the single life as a state chosen by an increasing number of adult Christians for significant portions of their lives. It is not sufficient to simply regard this state as a transitory phase prior to the fulfillment offered either by the choice of a spouse or of a religious or clerical vocation.

88. Von Hildebrand argues that the total gift of self within marriage and its bodily expression in sexual union has the power to shatter pride, overcome concupiscence, and heal the person's attachment to lower goods; see *Purity*, 121.

A personalist approach to the virtue of chastity can also bring into sharper relief the antithesis of this virtue: the vice of lust. Some of the Fathers struggled to distinguish between natural sexual desire and lust since all sexual desire was seen as tainted by the disorder of concupiscence. However, a personalist analysis can identify the difference between authentic sexual desire ordered to the gift of self and the cravings of lust. Desire informed by chastity is desire for the other as a person—it views the sexual qualities of the person in the light of his or her personal dignity. Lust abstracts the person's sexual traits and focuses on them apart from this dignity. It thus reduces the person so regarded to an object of use and enjoyment rather than viewing that person as worthy of respect and love.[89] Pope John Paul II notes that it is this propensity of fallen men and women to view one another as objects that is captured in Jesus' warning concerning committing adultery in one's heart in the Sermon on the Mount (Mt 5:27–28).[90] Chastity heals this fragmented desire, enabling it to once again be integrated into the service of self-giving love.

Another source that can contribute to a renewed understanding of chastity in the present context is psychology. An account of virtue always implies an understanding of human psychology in its depiction of moral growth and development. Contemporary psychology has both yielded new insights and confirmed ancient ones in regard to the acquisition of moral virtue in general and the virtue of chastity in particular.

V. Psychological Perspectives

It has been argued that the virtue of chastity, understood as the integration of the person's sexual drives in the service of love, is a key to psychological wholeness.[91] Chastity enables the person to respect the

89. This is captured in Wojtyla's "personalist norm" which states that "in its negative aspect that the person is the kind of good which does not admit of use and cannot be treated as an object of use and as such the means to an end. In its positive form the personalistic norm confirms this: the person is a good towards which the only proper and adequate attitude is love"; see *Love and Responsibility*, 41.

90. See the weekly general audiences of May 14, June 4, 18, 25, 1980, in *Theology of the Body*, 111–25.

91. This is the argument of Kraft in *Whole and Holy Sexuality*. For a more general con-

dignity of both him- or herself as well as that of others—a key for healthy interpersonal relationships. This virtue enables the person to integrate his or her physical, functional, spiritual, and aesthetic dimensions into sexual expression and growth over the course of life.[92] *Integration*, on these terms, means learning to accept one's sexual feelings and embodiment in the course of developing relationships with others based on mutual respect for their dignity. It affirms the worth of other persons rather than seeking to exploit or manipulate them. Chastity as integral to healthy psychosexual development is opposed to both repression (the denial of sex) and sexism (denigrating and seeking power over members of the opposite sex). In this respect, the contemporary appreciation of psychological integrity and growth reinforces ancient wisdom concerning chastity.

However, there are also ways in which contemporary psychological study can expand and enrich an understanding of the virtues. While there has always been a certain recognition of human growth and development within the moral tradition, at times this insight was hampered by an exaggerated importance attached to the notion of the "age of reason." This term seemed to function as a watershed in the passage to moral agency and hence responsibility. In regard to virtue, one would thus move from a prerational stage where virtues functioned in somewhat inchoate fashion to a context of full-blown culpability for one's acts.[93] In the case of chastity, the matter is complicated further by the fact that puberty emerges some time after the age of reason and by differing cultural evaluations of when an individual was sufficiently mature to commence a sexual relationship.

Modern developmental psychology has offered a helpful corrective to this apparent chasm between prerational innocence and moral responsibility. The work of Erik Erikson on human affectivity, Jean Piaget on cognition, James Fowler on faith, Robert Kegan on the self con-

---

sideration of the way in which classical virtue theory is congruent with modern psychological assessments of mental health, see Neal O. Weiner, *The Harmony of the Soul: Mental Health and Moral Virtue Reconsidered* (Albany: State University of New York Press, 1993).

92. Cf. Kraft, *Whole and Holy Sexuality*, 19–22.

93. Hence the Scholastic axiom that the first act of an individual after attaining the age of reason will either be an act of virtue or a mortal sin. For example, see Aquinas, *ST*, I–II, q. 89, a. 6.

cept, and Lawrence Kohlberg on moral reasoning have uncovered important patterns in human development over the course of the life cycle. It is true that approaches such as Kohlberg's, while particularly important from the standpoint of moral theory, are not without limitations imposed by certain philosophical presuppositions or a bias toward male experience.[94] Nevertheless, they make an important contribution toward uncovering some of the basic patterns of development within the human personality. For this reason some moralists have begun to use them to provide developmental perspectives on the moral life as a whole.[95]

This developmental perspective can also aid in the renewal of virtue-centered accounts of moral agency. The primary place where this integration has begun is in the elaboration of the theology of the fundamental option that often self-consciously draws on such developmental perspectives.[96]

In relation to sexuality, such perspectives can serve to provide a broader perspective on sexual acts. They can do so, first, by overcoming an isolated focus on individual sexual acts, abstracted from the whole of a person's growing moral character and the concreteness of the relationship in which they take place. Second, this perspective can serve to clarify and nuance the limitations placed on the moral agent's culpability by what was traditionally designated the impediment of ignorance due to immaturity.[97] Some have argued that these newer approaches would sug-

---

94. For an incisive critique of some of the philosophical presuppositions underlying Kohlberg's account of moral reasoning, see Meilaender, *Theory and Practice of Virtue*, 84–99. Cf. Craig Dykstra, *Vision and Character: A Christian Educator's Alternative to Kohlberg* (New York: Paulist Press, 1981), 7–29. For a critique of the androcentric bias of Kohlberg's data and some proposals that attempt to better integrate women's experience, see Carol Gilligan, *In a Different Voice: Psychological Theory and Women's Development* (Cambridge, Mass.: Harvard University Press, 1982).

95. See, e.g., Walter Conn, *Conscience: Development and Self-Transcendence* (Birmingham, Ala.: Religious Education Press, 1981), and *Christian Conversion: A Developmental Interpretation of Autonomy and Surrender* (New York: Paulist Press, 1986). These works also contain helpful overviews of the work of the various developmental theorists listed above.

96. See, e.g., Bernard Häring, *Free and Faithful in Christ*, Vol. 1: *General Moral Theology* (New York: Seabury Press, 1978), 164–222.

97. For a consideration of ignorance and other "enemies of the voluntary," see Cessario, *Introduction to Moral Theology*, 108–15.

gest some kinds of sexual acts at particular stages of personal development, such as masturbation by adolescents, may be more symptomatic
of an immature sexuality in need of integration rather than being in
themselves constitutive of one's moral character and goodness.[98]

However, in spite of the sometimes helpful perspective that they
provide, there are further questions that such developmental approaches
must address. Critics of fundamental option theory have rightly argued
that it tends to neglect the reflexive character of moral action highlighted by traditional virtue theory.[99] That is, particular moral acts not only
express one's developing moral character but also serve to shape it.
Hence, even at earlier stages of development attention must to be paid
to concrete acts such as masturbation by adolescents (although their developmental state may preclude full moral culpability) since these impact their developing moral freedom and agency. Bad moral choices,
even by immature persons, damage their character and thwart further
moral growth. There is therefore a need for further work to harmonize
the classical tradition of virtue with the insights of developmental psychology.[100]

Developmental perspectives do make clear, however, that the acquisition of chastity is closely interrelated with one's overall intellectual,
affective, and moral development. One cannot expect precisely the same
kinds of manifestations of the virtue from even two adults of the same
age and background if they are at very different developmental stages.
This awareness is particularly important for those engaged in pastoral
ministry in areas related to human sexuality, those who deal with the in-
terrelationship of sexuality and spirituality, and parents and religious
educators who attempt to instill values related to sexuality in the

98. On this point, see, e.g., Charles Curran, "Sexual Ethics: A Critique," in *Issues in
Sexual and Medical Ethics* (South Bend, Ind.: University of Notre Dame Press, 1978), 44–45,
49. Cf. Kraft, *Whole and Holy Sexuality*, 102–5.

99. See Lawler, Boyle, and May, *Catholic Sexual Ethics*, 94–95. Cf. the account of the
connection between action and freedom realized in growth in holiness provided by Cessario, *Introduction to Moral Theology*, 101–6, 151–56.

100. This need is recognized even by those who rather uncritically assume the superiority of these more modern approaches. See, e.g., Charles Curran, "The Historical Development of Moral Theology," in *Toward an American Catholic Moral Theology* (South Bend,
Ind.: University of Notre Dame Press, 1987), 14–15.

young.[101] Both the exercise and the acquisition of chastity is developmentally conditioned.

If the acquisition of chastity is conditioned by one's personal development, it is equally shaped by the cultural milieu in which one lives.

VI. Chastity and Culture

Even the most classical of approaches recognizes that not all of the particular moral excellences that produce human flourishing are rooted solely in human nature. The perception of many such values and even of human nature itself is shaped in part by the symbols and ideas of the culture in which they are viewed. Hence the effort to present or inculcate moral values must take into account this complex and far-reaching effect of cultural influence.

Modern proponents of virtue theory have recognized this cultural locus of virtue in describing the process of the passing on of a "tradition of virtue." Such a tradition is mediated by specific narratives that describe particular moral values and seek to engender specific practices that make possible their assimilation in differing cultural settings.[102]

If this is true for virtue in general, then it is also true of chastity in particular. To some degree or other chastity is a virtue mediated by moral and religious narratives whose acquisition will be shaped by particular cultural contexts and symbols. This observation suggests a few basic implications.

It will at times be the case that the Church in its teaching, preaching, and religious education has to attempt to offer prophetic criticism to deficient understandings of sexuality in specific cultures.[103] Thus, the

---

101. For a pastoral analysis of issues related to chastity in various states in life and its integration in spirituality, see Benedict Groeschel, *The Courage to Be Chaste* (New York: Paulist Press, 1985). For a further examination of some of these issues, see Chapter 7 of the present work.

102. See MacIntyre, *After Virtue*, 186–96. For a more thorough-going narrative approach to virtue theory, see Stanley Hauerwas, *The Peaceable Kingdom* (South Bend, Ind.: University of Notre Dame Press, 1983).

103. See the description of the sickness that can invade human culture in John Paul II, Letter to Families, *Gratissimam sane*, nos. 13–14. See also the indicators of a "culture of death" described in *Evangelium vitae*, nos. 10–17. The text can be found in *Origins* 24, no. 42 (April 6, 1995): 690f.

view of sex as a commodity for nothing more than pleasure or profit widespread in popular culture, the manner in which the media often undercuts any notion of chastity or sexual restraint,[104] or rigid and stereotypical understandings of gender roles are all examples of inadequate views of sexuality that deserve to be challenged and rejected.

How does one offer such a challenge? Obviously, this can be done through public critique and moral argument. However, it can also be done through concrete efforts to build and develop cultural practices that support a better understanding of sex and chastity. This can take the form of the development of alternative media that can effectively compete in the marketplace of ideas. It can occur through the effort to forge differing perceptions of sexual activity and more flexible gender roles through effective moral and religious catechesis. It can even be found in popular movements such as the efforts of many teens to offer a countercultural witness through signing a chastity pledge. All of this can contribute to what John Paul II has recently described as building a "culture of life" in which human sexuality is more adequately understood and respected.[105]

However, in this engagement with culture, whether through critical evaluation or the elaboration of alternative views and practices, care must be taken that this is not heard as mere prudery or the reintroduction of a more negative view of sex. Religious educators who focus only on the critical aspect of the engagement with culture run this very risk. The message of chastity, foreign as it may be in popular culture, will only be heard if it is linked to a compelling and positive vision of human sexuality and to the development of specific culturally attractive practices that can allow it to flourish. The Church, which in its teaching often proclaims its possession of the "truth" about the person and his or her sexuality, needs to allow this splendor to shine not merely in clarity of specific proscriptions, but in the radiance of a more compelling vision.

Finally, because human culture serves to mediate the particular values

104. On this effect of the media in undermining the efforts of parents and other religious educators, see Pontifical Council for the Family, *The Truth and Meaning of Human Sexuality*, no. 56. Unfortunately, the document's comments on the media are somewhat brief and predominantly negative.

105. See John Paul II, Encyclical Letter, *Evangelium vitae*, nos. 95–100.

that shape moral character, there must also be a profound respect for genuine autonomy of human cultures and authentic variations in regard to understandings of sexuality. Thus, various cultures might have differing estimates of the age or personal maturity necessary to enter into a stable sexual relationship or value motives for marriage other than romantic love or personal fulfillment often valorized in our own.[106] Such diversity of cultural perceptions can enrich and deepen an understanding of the mystery of human sexuality and its integration through chastity.

An appreciation and renewed understanding of the virtue of chastity indeed has much to offer contemporary culture. In a culture where sexual expression is routinely reduced to a narcissistic search for ecstatic release and personal satisfaction, it recalls the deeper values at stake in sexual relationships. Chastity enables sex to be understood within the context of human dignity, human growth, and human culture. In this way, it points toward and makes possible the human vocation to communion in love.

106. Thus the current code of canon law (can. 1083) specifies a minimum of 16 years of age for males to licitly enter marriage and a minimum of 14 years for females, but recognizes the power of local bishops conferences to set such limits at an older age depending on local custom (cf. can. 1072).

CHAPTER 5

Male and Female
Equality, Difference, Dignity

Moral virtues, of course, do not exist in the abstract. They exist within the persons who habituate themselves to them through repeated moral choices. By repeatedly choosing the good over time and in a variety of situations, a person's character becomes conformed to that specific form of moral goodness. The virtuous person develops a new power to act excellently that he or she did not previously possess.

Virtues, therefore, presuppose persons as their subjects. Virtue theory in turn demands an *anthropology*, an account of the person who develops and exercises the virtues. Given that the focus of the present work is on virtue as it pertains to matters of sexuality, it is crucial to note that human persons who acquire and exercise the virtues are necessarily embodied and therefore sexual beings. How one understands this embodiment and the place of sexuality in it is therefore an important question for an account of virtue—whether ancient or modern.

Some scholars will distinguish between "sex," "gender," and "sexuality."[1] In this view "sex" denotes our physicality, our embodiment as male or female. It encompasses the biological and relational aspects of the person's makeup. In part because of arguments put forward by feminist thinkers, "gender" has come to be understood in terms of the way in which education and environment condition us to understand the biological givens of sex.[2] It includes cultural expectations of what consti-

---

1. See, e.g., Kraft, *Whole and Holy Sexuality*, 15–18. Unfortunately, Kraft's own insistence on the unity of body and soul within the person's makeup is at odds with his Jungian view of the androgynous interior of the person.

2. For treatments of the emergence of the distinction between sex and gender in feminist theory, see Judith Van Herik, *Freud on Femininity and Faith* (Berkeley and Los Angeles:

tutes masculinity and femininity, as well as assumptions concerning which roles are appropriate for one sex or the other. On these terms "sexuality" refers to how individuals relate to others as men and women because of the dynamic interplay between nature and nurture within their personalities. Sexuality enters into all of the actions of the person. One is always an embodied and hence a sexual being.

While these distinctions might be useful, they are by no means un-controversial. The last thirty years have witnessed an intense debate across the spectrum of disciplines within the humanities and the sciences as to the relative impact of biology versus environment (nature vs. nurture) in shaping sexuality. Essentialists in this debate, while admitting some cultural influence on the way in which they are understood and expressed, lay primary emphasis on the biological givenness of sex differences.[3] The complex biological interplay of genital sex, biochemical sex, and genetic sex are the primary determinants of a person's sexual makeup. Constructionists, while admitting some impact on the part of biology, see both gender and sexuality as largely shaped and constructed out of cultural assumptions and influence.[4] On these terms it follows that sexuality can be deconstructed and understood far more individually. Gender too can be redefined to embrace new possibilities on the basis of alternative forms of sexual orientation and expression.[5]

It is beyond the scope of this study to adjudicate this complex and wide-ranging debate. It seems fairly safe to say that a balanced account of sexuality has to account for the impact of both biology and culture.[6]

University of California Press, 1982), 112–19; and John Archer and Barbara Lloyd, *Sex and Gender* (Cambridge, U.K.: Cambridge University Press, 1985).

3. See, e.g., Yves Christen, *Sex Differences: Modern Biology and the Unisex Fallacy*, trans. Nicholas Davidson (New Brunswick, N.J.: Transaction Books, 1991).

4. See, e.g., James Nelson, *Body Theology* (Louisville, Ky.: Westminster and John Knox Press, 1992), esp. 41–54; Rosalyn Diprose, *The Bodies of Women: Ethics, Embodiment and Sexual Difference* (London: Routledge, 1994); and Elaine Graham, *Making the Difference: Gender Personhood* (Minneapolis, Minn.: Fortress Press, 1996).

5. At the United Nations Habitat Conference held in Istanbul in 1996 some theorists argued strongly for five "genders" comprised of heterosexual men, heterosexual women, homosexual men, homosexual women, and transexuals. While this view was not adopted by the conference, it continues to be debated in the United Nations and elsewhere both as theory and social policy.

6. For a fascinating effort to account for the data of biology, psychology, and cultural

Extreme essentialism, especially in some sociobiological approaches, tends toward a determinism at odds with a Christian concept of freedom. Extreme constructionism tends to dualistically separate the subject from his or her embodiment. The body and sexuality have no intrinsic meaning—only that assigned by an autonomous and self-creating subject. This problem is exacerbated in postmodern approaches that solopsistically view all of reality in this fashion.

Yet the ongoing debate about sexual difference is by no means unimportant to considerations of sexual ethics approached from the standpoint of virtue. For at stake in much of this discussion are very basic issues of equality among persons that bear upon human dignity in fundamental ways. Much of the literature on sex differences and gender both inside and outside of feminist circles can be read as an attempt to account for both equality and difference between women and men. This chapter will locate the equality of the sexes in their possession of a shared human nature, while arguing that sexual difference may be understood as a fundamental relation constitutive of personhood.[7] It will develop this argument both in relation to Scripture and to contemporary theological reflection. The chapter will also consider some fundamental threats to the dignity of women and men as persons in the forms of interior acts of lust, pornography, masturbation, sex between unmarried persons, prostitution, sexual harassment and abuse, sexual misconduct by clerics and religious, and sexual violence.

I. Genesis Revisited

It is crucial to note some of the language used to describe the relationship of women and men in the opening chapters of Genesis, as these are foundational to subsequent biblical teaching both historically and canonically. The creation stories help to articulate a biblical perspective on how both equality and difference can be found between the sexes and in their mutual relationship to one another.

---

anthropology in identifying some of the key differences between the sexes, see Walter Ong, S.J., *Fighting for Life: Contest, Sexuality and Consciousness* (Ithaca, N.Y.: Cornell University Press, 1981).

7. Cf. John S. Grabowski, "The Status of the Sexual Good as a Direction for Moral Theology," *Heythrop Journal* 35 (1994):15–34.

Thus, the second account of creation (Gn 2:4b–3:24) after the dissonance created by the words of Yahweh in Genesis 2:18 that "It is not
good for the man to be alone," proposes as a solution to create an ʿēzer
for the man.[8] This term is sometimes translated rather freely as "suitable partner" (NAB) or more literally as a "helper suitable" (NIV).
While the latter translation more closely reflects the original Hebrew, in
contemporary English usage the term "helper" carries connotations of
inferiority and subservience. Current research has shown that the term
ʿēzer carries no such connotation. Lisa Sowle Cahill rightly observes
that the term ʿēzer is never used in the Old Testament to designate an
inferior. In fact, the term often refers to God as the one who gives aid
to Israel (cf. Ex 18:4; Dt 33:7, 29; Ps 20:3, 121:2, 124:8).[9] It thus serves to
underscore the equal dignity of women with men.

This contention is confirmed by the interlude that follows in which
God creates various animals and brings them to ʾādām who gives them
names. In biblical thought the giving of a name was a sign of authority.
It denoted the ability to grasp the essence of a thing and to express it.[10]
The narrator thus contrasts the dignity of woman with that of animals—an idea that seems offensive in its obviousness to the twenty-
first-century reader but that was far less obvious to many in the ancient
Near East of the tenth century B.C. The man only explicitly "names" the
woman in this sense after the sin of the couple and God's declaration
that the couple's relationship would be heretofore marred by domination and subservience (see Gn 3:16, 20).[11]

---

8. The dissonance is created by the contrast between this statement and the frequent
refrain of the first creation account that "God looked at everything he had made and
found it very good" (Gn 1:31). The author/redactor of the first account who juxtaposed
the two traditions presumably saw this disagreement but left it precisely because it serves
to highlight the importance of what it introduces.

9. See Cahill, *Between the Sexes*, 54. Cf. Phyllis Trible, *God and the Rhetoric of Sexuality*,
Overtures to Biblical Theology 2 (Philadelphia: Fortress Press, 1978), 90; and Westermann, *Genesis 1–11*, 227.

10. Cf. John McKenzie, S.J., "Name," in *Dictionary of the Bible* (New York: Macmillan,
1965), 603–5.

11. It might be argued that the woman is named by the man in 2:23, but it is not clear
that this should be read as the giving of a name in the same sense. For ʾādām recognizes
not only her but himself in a new way precisely through their mutual relation.

The covenant oath uttered by ʾādām in Genesis 2:23 is even more significant. For here the text uses not the generic term for "mankind" (ʾādām) but the for the first time the gender specific terms of ʾiššâ and ʾîš: "this one shall be called 'woman' for out of 'her man' this one has been taken." The point of this play on words, which works in English as well as in Hebrew, is to indicate that man and woman are of the same "stuff" or are the same kind of entity. Put more philosophically, it indicates that women and men have the same nature. It is noteworthy that both woman and man are made directly by God, man from the ʾădāmā (dirt or clay) and woman from the body of the man (see Gn 2:7, 22). Woman may be made *for* man as a partner and complement, but she is not made *by* him.[12] The marriage covenant is concluded by parties who are basically equal in dignity, even if not equal in legal standing in Israel's law.

Even more striking is the deliberate reversal of woman's legal status indicated by Genesis 2:24: "That is why a man leaves his father and mother and clings to his wife and the two of them become one body." In Israelite law, it was the woman who left her family to become part of the house (bêt) of the man.[13] Here, the description of the existing social order of tenth century B.C. Israel is reversed by the narrative and attributed to prelapsarian existence, implying that women's legally subordinate status was not part of God's original creative intent.

The first story of creation (Gn 1:1–2:4a), probably composed some centuries after the second, also highlights the basic equality of women and men, although in a somewhat different theological framework. This "Priestly" text describes ʾādām comprised of both sexes—male and female. And both are created in the image (ṣelem) and likeness (dĕmût) of God (see Gn 1:27). The term "image" in the text indicates not so much physical resemblance, but royal authority and representation in relation

12. Christopher Uehlinger points out that the Akkadian word for "rib" (ti) can also indicate "life." This and archeological evidence support the view that the woman derives both her life and her ability to give life as "mother of all the living" (Gn 3:20) directly from her Creator, not from the earlier prototype from whom she was built. See "Nicht nur Knochenfrau. Zu einem wenig beachteten Aspect der zweiten Schöpfungerszählung," *Bibel und Kirche* 53 (1998): 31–34.

13. Cf. Cahill, *Between the Sexes*, 55; and Paul Jewett, *Man as Male and Female* (Grand Rapids, Mich.: William B. Eerdmans, 1975), 124–28.

to the rest of the created world.[14] Women and men are given "dominion" over the rest of the creatures of the world (see Gn 1:26, 28) not to
dominate or exploit them, but to care for them as God does.[15] Unlike
the narrative progression of the older story, the creation of both sexes
is here described as simultaneous. Women and men are created by God
and have the capacity to relate to him directly. This fact provides an important foundation for the dignity of human persons.[16]

But the "image of God" in which men and women are created is not
exhausted in humanity's stewardship of creation. The text also under-
scores that it is through their mutual relation that men and women
comprise this image. Thus 'ādām is complete only in this dual version—
"male and female."[17] Human beings therefore are not created as disconnected monads, but as relational beings called to enter into communion and community with one another. The most fundamental of
these relations on the human level is that between male and female.[18]

14. For a detailed study of this text and its import for an understanding of the sexes,
see Francis Martin, "Male and Female He Created Them: A Summary of the Teaching
of Genesis Chapter One," Communio 20 (1993): 240–65; and Walter Vogels, "The Human
Person in the Image of God (Gn 1, 26)," Science et Espirit 46 (1994): 189–202.

15. A similar idea is expressed in the older creation story when God placed 'ādām in
the garder to "cultivate and care for it" (Gn 2:15b). On the compatibility of this kingly
role with responsible stewardship for the rest of creation, see Martin A. Klopfenstein,
"Was heisst 'Macht euch die Erde untertan?' Überlegungen zur Schöpfungsgeschichte der
Bibel in der Umweltkrise heute," in Leben aus dem Wort: Beiträge zum Alten Testament, Beataj 40,
ed. Walter Dietrich (Bern: Peter Lang, 1996), 275–83; Donald B. Sharp, "A Biblical Foun-
dation for an Environmental Theology," Science et Espirit 47 (1995): 305–13; and Manfred
Weippert, "Tier und Mensch in einer menschenarmen Welt. Zum sog. Dominium terrae in
Genesis 1," in Ebenbild Gottes—Herrscher über die Welt, Biblisch-Theologische Studien 33
(Neukirchen-Vluyn: Neukirchener Verlag, 1998), 35–55.

16. For a more general consideration of the significance of the imago dei for moral theology, see Cessario, Introduction to Moral Theology, 22–38.

17. Phyllis Trible argues that there is kind of parallelism between the phrases "image
of God" and "male and female" such that the latter statement develops the former; see
God and the Rhetoric of Sexuality, 17.

18. Cf. Westerman, Genesis 1–11: A Commentary, 142–61; and Karl Barth, Church Dogmatics,
trans. A. T. Mackay, T. H. L. Parker, Harold Knight, Henry A. Kennedy, and John Marks,
ed. G. W. Bromiley and T. F. Torrance (Edinburgh, U.K.: T. & T. Clark, 1961), 3:4:116–41.
For an overview of the implications of this understanding of the human person as relational for human sexuality as depicted in Genesis 1–3, see Epifanio Gallegeo, O.S.A., "La
sexualidad. Aporte de los relatos de la creación," Biblia y fe 18, no. 52 (1992): 21–36.

This relation is the basis of the broader human community in society.

These two fundamental meanings of the "image of God"—dominion and relation—are not disconnected from one another. The text itself links them through God's life-giving blessing on the union of the sexes: "God blessed them saying: 'Be fertile and multiply; fill the earth and subdue it. Have dominion over the fish of the sea, the birds of the air, and all the living things that move upon the earth'" (Gn 1:28). Through their shared fertility women and men exercise dominion over the created world. It is worth noting that here we have an intimation of what the Christian tradition would come to see as the two basic purposes of human sexuality: the union of the couple and the procreation and care of children.

But there is a relation even more basic to humanity's well-being than that between male and female in the marriage covenant—that is, humanity's relation to its Creator. The first account of creation is deliberately structured so as to include the creation of both humanity and animals on the sixth day (see Gn 1:24–30). In biblical thought, the number six denotes incompleteness and imperfection—it is the number of humanity apart from God.[19] Though all creation, including sexuality in all of its dimensions, is deemed "very good" (see Gn 1:30b), it is still radically incomplete. It is only in the Sabbath worship of the seventh day that creation and its human priest stewards are complete and whole.[20] And it is humanity that gives voice to this praise on behalf of the rest of material creation through worship. Human dominion for both women and men is priestly.[21] And human relationality is fully actualized

19. Thus in a comment on the significance of the number 666 which designates the beast of Revelation 13:18 in relation to biblical symbolism Adela Yarbro Collins notes that "'[s]ix' has connotations of incompleteness, imperfection, and even of evil"; see *The Apocalypse,* New Testament Message Series 22 (Wilmington, Del.: Michael Glazier, 1979), 97.

20. Seven in biblical thought is associated with completeness, with perfection, and ultimately with God himself; see John McKenzie, "Seven," in *Dictionary of the Bible,* 794. It is worth noting that when humanity fails to give voice to creation's praise, it becomes in a sense like the beasts with whom it was created on the sixth day. This is certainly the point of the story of Nebuchadnezzar in Dn 4:25–34.

21. By this is meant that both women and men have the capacity and responsibility to relate directly to God in worship—it does not suppose that this need be done in identical fashion.

only in communion—not just with fellow creatures, but even more with their transcendent Source.

Taken together, these two stories of creation offer a number of key theological insights into the equality and difference of the sexes. Both men and women are created by and for God as well as for each other. Both share a common humanity, in spite of their obvious differences. Both sexes are created in the image of God, indicating that they are given the role of priest-stewards in creation and called to communion with their Creator as well as with one another. The differences between the sexes are the basis of their covenantal union with one another. They are also attended by God's life-giving blessing in sexual reproduction, which is one expression of human stewardship within creation.

II. Other Biblical Teaching

The rather idyllic portrait of the prelapsarian relationship between the sexes was clearly quite different from the actual situation of women and of marriage in biblical times. Even the older story of creation offers some explanation for this disjunct through its etiological account of human sin (Gn 3:1–24). Because the couple listens to the words of the serpent and grasps at the shadowy illusions of pride in a vain attempt to "be like gods who know what is good and what is bad" (see Gn 3: 5), they find their relationships with God, with one another, and with the rest of creation broken and disordered. Overcome with shame and fear, the couple attempt to hide from God (see Gn 3:8) and are ultimately banished from the immediacy of his presence in the garden (see Gn 3:23–24).[22] Their nakedness now becomes a mark of vulnerability to

22. Though the Hebrew name of the garden (*'ēden*) carries connotations of sensual delight, it is striking that throughout the second creation account it is described in imagery that Israelite readers would easily associate with the Temple: its location in the east; its being a source of rivers (cf. Gn 2:10–14; Ezek 42); the tree of life (Gn 2:9, 3:22) which was depicted in the Temple as a candle (cf. Ex 25:31–35; Lev 24:1–9); the mention of onyx stone, which recalls its use in adorning the tabernacle and the Temple (cf. Ex 23:7; 1 Chr 29:2), and the vestments of the high priest (see Ex 28:9, 20); the cherubim stationed to guard the way to the tree of life, which evoke their use throughout the Temple (cf. Ex 25:18–22, 26:31; 1 Kgs 6:23–29); and the fact that God's presence is described as "walking about" in both the garden and the sanctuary (cf. Gn 3: 8; Lev 26:12; Dt 23:25, 2 Sam 7:6–7). All of this seems to indicate that the garden symbolizes a place of primordial

be concealed through veils in speech and dress (see Gn 3:7). The language of sexual union can now articulate not only fidelity and the gift of self within the marriage covenant, but the darker utterances of use and exploitation. And rather than the basic unity and equality in which the couple were created, their relationship, and thus that between the sexes, comes to be characterized by domination and subservience: "your urge shall be for your husband and he shall be your master" (Gn 3:16).[23] In a mysterious way, even humanity's relationship with the natural world is infected with antagonism (see Gn 3:17–18).

Thus the creation stories, particularly the second, make clear that the historical existence of humanity is lived within a diminished state. Once humanity is exiled from Eden, humanity's relationship with God, the relationship between the sexes, and the marriage covenant are all lived in a world marred by evil and sin. Yet the fact that Israelite women had fewer rights than their male counterparts or even in some cases women of surrounding countries does not give this condition the force of divine establishment.[24] Indeed, both canonically and theologically this situation stands as called into question by the opening chapters of Genesis.

---

communion and communication between humanity and God of which the Temple in tenth-century B.C. Israel was but a dim remembrance.

23. Pope John Paul II sees in this statement a depiction of male domination of and discrimination against women down through the ages. He notes, however, that Genesis calls this the effect of sin. See Apostolic Letter, *Mulieris dignitatem*, no. 10. Walter Vogels argues that the verse is better rendered "on the one hand you have a desire to dominate your husband, but he, on the other hand, is capable of dominating you," indicating how the mutual complementarity of the sexes often becomes a struggle for control. See "The Power Struggle between Man and Woman (Gen 3, 16b)," *Biblica* 77 (1996): 197–209. Cf. Adrien Janis Bledstein, "Was Eve Cursed? (Or Did a Woman Write Genesis?)," *Bible Review* 9, no. 1 (1993): 42–45.

24. It is overstated to hold that Israelite women were regarded as mere property of their husbands. Women could not be sold, unlike slaves or property, which could. They could not take vows or receive an inheritance without their husband's consent. On these matters, see Anthony Philips, *Ancient Israel's Criminal Law* (Oxford, U.K.: Blackwell, 1970), 117ff.; and Angelo Tosato, *Il matrimonio israelitico: Una teoria generale* (Rome: Pontifical Biblical Institute Press, 1982).

Historical study has found that Israelite women enjoyed less social and political freedom than women of neighboring cultures. However, in postexilic times the position of Jewish women outside of Israel tended to be comparable to that of the people with

There are indications in the Old Testament that even within the conditions of this diminished existence, women were honored either for their role in salvation history or for their position within their families.[25] The Scriptures record the deeds not only of Israel's patriarchs such as Abraham, Isaac, and Jacob, but also of its matriarchs such as Sarah, Rebekah, Rachel, and Leah.[26] Ancient Israel had women who ruled it as judges or queens.[27] It knew women who were gifted as prophetesses.[28] It celebrated women who were enabled by God to deliver the people of Israel.[29] But even ordinary women were honored in virtue of their position within their families as wives and particularly as mothers. It is also significant that biblical law so strongly condemned faults against one's mother (cf. Ex 21:17; Lv 20:9; Dt 21:18–21, 27:16) and that biblical literature enjoined children to respect and obey their mother equally with their father (e.g., Ex 20:12; Dt 5:16; Lv 19:3; Prv 19:26, 20:20, 23:22, 30:17; Sir 3:1–16).

Even more striking testimony to the dignity of women is Jesus' treatment of women depicted in the Gospels. In a culture that excluded women from many aspects of public life, Jesus showed himself to be very willing to break with many of these conventions.[30] Unlike other rabbis of his day, Jesus addressed women in his teaching. Indeed women were the subjects of a number of Jesus' parables. Women along with men were the recipients of his healings. They were included in his call

whom they lived. See Bernadette Brooten, *Women Leaders in the Ancient Synagogues* (Chicago and Atlanta: Scholars Press, 1982); and A. K. Bowman, *Egypt after the Pharoahs 332 B.C.–A.D. 642* (Berkeley and Los Angeles: University of California Press, 1986), 123–24.

25. For an overview of the Pentateuch's view of the family including the position of women within it, see Joseph Kottackal, "Family Life in Pentateuchal Traditions," *Bible Bhashyam* 20 (1994): 267–79.

26. For an overview of all of the women within the book of Genesis, see Toni Craven, "Women in Genesis," *The Bible Today* 35 (1997): 32–39.

27. See, e.g., the description of the judge and prophetess Deborah in Judges 4–5. There were also ruling women who were infamous as well as famous such as the vicious Queen Athaliah (see 2 Kgs 11).

28. In addition to Deborah one can look at the person and oracle of Huldah described in 2 Kings 22:14–20.

29. Thus Jael was celebrated for slaying Sisera, the general of the Canannite king Jabin (cf. Jdg 4:17–24, 5:24–27). The books of Judith and Esther, whether or not they are historical accounts, celebrate the exploits of particular Israelite women.

30. The following summary is based upon Collins, *Christian Morality*, 185, 189–90.

to conversion and discipleship, and some wealthy women actually traveled with Jesus as disciples and provided for him out of their means (see Lk 8:1–3). It was to women that the risen Jesus first appeared, commissioning them to bring the good news of the Resurrection to the grieving, fearful Apostles. In all of these respects Jesus' treatment of women was a novelty from the perspective of his culture. Rather than treating them as second class or subservient, he treated them as persons equal in dignity to their male counterparts.[31]

There is clearly some tension and ambiguity in the biblical portrayal of the respective positions of women and men. On the one hand, much biblical literature includes legislation and teaching that presupposes a subordinate status for women. On the other hand, the opening chapters of Genesis raise very basic theological questions as to whether this situation is the result of divine mandate or human sinfulness. These questions are underscored by the novelty of Jesus' treatment of women and his inclusion of them in his call to conversion and discipleship, as well as by the insistence of other New Testament texts on the basic baptismal equality of women and men (see Gal 3:27–28). Yet the New Testament authors also maintain that there are specific positions in the church (e.g., 1 Cor 14:33b–36) and family (e.g., Eph 5:21–33) appropriate to women and men and that leadership roles in them should be reserved for men. Scholars continue to debate the precise meaning of these texts and the degree to which they are shaped by their cultural horizon. It is beyond the scope of this study to attempt to sort out all of the complicated exegetical and ecclesiological questions raised by such texts.

In regard to the position of men and women within the family, however, it is possible to read the New Testament as calling for a transformation of the way in which men's and women's roles were lived within Christian households, even while accepting the larger pattern of Hellenistic culture. For example, Ephesians 5:21–33, the most elaborate and theologically important of the so-called household order texts *(Haustafeln)* in the New Testament, contains important indicators of mutuality between the couple. The text begins with the injunction given to couples to "subordinate yourselves to one another out of reverence for

31. Cf. John Paul II, *Mulieris dignitatem*, nos. 13, 24.

Christ" (Eph 5:21).[32] Furthermore, the "headship" of the husband is invested with a radically different meaning through its being superimposed onto the model of Christ who "handed himself over" *(paredōken)* for the Church. To describe a husband's love for his wife in this way is to indicate that "[t]he husband becomes the chief servant, like Christ, and the wife an example of one who responds to her serving lover with loving submission as the Church does to Christ."[33] Hence even though the text uses language and ideas intelligible within the Hellenistic culture from which it emerged, the text seeks to transform the concept of male authority within the patriarchal household from within.[34] It is in part on this basis that Pope John Paul II has taught that this text "is to be understood and carried out in a new way: as a *'mutual submission out of reverence for Christ.'"*[35] Though it has taken some centuries to articulate such an understanding of mutual authority within the marriage covenant, this development is a reflection of the way in which the grace of the redemption overcomes the antagonism between the sexes wrought by sin.

III. Contemporary Reflections

The complexity of the biblical witness and the urgency of contemporary questions concerning the equality of women suggest the need for more systematic theological reflection on the topic. The Scriptures point toward the equal dignity of women and men as persons, even while recording the fact that this was imperfectly realized in differing

32. *Hypotassomenoi allelois en phobo Christou;* my translation. Stephen Miletic notes that this verse also elliptically supplies the verb for the specific submission of the wife to her husband enjoined in verse 22. Because the verb itself only appears in Christological formulations (as in 5:21 and in the description of the submission of the Church to Christ), Miletic argues that it should be read "in the middle voice with an imperative force," implying that it describes the voluntary act of a free agent. See *"One Flesh,"* 28–29.

33. Ben Witherington, *Women in the Earliest Churches,* Society for New Testament Studies 59 (Cambridge, U.K.: Cambridge University Press, 1988), 74.

34. Cf. Witherington, *Women,* 220, 243 n.157; Miletic, *One Flesh,* 116.

35. John Paul II, *Mulieris dignitatem,* no. 24. The citation is from *On the Dignity and Vocation of Women,* Vatican Translation (Boston: St. Paul Books and Media, 1988); emphasis in original. For an examination of the theological basis and practical import of this teaching, see John S. Grabowski, "Mutual Submission and Trinitarian Self-Giving," *Angelicum* 84 (1997): 489–512.

historical and cultural settings. Yet the Scriptures also underscore the differences between the sexes as the basis for the covenant of marriage and as necessary for the exercise of human dominion in the procreation and care of children.

Contemporary philosophical and theological reflection has also wrestled with both the equality and the difference of the sexes. The problem is not unlike that of the one and the many which vexed many of the greatest minds of the ancient world.[36] Is unity or diversity the most basic component of reality? And is it the unity and equality of the sexes or their mutual differences that are more important?

Some approaches to this difficult set of issues seem to minimize the differences between the sexes in order to emphasize their equality. Real sexual difference is seen as a basic biological minimum. In this vein one can find the opinion of Rosemary Radford Reuther written some years ago: "[M]aleness and femaleness exist as reproductive role specialization. There is no necessary (biological) connection between reproductive complementarity in either pyschological or social role differentiation. These are the works of culture and socialization, not of 'nature.'"[37] More starkly, some more radical theorists have seen such minimal biological differences as mere obstacles to be overcome on the road to real sexual equality—that is, equality will only be achieved when all human reproduction takes place within a laboratory.[38]

There are significant problems with this approach. The first is its underlying philosophical presupposition that equality is identical to sameness. This is an idea with roots as ancient as the monism of Anaximander and buddings as recent as Marxism and modern Western liberalism.[39] This is not so much an answer to the problem of the one and the many as it is a denial of it through an embrace of half of its dialec-

36. On the parallel between this ancient philosophical problem and the contemporary debate over the unity and diversity of the sexes, see Patricia Wilson Kastner, *Faith, Feminism and the Christ* (Philadelphia: Fortress Press, 1983), 55–60.

37. Reuther, *Sexism and God-Talk: Toward a Feminist Theology* (Boston: Beacon, 1983), 228.

38. Cf. Shulamith Firestone, *The Dialectic of Sex: The Case for Feminist Revolution* (New York: William Morrow, 1970).

39. In his work *Peri physeôs* Anaximander argued that all motion in the cosmos is generated by the injustice of difference. That is, all things move in order to reach the state of entropy conceived of as a static sameness. For an examination of the textual and

tic. Furthermore, the minimization of difference in the name of equality seems very difficult to square with the wide array of empirically
measurable difference between the sexes. This includes not just the
enormously complex range of differences on the biological level—genital, hormonal, and genetic sex with the concomitant secondary sex characteristics that they produce—but evidence for an array of cognitive
and emotional differences between the sexes as well.[40]

Conversely, other approaches seem to so exaggerate the differences
between the sexes that they undermine their equality in the name of
preserving difference. This is the case with views that locate sexual difference on the level of human nature itself, holding that women and
men have distinct "natures." An approximation of such a view can be
found in the thought of Louis Bouyer. Bouyer holds that the nuptial
imagery found within the Scriptures, the theological tradition of the
Church, and in the liturgy "rests on what is fundamentally symbolic in
that creation itself, and particularly in human nature."[41] This is
butressed by Bouyer's view of the ontological connection between the
body and soul, which is such that an individual's "physical being will reveal and define his metaphysical being itself."[42] The result is that men
and women are understood to have sharply defined (though equally important) roles in the Church, in society, and within the family.[43]

To locate the differences between the sexes on the level of nature is
fraught with problems of a different kind. While this approach pre-
serves the differences between the sexes as ontologically and theological-

historical basis of Anaximander's thought, see Charles H. Kahn, *Anaximander and the Origins of Greek Cosmology* (New York: Columbia University Press, 1960; rpt., Philadelphia:
Centrum, 1985).

40. For overviews of some of this evidence, see James A. Monteleone, "The Physio-
logical Aspects of Sex," in *Human Sexuality and Personhood* (St. Louis: Pope John XXIII
Medical-Moral Center, 1981), 71–85; Ong, *Fighting for Life;* Gilligan, *In a Different Voice;*
Michael Levin, *Feminism and Freedom* (New Brunswick, N.J.: Transaction Books, 1987); and
Cornelius F. Murphy Jr., *Beyond Feminism: Toward a Dialogue on Difference* (Washington, D.C.:
The Catholic University of America Press, 1995), 75–88.

41. Bouyer, *Woman in the Church,* trans. Marilyn Teichart (San Francisco: Ignatius Press,
1979), 89.

42. Ibid., 53.

43. For a more thorough analysis of Bouyer's thought in this regard, see Grabowski,
"Status of the Sexual Good," 23–25.

ly significant, it seems to risk undermining their basic unity and equality. If there are distinct "natures" of the sexes, then in what does their common humanity consist? Are there, in fact, two different human species? Others have pointed out that this view creates acute soteriological problems as well. For if, as many of the Fathers of the Church held, "that which is not assumed is not redeemed," how can Christ's assumption of a "male human nature" redeem women?[44] It also raises questions for Christian morality. If men and women differ on the level of nature, are there different goods to which they are inclined and hence different norms by which they should live? Does moral virtue and its acquisition differ between men and women?[45]

The way forward from this conundrum is illumined through reflection on the most basic mystery of Christian faith: the Trinity. Just as the revelation that God is both a Trinity of Persons and yet utterly one in nature provided an unexpected solution to the problem of the one and the many that so baffled ancient thought, it can shed light on the debate on sexual difference. In the Trinity, each person is utterly equal in his possession of the divine nature and yet utterly irreducible to one another as Persons. Divine Personhood is known through the relations that are constitutive of it. Only the Father begets, only the Son is begotten, and only the Holy Spirit is breathed forth as the bond of their mutual love. Personal difference exists within the unity of nature.

So too with men and women created in the image of God. The sexes share a common humanity—the same nature.[46] Yet they are irreducibly different as persons. They are the "two equally valuable but different expressions of the one nature of humanity," as Walter Kasper has aptly ex-

44. See Rosemary Radford Reuther, "Can a Male Savior Save Women?," in *To Change the World: Christology and Cultural Criticism* (London: SCM, 1981), 45–56; Anne Carr, *Transforming Grace: Christian Tradition and Women's Experience* (San Francisco: Harper & Row, 1988), 52, 112; and Elizabeth Johnson, "The Maleness of Christ," in *The Special Nature of Women?*, Concilium 1991–1996, 108–16, esp. 109.

45. This is an interesting and important question even if one does not locate sexual difference on the level of nature. For a good initial study, see Christopher Klofft, "Moral Development, Virtue, and Gender: A Comparison of the Differing Accounts of Lisa Sowle Cahill, Servais Pinckaers, and Paul Evdokimov" (S.T.D. diss., The Catholic University of America, 2000).

46. On human nature as an image of the Trinity, see Cessario, *Introduction to Moral Theology*, 27–29.

pressed it.[47] Put more technically, sexual difference is accidental on the level of human nature but essential to actually existing persons.[48] Sexual difference can thus be understood as a relation that along with other relations is constitutive of personhood.[49] It is an aspect of the uniqueness or "originality" of each person inscribed in the very fabric of his or her being.[50] Yet it is also at the same times a summons, a task, and a call to communion for "it is not good for the man to be alone" (see Gn 2:18b). Communion is indeed a "way toward personality" and the call to communion is inscribed in one's makeup as male or female.[51] Pope John Paul II has described this as the "nuptial meaning of the body."[52] For in his or her somatic makeup, each person gives testimony to the fact that he or she is called to learn to give themselves as a gift. The dynamism and vocation of human sexuality is love.

IV. Ethical Import

A. The Dignity of the Person and Sexuality

Because each person is created in the image of God, he or she possesses an inalienable and nontransferable dignity. Sexuality, which is one dimension of a person's relational uniqueness and integrally connected to his or her vocation to love, participates in this personal dignity. Hence sexuality, like the person, should not be trivialized or misused.

As possessed of such dignity, every person is in justice owed respect and reverence. In light of Christian revelation and Jesus' gift of himself on the cross for the whole of humanity, it becomes apparent that each human being is also worthy of unconditional love. It is God's redemp-

47. Walter Kasper, "The Position of Women as a Problem of Theological Anthropology," trans. John Saward, in *The Church and Women: A Compendium*, ed. Helmut Moll (San Francisco: Ignatius Press, 1988), 58–59.

48. Cf. Grabowski, "Status of the Sexual Good," 25–28.

49. Other such relations might include one's being a creature, a son or daughter, a brother or sister, a husband or wife, a mother or father—both on the natural plane and through grace.

50. Cf. Pope John Paul II, Apostolic Letter, *Mulieris dignitatem*, no. 10.

51. The citation is from Romano Guardini, *La realtà della Chiesa* (Brescia: Morcelliana, 1973), 63. The translation is my own.

52. See the weekly general audience of January 9, 1980, in *Theology of the Body*, 60–63.

tive love for humanity that informs and enables the "great commandment" of love described in the Gospels. Ethically, then, every person should be treated as both an *alter ego* and an *alter Christus*. Minimally, this requires that in the gift of self in love each person should not be used as a mere means to one's own ends in utilitarian fashion.[53] Self-donation, including bodily self-donation, on the part of persons must be offered and received in unconditional respect and love.

Furthermore, though much modern ideology has trumpeted the liberation of sexuality from the repressive confines of commitment, this proclamation can be challenged on a variety of grounds: empirical observation of the havoc wreaked on familial and social relationships by this ideology; the biblical paradigm of sexual intimacy as a covenant ratifying gesture; the sacramental theology of marriage that grew from this paradigm; and faithfulness as a dimension of Christian character. For Christians, respect for persons as male and female also requires respect for the meaning of sexual union discerned within the Scriptures and an understanding of how it relates to their call to follow Jesus as disciples. This false concept of sexual freedom is also fundamentally at odds with the virtue of chastity as understood within the Christian tradition.

B. Lust and Practices Opposed to Chastity

Just as classical virtue theory specified certain vices that opposed each virtue, these anthropological reflections have still further implications with regard to the vice of lust and specific practices opposed to chastity. Such vicious practices distort and impede the person's capacity for self-donation. These acts can be internal to the mind and heart or externalized in action and behavior.

1. Interior Acts of Lust

As noted in the previous chapter, the Church's theological tradition has understood lust to be disordered desire for sexual pleasure or a fixation on sexual pleasure to the exclusion of other purposes of human sexuality (i.e., procreation and interpersonal union). Within the interior of the person this vice often takes the form of lust-inspired sexual fan-

53. See Wojtyla, *Love and Responsibility*, 40–44;. cf. the helpful discussion of the various ends of human action offered by Cessario, *Introduction to Moral Theology*, 36–37.

tasy—choosing to dwell upon sexual images or acts for the purpose of enjoying the pleasure that they produce. Such fantasies often abstract sex from any interpersonal context, from the dignity of persons, and from the real moral values at stake in sexual activity—for example, the unmarried person who fantasizes about sexual acts, the married person who fantasizes about romantic or sexual involvement with someone other than his or her spouse.[54] These kinds of thoughts, even if never acted upon, undermine the person's freedom to perceive and live the good as an embodied, sexual being.[55] They undercut the self-possession necessary to make a gift of oneself in love.

But this is not to say by any means that all thought about sexual matters is lustful. From an ethical perspective, a decision to stir up lust through sexual fantasy should be distinguished from fantasies produced by the unconscious (i.e., dreams) or spontaneous sexual thoughts.[56] It should also be distinguished from chaste sexual desire or use of the imagination which perceives the sexual attractiveness of others as integral persons. Finally, it should be noted that there are many reasons for which one might legitimately think about sex that are not in themselves opposed to chastity—for example, doctors and therapists attempting to help patients overcome sexual problems, educators attempting to impart a deeper understanding of authentic human sexuality, spouses seeking to better integrate their sexual relationship into the fabric of their mutual love.

2. Pornography

Fuel for interior acts of lust can be provided by pornographic words or images. Pornography takes real or simulated sexual acts and displays

54. It is possible, of course, for a married person to be guilty of lust in relation to his or her spouse—even interiorly. To do so would be to view him or her as merely an object of sexual gratification rather than as a person to be respected and loved through the means of bodily union. It is for this reason that Pope John II observed (using the biblical idiom) that spouses can "commit adultery in their hearts" in relation to one another. See his weekly general audience of October 8, 1980, in *Theology of the Body*, 156–59.

55. On the impact of lust on free moral choice, see Cessario, *Introduction to Moral Theology*, 111–12.

56. The former is a human act and thus the subject of moral evaluation. The latter are involuntary acts of a human. For a more complete discussion of the role of the voluntary in the moral life, see Cessario, *Introduction to Moral Theology*, 100–115.

them for third parties for purposes of entertainment or profit.[57] The rapid access to information made possible by the growth of the Internet has also made pornographic materials far more widely available—at least in wealthier areas of the world. This growth of information technology has also made it harder for civil authorities to prevent the production and distribution of such materials or even to restrict access to them by the young or by sexual predators.

Production or use of pornographic materials is contrary to both chastity and justice. They are a demonic icon of fallen sexuality, distorting the beauty of the body and the mutual self-gift of the conjugal act to a form of voyeuristic fixation on anonymous body parts. They fail to respect the dignity and subjectivity of those whom they portray. Even if they participate in them willingly, persons who engage in the production of pornographic materials are stripped not just of their clothing, but of their dignity as persons. They are treated as mere objects for the sexual consumption and enjoyment of others.[58] Particularly grave harm is done to vulnerable persons such as children or disadvantaged women who are coerced into participation in the making of these materials. Those who produce and distribute pornography violate justice by profiting from the exploitation of others and by being an occasion of scandal to the public. Those who buy or use pornography formally cooperate in this degradation of other human beings and thus sin not only against chastity, but against justice and love as well.

3. Masturbation

Often those who feed sexual fantasy with pornographic materials seek to heighten the pleasure they seek through masturbation—that is, genital stimulation to the point of orgasm outside the context of intercourse. Indeed, these practices often form an unhealthy cluster of mu-

57. Cf. *CCC*, 2354.

58. Pope John Paul II uses this line of argument to draw a subtle distinction between authentic art that happens to involve nudity and pornography. Art, the pope argues, always portrays the subjectivity and hence the dignity of those it portrays. Pornography, on the other hand, isolates the sexual characteristics of the person from his or her total personal reality and therefore presents those it portrays as objects for the use and satisfaction of others. See the weekly general audiences of April 15, 22, and 29, and of May 6, 1981, in *Theology of the Body*, 218–29.

tually reinforcing behaviors that can become addictive for who practice them.[59] Lustful fantasy inspired by pornography frequently seeks release through masturbation. A person trapped in such a pattern may seek to increase his or her level of sexual pleasure by engaging in other kinds of sexual acting out—having recourse to prostitution, or engaging in clandestine affairs. Conversely, a person in the grip of these vicious habits may withdraw from others, solopsistically preferring the pleasure derived from fantasies without the vulnerability of interpersonal exchange necessary to real relationships. As William Kraft expresses it, "Masturbation can lead to an affair with oneself."[60]

Though it is not an uncommon practice among adults and adolescents, the Catholic tradition has generally regarded masturbation as seriously disordered.[61] This is because it seeks sexual pleasure in isolation from the basic purposes of sexuality—an interpersonal union of love and the procreation and education of children. Masturbation can achieve neither of these ends. As such it does not enable a Christian to realize his or her vocation to love—whether as single, celibate, or married. The fixation on genital pleasure and release in isolation from the transcendent meaning of human sexuality frustrates the capacity to freely give oneself in love that is the hallmark of chastity. Instead, it accords well with the current ideology dominant in Western culture which truncates the meaning of sex to personal pleasure through ecstatic release.

While the practice of masturbation is itself a grave violation of chastity, the Church's tradition has also increasingly recognized that one's culpability for such an act might be greatly impacted by age, psychosexual maturity, and other circumstances. Such factors can lessen or

59. See Mark Laaser, *Faithful and True: Sexual Integrity in a Fallen World* (Grand Rapids, Mich.: Zondervan, 1996), 25–29. It is interesting to note that many of Laser's descriptions of the compulsion generated by sexual addiction bear a great deal of resemblance to the classical moral tradition's understanding of the vice of lust.

60. Kraft, "A Pyschospiritual View of Masturbation," *Human Development* 3 (1983): 79–85. The citation is from p. 80.

61. On the consistency of the Catholic tradition on this issue, see Gerald Coleman, S.S., *Human Sexuality: An All-Embracing Gift* (New York: Alba House, 1992), 301–3; and Lawler, Boyle, and May, *Catholic Sexual Ethics*, 177–78. On the statistical frequency of the practice, see Coleman, *Human Sexuality*, 306–8.

even minimize a person's culpability for engaging in such an act.[62] Thus the moral culpability of an adolescent who uses masturbation to relieve hormone-induced sexual tension or the psychological pain and pressure experienced by a man struggling with infertility who engages in masturbation as part of a medical procedure designed to diagnose or treat this condition will be different from that of a relatively mature adult who engages in the practice out of boredom or curiosity. But even when a person's culpability is minimal, the act itself remains morally bad and therefore in no way contributes to growth in chastity.

4. Extramarital Sex

Another fundamental distortion of the meaning of human sexuality and the dignity of person is sexual activity between persons who are not irrevocably committed to one another in marriage. When two unmarried persons engage in sex the biblical and theological tradition has named it fornication. When one or both parties are married to another, the tradition has termed it adultery. Throughout its history, the Church has condemned these practices and institutions that have attempted to legitimize them such as concubinage. Today this opposition is often directed against "trial marriages" and "free unions" (i.e., the various forms of cohabitation) as well as casual sexual encounters.[63] The fact that these practices have become more widespread and socially acceptable in many Westernized societies is undoubtedly one of the legacies of the sexual revolution.[64] If the pill and other modern contraceptives removed the burden of children from marriage, practices such as casual sex and cohabitation have removed the obligation of marriage from the pursuit of sex and companionship.

In light of the understanding of sexual union as a covenantal and

---

62. Cf. CCC, 2352.

63. Cf. John Paul II, Apostolic Exhortation, Familiaris consortio, nos. 80–81.

64. Within the United States, across all age groups, there has been a 45 percent increase in cohabitation from 1970 to 1990. While 11 percent of couples cohabited in the United States between 1965 and 1974, at present 50 percent of marriages are preceded by cohabitation (and many cohabiting couples never marry). See the statistics and sources summarized in Secretariat for Family, Laity, Women and Youth, Marriage Preparation for Cohabiting Couples: An Informational Report on New Realities and Pastoral Practices (Washington, D.C.: United States Catholic Conference, 1999), 3–7.

sacramental activity described above, the moral evil of these actions is evident. To engage in sexual activity is to imply an unconditional and faithful gift of self within the covenant of marriage. It is to somatically articulate a particular kind of language of unconditional fidelity and self-donation, reflective of Christ's self-offering to the Church. However, when no such covenant exists between the two persons, such a language, whether spoken with the body or verbally, becomes an untruth, a falsehood.[65] The words or deeds of sexual expression are not adequate to the truth of the relationship between the two persons. It therefore violates the dignity of both parties and undermines their capacity to give themselves in love and truth. It also risks committing a grave injustice to children who might be conceived through such a union and born to unmarried parents, or worse, destroyed within their mother's wombs. Sex between persons not married to one another thus violates justice, truth, and chastity. When such persons are married to another there is an even more grave breach of fidelity through the violation of the marriage covenant.

Some authors have attempted to argue for a distinction between casual sex and so-called preceremonial sex (sex between persons who are not married but committed to one another in some way—e.g., through engagement).[66] While the former is almost always morally evil, the latter, it is asserted, though a disvalue (i.e., "ontic evil") may not be morally evil in every case. This argument is faulty for a number of reasons. It ignores the fact that sexually active couples with only an emotional or an intentional commitment may never marry. It assumes that choosing evil (of whatever kind) has no impact on the character of the couple. And it suggests that marriage is nothing but a mere ceremony—a ritual devoid of efficacy. This assumption is contrary to the whole of the Church's sacramental theology, which insists on their being acts of Christ within the Church. To worship the eucharistic elements prior to the consecration is to engage in idolatry. To do so after is to recognize

65. See John Paul II, Apostolic Exhortation, *Familiaris consortio*, no. 11. This bears upon not only bodily sexual activity but also simulated sex through conversation (e.g., "phone sex") or through electronic means of communication (e.g., "cybersex" in an Internet chatroom).

66. See, e.g., Philip Keane, S.S., *Sexual Morality: A Catholic Perspective* (New York: Paulist Press, 1977), 100–110.

the presence of Christ. So too with marriage. Sexual union prior to marriage is a travesty. Afterward it is a renewal and remembrance of the sacrament celebrated.

5. Prostitution

Another profound degradation of human sexuality and human persons can be found in prostitution and other forms of commercial sexual activity. Known as the "world's oldest profession" because of its presence in both cultic and commercial forms in the ancient world, currently prostitution has become increasingly connected with pornography and the sex industry in many Western countries and has expanded in new forms of sexual slavery in the third world.[67] In both cases the practice generally targets those who are vulnerable because of socioeconomic conditions and age—particularly women and children.[68]

Even more than sex between unmarried persons, prostitution and paid sexual performances depersonalize their participants. For in this case there is no friendship, emotional attachment, or knowledge of one another between those paid to perform sex acts and those who pay them. The prostitute or performer becomes nothing but an anonymous body to be bought and sold, a commodity to be consumed with no recognition of her or his personal dignity. Those who pay for these sexual services violate not only the dignity of the prostitute as a person but sin against themselves as body persons called to imperishable life.[69] The practice is thus a violation of both chastity and justice. Those who force others into prostitution or profit from it commit an even more grave injustice, scandalizing others (particularly when they use children, adolescents, or other vulnerable persons) and poisoning communities in

67. On the links between prostitution and other forms of commercialized sex, see Ronald Weitzer, *Sex for Sale: Prostitution, Pornography, and the Sex Industry* (New York: Routledge, 2000). On the growth of traffic in women and children as sexual slaves, see Sietske Altink, *Stolen Lives: Trading Women into Sex and Slavery* (London: Scarlet Press, 1995).

68. Some see current Western cultural patterns of prostitution as an outgrowth of established patterns of sexual inequality. See, e.g., Jo Ann L. Miller, "Prostitution in Contemporary American Society," in *Sexual Coercion: A Sourcebook on Its Nature, Causes and Prevention*, ed. Elizabeth Grauerholz and Mary Koralewski (Lexington, Mass.: Lexington Books, 1991), 45–57.

69. Cf. 1 Cor 6:15–20; *CCC*, 2355.

which the practice takes place. It should be noted that the moral culpability of those who sell themselves as prostitutes can be minimized by force, the threat of violence, poverty, addiction, or other constraints upon their freedom.[70]

6. Sexual Harassment and Abuse

When the deformation of sexual activity into an assertion of power and control takes place in a public or professional arena, it is often identified as sexual harassment. Sexual harassment has come to be understood legally and ethically as taking a number of forms: unwelcome sexual advances; requests for sexual favors as a condition of employment, academic status, or treatment; or the creation of a hostile environment through conduct that interferes with another's ability to work or study.[71] Usually in such cases there is a power differential between the two parties involved—a supervisor and a subordinate, a teacher and a student, a pastor and a parishioner, a doctor and a patient, a politician and an intern. This practice not only voids the meaning of sex as self-giving, it is fundamentally unjust because the misuse of power on the part of the person in the higher position breaches the integrity of his or her profession. It too therefore is opposed to both chastity and justice. Doctors, teachers, clerics, and even politicians undertake their profession to serve and help those entrusted to their care. When this position is used to prey on others for one's own sexual gratification, it is a betrayal of professional integrity and interpersonal justice.

When this conduct goes beyond merely creating a hostile environment or making unwanted sexual advances to sexual activity between a person in a superior position and one in a subordinate position, it can be described as a form of sexual abuse. The more the person preyed upon is vulnerable because of socioeconomic factors, mental illness, or age, the greater the violation of justice. The worst forms of sexual

70. See CCC, 2355.
71. On this topic, see I. Landau, "On the Definition of Sexual Harassment," *Australasian Journal of Philosophy* 77, no. 2 (1999): 216–23; and Anne E. Patrick, "Sexual Harassment: A Christian Ethical Response," *Annual of the Society of Christian Ethics* 19 (1999): 371–76. For an overview of the legal basis of sexual harassment claims, see Richard H. Hiers, "Sexual Harassment: Title VII and Title IX Protections and Prohibitions—The Current State of the Law," *Annual of the Society of Christian Ethics* 19 (1999): 391–406.

abuse are directed against those incapable of full moral agency: the
mentally ill, the mentally handicapped, and children.

Traditional moral analysis has treated such sins under the rubric of
"seduction."[72] However, such a designation risks ascribing too much
moral agency to the abused party and obscuring the impact of the power differential in the relationship highlighted by more recent reflection
on sexual harassment. When one adult with relatively equal status and
authority (of whatever kind) manipulates another to whom he or she is
not married to engage in sex, the designation of seduction is apt. When
an adult in a position of authority (e.g., a parent, a cleric, a doctor)
preys upon a child or mentally ill person, he or she is legally and
ethically guilty of something closer to rape—even if no violence or
physical coercion is involved. There are also a variety of cases in between—for example, the employer who requires sexual favors from an
employee.

There are specific disorders that predispose individuals toward the
sexual abuse of children. When an adult has recurrent and intense sexual urges and sexual fantasies (whether acted upon or not) involving pre-
pubescent children, he suffers from *pedophilia*.[73] When such urges and
fantasies (and actual abuse) are directed toward postpubescent children
(i.e., adolescents), the disorder is described as *ephebophilia*. Clinicians
sometimes further divide these disorders into *regressed* and *fixated* forms.[74]
The former refers to those whose primary sexual attraction is to adults
of the opposite sex but who in situations of extreme stress regress psy-
chosexually and become attracted to children. The latter refers to those
whose primary sexual attraction is to children. Those with the regressed
form of these disorders are far more responsive to clinical treatment
than those with the fixated forms. It also appears that ephebophiles in

72. See, e.g., St. Thomas's treatment of seduction as one of the parts of lust in his *ST*
II–II, q. 154, a. 6.

73. For helpful overviews of these disorders, see Coleman, *Human Sexuality*, 79–89;
and Peter Cimbolic, "The Identification and Treatment of Sexual Disorders and the
Priesthood," *The Jurist* 52 (1992): 598–614. The masculine pronoun is used here because, as
Cimbolic notes, "the sex ratio is thought to be at least twenty males to every female with
this class of disorders [paraphilias]" (p. 603).

74. See Coleman, *Human Sexuality*, 80, 85; Cimbolic, "Identification and Treatment,"
600–601.

general are more responsive to treatment than pedophiles.[75] Generally, these disorders are classified as *paraphilias*—that is, psychosexual disorders.[76] The exact relationship of these disorders to more recognizable sexual orientations is both complex and controversial.[77]

While the presence of these disorders might lessen the culpability of those who engage in them, sexual abuse of children remains a monstrously evil and destructive act that requires decisive action from those who become aware of it. Children who are victims and their families are often devastated by this abuse and suffer lasting harm psychologically, morally, and spirituality. Because of this and because adults who molest children may have scores of victims, it is morally imperative that responsible parties who become aware of such acts report this abuse to civil authorities immediately. As one clinician notes, "A single child molester may commit hundreds of sexual acts on hundreds of children. To report one abuser is to perhaps save scores of future victims."[78]

7. Sexual Misconduct by Clerics and Vowed Religious

The Church, though it is the community of salvation constituted by the death and Resurrection of Jesus and the outpouring of the Holy

75. See Stephen J. Rossetti, *A Tragic Grace: The Catholic Church and Child Sexual Abuse* (Collegeville, Minn.: Liturgical Press, 1996), 88.

76. Currently recognized paraphilias include exhibitionism, fetishism, frotteurism, pedophilia, sadomasochism, sexual sadism, transvestic fetishism, voyeurism, and other less-defined disorders such as ephebophilia. For a description of these disorders, see Cimbolic, "Identification and Treatment," 602. However, some classify the fixated forms of them as sexual orientations akin to a heterosexual or homosexual orientation. Melvin Blanchette, S.S., and Gerald Coleman, S.S., in a recent article argue for five sexual orientations: heterosexuality, homosexuality, bisexuality, fixated pedophilia, and fixated ephebophilia; see "Priest Pedophiles," *America* 186, no. 13 (April 22, 2002): 18–21. It is not clear on what clinical or theological basis these disorders are thus reified into sexual orientations.

77. Many pedophiles who abuse boys are in fact heterosexual in their sexual orientation. Ephebophilia is a less defined condition clinically, but it seems that ephebophiles are attracted to adolescents who correspond to their basic sexual orientation (heterosexual or homosexual), leading some to speak of a "regressed" or "stunted" form of these orientations. See Stephen Rossetti, "The Catholic Church and Child Sexual Abuse," *America* 186, no. 13 (April 22, 2002): 8–15, esp. 11.

78. A. Kenneth Fuller, "Child Molestation and Pedophilia: An Overview for the Physician," *Journal of the American Medical Association* 261 (1989): 602–96, cited in Cimbolic, "Identification and Treatment," 604.

Spirit, is nonetheless made up of sinners. Few things make this point more clearly and tragically than sexual misconduct on the part of clerics and vowed religious. Such persons undertake promises of celibacy as a sign of the inbreaking of eternity into time in Christ and the eschatological union of the Church with her Bridegroom. Breaking these promises cannot but cast doubt on the reality of the mysteries that the celibate state is meant to signify. That is, these actions scandalize those in the Church and the broader society. Though not unknown throughout the Church's history, cases of sexual misconduct by clerics and religious have received intensive treatment by the media in recent years—particularly instances of sexual abuse of children and adolescents.

The immorality of these acts by clerics and religious is evident. For the reasons described above, genital activity between unmarried persons violates both chastity and justice. When one of these individuals has made a promise of celibacy for the sake of the Kingdom of God there is a further violation of truthfulness and fidelity to this promise as well as the evil of scandal given to others by this failure. In most cases such actions may also be considered a form of sexual abuse—even when the victim is a "consenting adult"—since the state of the cleric or religious puts him or her in a position of spiritual authority over the other. When the victim is a mentally ill or handicapped person or a child, the betrayal by the cleric or religious is particularly heinous. The person who has promised him- or herself to God and the service of the Church who preys upon the vulnerable to satisfy emotional or sexual needs truly acts as a "wolf in sheep's clothing." Such acts do incalculable harm to victims, their families, parishes, and to the Church's ability to evangelize and teach within a skeptical society.

Those in positions of pastoral authority (i.e., bishops and religious superiors) have moral obligations to both the clerics and religious under their authority and those whom they serve.[79] If there is credible evidence that sexual misconduct has occurred, they have a responsibility to act to prevent further actual or potential harm to victims and further scandal to the community (usually this means removing a person from active

79. For a balanced consideration of some of the canonical and moral issues at stake, see James H. Provost, "Some Canonical Considerations Relative to Clerical Sexual Misconduct," *The Jurist* 55 (1992): 615–41.

ministry until such evidence can be thoroughly examined). If such misconduct has violated civil law (e.g., cases involving sexual abuse of children), civil authorities should be notified so that appropriate criminal investigations and procedures can be undertaken. At the same time, those in pastoral authority must respect the rights of accused clerics and religious to be treated fairly and receive some form of due process so that they are not treated as guilty on the basis of even spurious accusations.[80]

While cases of sexual misconduct by clerics and religious, particularly those involving the abuse of minors, rightly evoke horror, some further observations are in order. Studies have found that disorders such as pedophilia are no more prominent among clergy and religious than among the population as a whole. Celibacy does not predispose those vowed to it to the abuse of children or other forms of aberrant sexual behavior.[81] The vast majority of celibates live their vows and find them a means to grow in both chastity and love. Less clear is whether seminaries and the religious life attract a disproportionate number of those who have unresolved sexual problems and how to deal with this phenomenon if this proves to be the case.[82]

8. Sexual Violence and Coercion

Fundamentally contrary to the meaning of sexuality and its orientation toward love as well as to the dignity of persons is any form of sexual violence. Unfortunately, rape has had a long and ugly history as an expression of fallen human sexuality. It has been used not only as an outlet for individual lust, but as an expression of power individually and

80. For an overview of what such "due process" should involve from the perspective of canon law, see John P. Beal, "Doing What One Can: Canon Law and Clerical Sexual Misconduct," *The Jurist* 55 (1992): 642–83.

81. See Rossetti, "Catholic Church," 9–10.

82. Many have called for psychological testing of those in seminaries to identify and weed out pedophiles and ephebophiles since these disorders create observable and shared cognitive distortions. It is fairly clear that those who have these disorders are not fit for ordination or for religious life. Others have argued that the same holds for persons with homosexual orientations. However, this seems to overlook the complex relationship between sexual orientation and the abuse of children noted above and the fact that many persons with a homosexual orientation are able to live chastity in continence. For some initial discussions of these issues, see Rossetti, "Catholic Church," 9–11; and Blanchette and Coleman, "Priest Pedophiles," 18–21.

corporately–for example, when used on a mass scale to induce terror during war. The victims of rape are typically those members of a community who are most vulnerable, particularly women and children.

There is some debate as to how to best understand and classify the evil involved in sexual violence. Much of the contemporary literature on sexual assault has argued that rape is fundamentally an assertion of power or dominance over another—it is not primarily a sexual act.[83] While there is undoubtedly truth in this claim, it is undeniable that this particular form of violence is aimed at and experienced by the victim not just in the pysche but in her or his bodiliness. Because sexuality touches the very core of the person and therefore is a particular way in which the person is vulnerable to others, such violence is especially devastating.[84] Even more destructive is when sexual violence takes place between persons who purport to be friends (e.g., "date rape"). More heinous still is when sexual assault occurs between spouses—for it violates the heart of the trust and mutual respect/love on which marriage is built.[85] These practices are utterly incompatible with any form of interpersonal justice—let alone love.

Practices that use controlled forms of violence or simulated violence for purposes of sexual arousal (i.e., sadomaschochism) are also morally objectionable. Even if employed between spouses, it is difficult to see how real or simulated violence is compatible with the gift of self in love that sexual union signifies. Pleasure derived from interpersonal love and that derived from one's own or another's pain are qualitatively different. It is therefore better to understand sadomasochistic practices as a disordered expression of sexuality.[86]

83. See, e.g., Marie Fortune, *Sexual Violence: The Unmentionable Sin* (New York: Pilgrim, 1983). For an overview of different explanations for rape, see L. Ellis, *Theories of Rape: Inquiries into the Causes of Sexual Aggression* (New York: Hemisphere, 1989).

84. For an overview of some of the pastoral and spiritual dimensions of the trauma inflicted by rape, see Mary D. Pellauer, "A Theological Perspective on Sexual Assault," *Christianity and Crisis* 44 (1984): 250–55.

85. Unfortunately, the Catholic tradition's understanding of the marital *debitum* owed by spouses to one another has at times made it difficult to discern the tragic fact that sexual assault can and does occur between spouses. For an ethical analysis of marital rape, see Edward J. Bayer, *Rape within Marriage: A Moral Analysis* (Lanham, Md.: University Press of America, 1985). For an overview of the phenomenon, see Diana E. Russell, *Rape in Marriage*, rev. ed. (Bloomington: Indiana University Press, 1990).

86. For those who require such practices to become aroused sexually, this may

A still more subtle distortion of sexual activity into a statement concerning power occurs in sexual coercion or manipulation. This takes place when sex becomes a bargaining tool in a struggle for power between persons. This can happen, for example, when spouses use sex as a reward or withhold it as a punishment in return for certain behaviors on the part of their partner. Obviously, there can be many legitimate reasons why a spouse might defer a request for sexual relations on the part of his or her partner (e.g., illness, fatigue, concern about pregnancy when a couple has good reasons to avoid becoming pregnant), but when this is done for reasons of vengeance or to make a power statement, it too undercuts the mutual respect and love of spouses.[87] In such cases, the language of control overwrites and deforms the word of love.

V. Conclusion

An appreciation of the human person as male or female created in the image of God can serve to deepen an understanding of the virtue of chastity and its requirements. Men and women are created for love, and this fundamental vocation is writ within their differences as embodied persons. Because they are fulfilled in the self-donation of love, men and women need to be accepted unreservedly and loved unconditionally in ways appropriate to their state in life. To engage in sexual practices that do nothing more than use persons as objects for sexual enjoyment, control, or an outlet for various psychological needs undercuts their dignity and belies their destiny in the eternal communion of love which is God's triune life. Hence lust-inspired sexual fantasy, masturbation, pornography, fornication, adultery, prostitution, sexual harassment and abuse, sexual misconduct by celibates, and sexual violence and coercion in differing degrees all deny the dignity of human persons and their vocation to love. These practices also coursen those who engage in them, deadening their perception of the real values at stake in human sexuality and thwarting their growth in the self-possession that makes the gift of self in love possible.

---

indicate a psychological disorder (one of the paraphilias akin to pedophilia). See Cimbolic, "Identification and Treatment," 599–604.

87. It also often indicates deeper problems in the marriage such as long-term resentment, hostility, or bitterness.

But these practices do more than harm individuals. They scandalize others who observe them, harming families, communities, and society as a whole. Particular harm is done to those who are victims of these acts on the part of others. For example, those who are sexually abused as children are themselves more likely to abuse others upon reaching adulthood. Hence cycles of destructive behavior are passed across generations of fallen human beings. When Christians engage in these disordered practices, they do harm to the bonds of love within the Body of Christ and diminish the Church's ability to give witness to the gospel.

It is the role of the virtue of chastity to enable men and women to see and treat one another as equal yet irreducible persons, sharing together the calling to an imperishable life. One crucial dimension of human embodiment is fertility. Much of the Church's tradition has seen the shared fertility of husband and wife as the primary purpose for sexual expression. How can this insistence be related to the covenantal understanding of sexuality, the account of virtue, and the anthropology developed thus far? What further bearing does it have upon issues of sexual ethics? What are the implications of this insistence on the importance of procreation for the relationship of a man and a woman within marriage? These questions will be the focus of the next chapter.

CHAPTER 6

Covenant Fidelity, Fertility, and the Gift of Self

The virtue of chastity is ordered to more than respect for the dignity of persons and the unique capacity of sexuality to express the human vocation to self-giving love within marriage or consecrated virginity. Virtually the whole of the Christian tradition has also insisted on openness to life or respect for the procreative aspect of sexual union as a fundamental value toward which chaste sexual expression is ordered.

However, one of the most striking features of contemporary Western thinking regarding sexuality is precisely its jaundiced view of procreation. Unlike the ancient world or medieval society, many contemporary observers see human fertility as a problem in need of a solution. For some, this is because it is seen as a biological constraint that interferes with pursuit of personal fulfillment and pleasure within sexual activity. For others, it is because sexual reproduction is seen as a threat to a planet with a growing population and limited resources.[1] These suspicions are articulated not only by the icons of popular culture or alarmist demographers, but by an increasing number of ethicists as well.[2]

---

1. This is the argument of Paul Erlich's *The Population Bomb* (New York: Ballantine Books, 1971) and *The Population Explosion* (Brookvale, New South Wales.: Simon & Schuster, 1990). For a critique of Erlich's views and their presuppositions, see Mercedes Arzú Wilson, *Love and Family: Raising a Traditional Family in a Secular World* (San Francisco: Ignatius Press, 1996), 162–95. See also the recent report "World Population Monitoring 2001," prepared by the Population Division of the Department of Economics and Social Affairs of the United Nations (2001), which challenges the assumptions and projections of many population studies. The report is available at *http://www.un.org/esa/population /unpop.htm*.

2. Thus Don Marietta argues against seeing procreation as the purpose of sex, holding that the only constraints on sexual activity should be if it causes harm to persons; see

This chapter will consider the primacy of procreation within the Christian tradition's ethical reflection on sexuality, and how this can be integrated within an understanding of chastity's role in the Christian vocation to love that has been developed thus far. It will then apply this to some specific questions of sexual ethics: reproductive technologies and homosexual activity and partnerships. It will also consider some questions in need of further reflection in regard to marital sexual expression. Finally, the chapter will consider a "test case" for the application of a virtue-based approach to such questions in regard to the existence of a moral difference between natural and artificial means of family planning.

I. Fertility and the Gift of Self

The contemporary Western view of human fertility as a problem in need of a solution stands in marked contrast to the witness of the Scriptures and the Christian theological tradition. From their opening chapters, the Scriptures indicate that God's blessing attends the union of male and female and that through sexual reproduction a couple shares in the mandate to exercise priestly dominion over the earth (see Gn 1:28). As seen in the last chapter, this expression of human dominion is identified by the biblical text as one aspect of humanity's being created in the image of God. Throughout the Old Testament, children are uniformly seen as a blessing, whereas sterility is regarded as a curse.[3] Of course, this theological conviction emerges out of a culture in which children were necessary for political and economic security and well-being. The larger one's family, the better chance that one would be able to live in peace with others and be provided for in sickness and in old age. This situation remained true in premodern agrarian societies and it remains the case in contemporary agrarian societies. However, this does

---

Philosophy of Sexuality (Armonk, N.Y.: M. E. Sharpe, 1997), 32–37. More strongly Christine Gudorf argues against what she calls "procreationism" and sees mutual sexual pleasure within voluntary relationships as the only necessary criteria for evaluating sex. In this view, it is the decision to *have* children that must be morally justified; see *Body, Sex, and Pleasure: Reconstructing Christian Sexual Ethics* (Cleveland: Pilgrim, 1994), esp. 18–50.

3. On the value of fertility and procreation in the sexual ethic of the Old Testament, see Collins, *Christian Morality*, 175–78.

not mean that children cannot be understood as a blessing within present-day industrial and infomational societies in which children can still be regarded as the personification of the couple's union.[4]

If, in fact, each human being is created in the image of God, then procreation is a privileged form of cooperation with God in which men and women together help bring new life into being in that same image and likeness. It is, in the words of Pope John Paul II, a renewal of "the mystery of creation."[5] Up to the twentieth century, the whole of the Christian theological tradition has understood procreation to be either a or the primary purpose of sexual activity and deliberate efforts to frustrate this purpose as sinful. While not without some differences of emphasis and expression, this was the view of the Fathers of the Church, of the Christian East, of the Protestant reformers, as well as of the Catholic West.[6] The 1917 Code of Canon Law summarized the thrust of this tradition in paragraph 1 of canon 1013: "The primary end of marriage is the procreation and education of children; its secondary end is mutual help and the allaying of concupiscence."[7] The Church's tradition has held that any deliberate action contrary to either the procreative purpose of sexuality or the fidelity of marriage is gravely disordered.[8]

While various social and intellectual developments over the course of the twentieth century would raise questions about the principle of family limitation, theological developments such as personalism would give increasing weight to the interpersonal and affective dimensions of human sexuality.[9] As seen above, early personalist thinkers such as Dietrich von Hildebrand worked to create a new axiology for love within marital sexuality, insisting on it being the meaning of marriage even while acknowledging procreation as its primary purpose.[10] Others raised even

---

4. Cf. Murphy, *Beyond Feminism*, 154.

5. See John Paul II's weekly general audience of March 12, 1980, in *Theology of the Body*, 80–83.

6. The most comprehensive study of the Western tradition is still Noonan's *Contraception*; see also Lawler, Boyle, and May, *Catholic Sexual Ethics*, 46–67.

7. The citation is from John Gallagher, C.S.B., "Magisterial Teaching from 1918 to the Present," in *Readings in Moral Theology*, No. 8: *Dialogue about Catholic Sexual Teaching*, 71–92, at p. 71.

8. Cf. *CCC*, 2370, 2400.

9. See the summary of these developments provided in Chapters 1 and 4.

10. See Von Hildebrand, *Marriage*, 6–7, 19–27.

more fundamental questions about the primacy of procreation over other ends of marriage.[11]

The Second Vatican Council avoided hierarchical language in framing the relationship between the ends of marriage.[12] This silence has sparked an ongoing debate among scholars. Some see it as indicating a change in the Church's understanding regarding the equal importance of both conjugal love and procreation.[13] Others argue that the older hierarchy was never explicitly repudiated and that Vatican II merely avoided this technical formulation in its Pastoral Constitution.[14]

In some respects this interpretive debate has been rendered moot by more recent teaching that has insisted on the "inseparable connection" between the unitive and procreative meanings of human sexuality. This was, of course, the assertion of Paul VI in *Humanae vitae*.[15] However, the encyclical never fully explained the basis for this connection, and its appeals to the natural law were found by many to be insufficient.

Given the crisis sparked by the debate over *Humanae vitae*, it is not surprising that Pope John Paul II has devoted much of his teaching in the areas of marriage and sexuality to explicating the exact nature of this connection. Thus, in his Apostolic Exhortation *Familiaris consortio*, he writes: "Fecundity is the fruit and sign of conjugal love, the living testi-

11. See Doms, *Meaning of Marriage*, 67–69, 85–88, 93–94, 119.

12. Thus *Gaudium et spes* spoke merely of the "various benefits and purposes of marriage" (no. 48) and framed its description of procreation in this way: "Hence while not making the other purposes of matrimony of less account [*non posthabitus ceteris matrimonii finibus*], the true practice of conjugal love, and the whole meaning of family life which results from it, have this aim: that the couple be ready with stout hearts to cooperate with the love of the Creator and Savior, who through them will enlarge and enrich His own family day by day" (no. 50). The citations are from *Documents of Vatican II*, 250, 254.

13. See, e.g., Theodore Mackin, *What Is Marriage?* (New York: Paulist Press, 1982), 235–37; Michael Lawler, *Secular Marriage, Christian Sacrament* (Mystic, Conn.: Twenty-Third Publications, 1985), 53; and Joseph Selling, "Magisterial Teaching on Marriage 1880–1986: Historical Consistency or Radical Development?," in *Readings in Moral Theology, No. 8: Dialogue about Catholic Sexual Teaching*, 93–97, esp. p. 96.

14. See, e.g., Francisco Gil Hellin, "El lugar propio del amor conyugal en la estructura del matrimonio segun la 'Gaudium et spes,'" *Annales Valentinos* 6 (1980): 1–35; Ramón García de Haro, *Marriage and Family in the Documents of the Magisterium*, 2nd ed., trans. William E. May (San Francisco: Ignatius Press, 1993), 234–56; and William E. May, *Marriage: The Rock on Which the Family Is Built* (San Francisco: Ignatius Press, 1995), 110–11.

15. *Humanae vitae*, no. 12.

mony of the reciprocal self-giving of the spouses."[16] Sexual intercourse is, for John Paul II, as noted above, a "language of the body" that communicates complete fidelity within the marriage covenant and total self-donation. To choose to eliminate or suppress one's fertility negates part of the meaning of the gift; it is a "falsification of the inner truth of conjugal love."[17] This is because fertility is not merely viewed as a biological aspect of the person that can be altered at his or her discretion, but like sexuality itself it is an existential reality (i.e., rooted in the order of existence) and pertains to the person as a whole.[18] The procreative meaning of human sexuality is thus wedded to the expression of love by means of the personalist concept of self-donation and an anthropology that sees fertility as integral to the person.

Equally striking is that John Paul II has insisted that this norm does not rest simply on a personalist reading of natural law or even on the consistency of the Church's tradition on this question; rather it flows from biblical revelation itself.[19] For he discerns this same pattern of sexual union as embodied self-giving and procreation as cooperation with God's creative act in the "original experiences" of the opening chapters of Genesis. This same locus for understanding human sexuality makes clear that motherhood and fatherhood are not mere biological functions, but personal and experiential participations in the mystery of God's creative design.[20]

To understand respect for the shared fertility of husband and wife as implied by the totality of bodily self-donation is a significant develop-

---

16. *Familiaris consortio*, no. 28.

17. *Familiaris consortio*, no. 32. For other instances of this line of argument in the papal teaching of John Paul II, see Letter to Families, *Gratissimam sane* (1994), no. 12. Cf. the weekly general audiences of July 11, August 8, and August 22, 1984, in *Theology of the Body*, 386–88, 395–96, 396–99. The philosopher Karol Wojtyla had already made a similar claim in his exposition on Catholic sexual ethics in *Love and Responsibility*, 234.

18. Cf. Wojtyla, *Love and Responsibility*, 57, 230. In *Familiaris consortio*, Pope John Paul II suggests that the view of human fertility implicit in contraceptive technologies and that underlying natural methods of birth regulation represent "two irreconcilable concepts of the human person and of human sexuality" (no. 32).

19. See the weekly general audience of July 18, 1984, in *Theology of the Body*, 388–90.

20. See the weekly general audiences of March 5, 12, and 26, 1980, in *Theology of the Body*, 77–86. The pope argues for a connection between the "knowledge" that spouses gain of concerning one another in sexual self-donation and procreation (cf. Gn 4:1).

ment within Catholic theological reflection on sexuality.[21] It offers an explication of the "inseparable connection" advanced, but not fully explicated, in *Humanae vitae* and it does so not just on the basis of new personalist arguments, but on the grounds of biblical revelation as well. This personalist idea of intercourse bespeaking a complete offering of self is congruent with the biblical understanding of sexual intercourse as a covenant ratifying gesture, considered in Chapter 2, as well as with the person's vocation to make a gift of him- or herself in love, developed subsequently. Such an approach makes it clear that the two meanings of human sexuality cannot be dichotomized or played off against one another. Just as it is wrong to willfully negate one's fertility in the name of fostering mutual love, it is wrong to seek to use one's spouse to achieve procreation to the detriment of mutual love.[22] Conjugal chastity is ordered to both loving self-donation and the gift/acceptance of fertility as an aspect of the totality of the person.

II. Some Implications

The developing understanding of the "inseparable connection" between the unitive and procreative meanings of human sexuality is not merely the basis for the exclusion of virtually every case of contraception by the Church.[23] It also provides a framework in which to understand Catholic teaching on a range of other issues in sexual and medical ethics.

21. For an overview of the historical development and theological significance of this development, see George John Woodall, "The Principle of the Indissoluble Link between the Dimensions on Unity and Fruitfulness in Conjugal Love: A Hermeneutical Investigation of Its Theological Basis and of Its Normative Significance" (S.T.D. diss., Gregorian University, 1996).

22. Cf. Wojtyla, *Love and Responsibility*, 58–59, 61–63, 233.

23. The Church does allow for contraceptive, though not abortifacient, means to be used in Catholic healthcare facilities to treat victims of rape. See Bohr, *Catholic Moral Tradition*, 300–301. See also Directive 36 of the United States Conference of Catholic Bishops *Ethical and Religious Directives for Catholic Health Care Services (ERDs)*. This seems to create tension with the designation of contraception as an "intrinsic evil" in magisterial teaching (e.g., *Humanae vitae*, no. 14; *CCC*, 2370). This apparent contradiction between the Church's teaching and praxis can be resolved if one understands the teaching as insisting that it is intrinsically evil to contracept a *conjugal act*. Acts of rape (even if they occur within marriage) are in no sense conjugal acts for the reasons described in the previous chapter.

A. Reproductive Technologies

The past century has witnessed an explosion of medical knowledge and technology, including in the treatment of infertility. Given the importance that the biblical and theological tradition places on procreation, one might assume that the Church would laud any such developments. However, insofar as many of these procedures divorce the effort to achieve conception from a conjugal act and, in some cases, from the marital relationship itself, the Church has stated its opposition to many of them.[24] This includes relatively simple procedures such as artificial insemination in which previously collected semen or a sperm preparation is introduced into a woman's vagina, cervix, or uterus.[25] It also includes more technologically sophisticated interventions that attempt achieve conception in vitro and then transfer some or all of the embryos conceived to a woman's body in the hope that implantation will occur (in vitro fertilization–embryo transfer [IVF-ET]). Initially developed in the mid-1940s as a way to bypass blocked or diseased fallopian tubes, IVF-ET is now used to treat virtually any form of infertility (except azoospermia in men). More recent variants of the procedure attempt to more closely mimic the physiological processes of natural gestation.[26]

These procedures are morally problematic on a variety of grounds. For these procedures too sunder the connection between the mutual

24. See the Congregation for the Doctrine of the Faith's Instruction on Bioethics, *Donum vitae,* issued on February 22, 1987. For an overview of the principle arguments of the Instruction, see May, *Marriage,* 85–99. For an application of these and other arguments to more recent forms of "assisted reproductive therapy" (ART), see John S. Grabowski, "The New Reproductive Technologies: An Overview and Theological Assessment," *Linacre Quarterly* 69 (2002): 100–119. A more complete discussion of these issues in reference to the *Ethical and Religious Directives for Catholic Health Care Facilities* can be found in the volume on medical ethics in this series.

25. See Coleman, *Human Sexuality,* 365.

26. Thus zygote intrafallopian transfer (ZIFT) is similar to IVF except that the fertilized eggs (zygotes) are transferred to the fallopian tubes one day after fertilization in the laboratory. Tubal embryo transfer (TET) follows the same procedure as ZIFT except that the embryos are transferred to the fallopian tubes two days after laboratory fertilization. The greater maturity of these embryos when they reach the uterus more closely corresponds to conception *in vivo* after intercourse.

love and the procreation of new human life in a manner inverse to that within contraception.[27] Most forms of "assisted reproductive therapies" aim to produce children apart from conjugal union, while contraception aims to exclude children that might result from such union. As a result they fail to respect the basic meanings of conjugal love in concrete actions. They also depersonalize the children "produced" through them, since it is the bodily gift of self on the part of husband and wife that is the context created by God to receive the gift of children.[28] Heterologous forms of such procedures (i.e., those that use gametes from persons not married to one another) are additionally objectionable because they strike at the exclusivity and fidelity of marriage which intercourse recalls and signifies as a covenant-ratifying gesture.[29]

Clearly, infertility is a significant problem that can cause great suffering to couples who experience it. It is no doubt true that the Church needs to do more by way of providing pastoral care and support to such couples. However, compassion in the face of suffering cannot justify deforming human sexuality or reducing children to commodities. Children remain a gift from God—not a right that can be acquired at any cost.[30]

This does not mean that scientific research or medical intervention in regard to infertility is without value. Procedures that assist the possibility of procreation within the context of the conjugal act are viewed by the Church as morally good.[31] The same may be said of efforts to

27. Cf. *Donum vitae* I, B, 4.

28. See *Donum vitae* II, A, 1. Cf. James Burtchaell, C.S.C., *The Giving and Taking of Life: Essays Ethical* (South Bend, Ind.: University of Notre Dame Press, 1989), 134f.

29. See *Donum vitae* II, A, 2. Some authors attempt to distinguish the more objectionable heterologous forms of these procedures and their homologous counterparts, arguing that the "simple" cases of AIH or IVF-ET that avoid the destruction of embryos could, in some cases, be morally licit. See, e.g., John Mahoney, S.J., "Human Fertility Control," in *Readings in Moral Theology*, No. 8: *Dialogue about Catholic Sexual Teaching*, 251–66; and Cahill, *Sex, Gender and Christian Ethics*, 217–54. However, this position does not adequately address the argument based on the inseparability principle, nor the arguments concerning the depersonalization of children produced through these procedures.

30. See *Donum vitae* II, B, 8.

31. On this point *Donum vitae* II, B, 7 echoes Pope Pius XII: "medical intervention respects the dignity of persons when it seeks to assist the conjugal act either in order to facilitate its performance or in order to enable it to achieve its objective once it has been

surgically repair some impediments to human fertility that underlie cases of partial or complete sterility affecting couples.[32]

B. Homogenital Activity and Partnerships

The same framework is also relevant to the highly complex issue of homosexuality. A *homosexual orientation* is the term often used to refer to a predominant and persistent pyschosexual attraction to members of one's own sex not chosen or created by the person.[33] Such an orientation is not completely indicated by sexual attraction, fantasy, or even genital activity since some individuals in same-sex environments (such as prisons or same-sex boarding schools) engage in homogenital behavior but return to heterosexual practice when they leave them.[34] Though debated

---

normally performed." The citation is from *Respect for Human Life*, Vatican translation (Boston: Daughters of St. Paul, 1987), 32–33. The document is quoting Pius XII, "Discourse to Those Taking Part in the 4th International Congress of Catholic Doctors, September 29, 1949." Other methods such as GIFT have created confusion among Catholic authors since they do in fact aim to produce conception *in vivo*. However, it is difficult to reconcile the typical GIFT procedure with the framework of *Donum vitae* insofar as it relies on medical masturbation—not intercourse—to obtain sperm; see Coleman, *Human Sexuality*, 362. There are also modified versions of GIFT that collect sperm through various means from an act of intercourse prior to washing and repositioning it in the fallopian tubes. David Bohr prudently concludes regarding such procedures: "As long as the husband's sperm are collected by a morally acceptable method and the repositioning of the gametes are within the context of the conjugal union of husband and wife, the process is not morally objectionable"; see *Catholic Moral Tradition*, 289; cf. Coleman, *Human Sexuality*, 363–64. Other authors are critical even of modified versions of GIFT; see, e.g., Donald DeMarco, *Biotechnology and the Assault on Parenthood* (San Francisco: Ignatius Press, 1991), 219–35.

32. For examples of such procedures, see E. Cofino et al., "Transcervical Balloon Tuboplasty: A Multicenter Study," *Journal of the American Medical Association* 264, no. 16 (1990): 2079–82; J. M. Kasia et al., "Laproscopic Fimbrioplasty and Neosalpingostomy: Experience of the Yaounde General Hospitial, Cameroon," *European Journal of Obstetrical Gynecological Reproductive Biology* 73, 1 (1997): 71–77; and K. Sueoka et al., "Falloposcopic Tuboplasty for Bilateral Tubal Occlusion: A Novel Infertility Treatment as an Alternative to In-Vitro Fertilization?," *Human Reproduction*, 18, no. 1 (1998): 71–74. I am indebted to Dr. Hanna Klaus for these references.

33. See Gerald Coleman, S.S., *Homosexuality: Church Teaching and Pastoral Practice* (New York: Paulist Press, 1995), 15–17. Coleman's book is exceptional in its clarity and balance in treating this subject. I am dependent on his treatment in much of what follows.

34. This is one reason why some researchers hold that sexual orientation is best understood as a continuum of 0–6 with 0 being an exclusive heterosexual orientation and 6

widely, the number of homosexual persons in the population as a whole is perhaps about 4 percent.[35]

Equally controversial is the effort to locate the cause or causes of a homosexual orientation.[36] Until 1973 the American Pyschiatric Association classified homosexuality as a mental disorder. In spite of opposition from a significant minority of its membership, the group changed this classification so that only ego-dystonic homosexuality (i.e., the condition of those individuals who do not accept their sexual orientation) was subsequently classified as a disorder.[37] The controversy has continued in that some have attempted to find a biological basis for a homosexual orientation, while others identify it as stemming from a problem within psychosexual development. There is some evidence for a biological basis or at least predisposition toward a homosexual orientation which has been discovered through studies of genetics and of the impact of hormones on prenatal development.[38] Yet there is also strong evidence on the pyschological side, particularly pyschoanalytic theory's view that a problem in one's relationship to one's parents might interfere with the formation of gender identity that is one of the components of sexual orientation. This developmental explanation is taken still further by those who argue that it is possible for homosexual persons through counseling and prayer to actually change their sexual orientation. Others dispute this claim, arguing that those who through these means appeared to "cross over" were simply confused about their orientation and that such claims cause further confusion and pain for homosexual persons.[39] As Gerald Coleman prudently concludes, "[N]o one theory of homo-

---

being an exclusive homosexual orientation. On this view, most heterosexual persons are actually a 1 or 2 and most homosexual persons are actually a 4 or 5. This explains why one can have impulses or even sexual experiences contrary to one's orientation without calling it into question. See Coleman, *Homosexuality,* 23.

35. See ibid., 28–30.

36. For good overviews of these various theories, see John Harvey, *The Homosexual Person* (San Francisco: Ignatius Press, 1987), 37–63; and Coleman, *Homosexuality,* 33–55.

37. Ego-syntonic homosexuality (i.e., the state of those homosexual persons who accepted their sexual orientation) was no longer classified as a disorder in the third edition of the *Diagnostic and Statistical Manual of Mental Disorders.* On this change and the controversy surrounding it, see Coleman, *Homosexuality,* 24–25.

38. Cf. John Bancroft, "Homosexual Orientation: The Search for a Biological Basis," *British Journal of Psychiatry* 164 (1994): 437–40.

39. For an overview of this debate, see Coleman, *Homosexuality,* 48–55.

sexuality can explain such a diverse phenomenon," and thus caution and humility are needed in the face of the data concerning its cause.[40]

In recent teaching, the Church has acknowledged the existence of a homosexual orientation or deep-seated homosexual tendencies, without attempting to adjudicate the current debate over its causes.[41] The Church has also held that, however this orientation comes into being, it is not morally equivalent to a heterosexual orientation. It is, in the Church's understanding, "an objective disorder" insofar as it inclines persons to activity that is in itself disordered.[42] This does not mean that homosexual persons are culpable for an orientation that they did not choose, or that they are possessed of less human dignity and worth, or that they are incapable of growth in virtue and holiness. Indeed, as fallen, all men and women have inclinations that are disordered. What is morally relevant is whether a person acts on such disordered inclinations.[43]

On the basis of the biblical witness as well as the importance of procreation as understood within its tradition, the Church has consistently taught that homogenital activity is morally evil.[44] Even for persons who have a homosexual orientation, it is always and everywhere morally wrong to engage in genital activity based upon it.[45]

There are reasons for this teaching that go beyond the nonprocre-

40. Coleman, *Homosexuality*, 54.

41. See, e.g., Congregation for the Doctrine of the Faith, Declaration on Sexual Ethics (*Persona humana* [1975]), no. 8; Congregation for the Doctrine of the Faith, *Letter to the Bishops of the Catholic Church on the Pastoral Care of Homosexual Persons* (1986), no. 3; *CCC*, 2357–58.

42. Congregation for the Doctrine of the Faith, *Letter*, no. 3; *CCC*, 2358.

43. It must be acknowledged, however, because of the existential weight of sexuality (and sexual orientation) for personhood, a person with a homosexual orientation faces a more difficult struggle than one with a propensity toward anger.

44. Many contemporary authors attempt to discount biblical treatments of homosexuality on the basis that such texts are culturally conditioned and that biblical authors are unaware of the existence of a homosexual orientation. See, e.g., Margaret Farley, R.S.M., "An Ethic for Same-Sex Relations," in *A Challenge to Love: Gay and Lesbian Catholics in the Church*, ed. Robert Nugent (New York: Crossroad, 1983), 93–106. However, in its 1986 *Letter* the Congregation for the Doctrine of the Faith replied that, whatever cultural conditioning may be found within individual biblical texts, they are relevant to this question especially when read within the overall biblical theology of the covenantal unity of male and female in marriage as the normative context for sex. Biblical authors clearly prohibit homogenital activity (even if they are unaware of a homosexual orientation). See no. 7.

45. See, e.g., Congregation for the Doctrine of the Faith, *Letter*, nos. 8, 11. The same

ative character of homosexual activity. The biblical understanding of the marriage covenant is quite clearly predicated on the union of persons who are irreducible to each other as *male and female.* Thus a truthful expression of "the language of the body" depends in part on "the nuptial meaning of the body." It is this same union in difference that underlies the nuptial imagery for the union between Christ and the Church integral to much Christian soteriology, sacramental theology, ecclesiology, and eschatology. The gift of self to which conjugal chastity is ordered is a union of persons who are equal in nature and dignity, yet distinct as sexual and embodied persons. This same conclusion is reinforced by the Trinitarian anthropology considered above. Human beings as male and female are created in the image of the God who is both a Trinity of relationally irreducible Persons and yet utterly equal in their possession of the one divine nature. This potentially life-giving union in difference cannot be reflected either symbolically or actually in the union of a same-sex couple.[46]

For these reasons, the Church continues to conclude that homosexual persons, like all unmarried Christians, are called to live chastity in the form of continence.[47] Yet it is also clear that homosexual persons face particular obstacles to growth in chastity. Some of these come from being the subjects of prejudice, hatred, and violence in civil society and, at times, within the Church itself. Some of these come from the fact that it is difficult to quickly change long-standing patterns of relating to

---

document rejects the idea that because some persons have this orientation, they must act upon it, for this undercuts the Christian concept of freedom (cf. no. 11).

46. In a 1991 article Xavier John Seubert, O.F.M., argues that the traditional all-male imagery of the Trinity as the most basic mystery of Christian faith overrides considerations of biological complementarity between the sexes and might be used to justify genital relations between homosexual persons; see "The Sacramentality of Metaphors: Reflections on Homosexuality," *Cross Currents* 42 (1991): 52–68. While a novel theological argument, this view suffers from at least two significant problems. First, it reduces sexual difference to a merely biological phenomenon rather than a relation that (along with others) shapes human personhood. Second, it neglects the irreducibility of the divine Persons to one another through their mutual relations in the midst of their shared possession of the one divine nature. The irreducible relational difference has its created counterpart in the irreducible personal difference of male and female who are created in the image of the Triune God.

47. See Congregation for the Doctrine of the Faith, *Letter*, no. 12.

others as sexual persons.[48] A young man or woman who has lived an active homosexual life-style will not find it easy to practice continence overnight—particularly in close relationships. Yet such a person needs the friendship and love of others (though not genital sex) to be happy and fulfilled.[49]

As a continuation of the teaching of Jesus, authentic Church teaching is not a set of abstract rules or a club to be used to beat others with different points of view; it is a summons to conversion.[50] As such, it is addressed to all persons, to those of homosexual orientation as well as those of heterosexual orientation. The same teaching that calls homosexual persons to grow in chastity and their capacity to love through the practice of continence also calls heterosexual Christians to seek moral change and growth. Heterosexual Christians are called to abandon their own fears, prejudice, and hatred in accepting their homosexual brothers and sisters in the communion of love and truth.[51] They too are called to face their own sexual sins and to grow in chastity and love in a manner appropriate to their state in life. By accepting this challenge, members of parishes and Christian communities can create a loving and hospitable environment that makes change and conversion possible for all of their members.

Some persons find inconsistency in the Church's opposition to "unjust discrimination" against homosexual persons, on the one hand, and its opposition to "same-sex marriage," on the other.[52] Why, it is asked, should not homosexual persons have the same opportunity to find happiness in a legally recognized lifelong partnership with another person? Is the Church guilty of advocating discrimination? A closer examina-

---

48. See the discussion of the law of gradualness in the fourth section of Chapter 7.

49. A person who engages in genital behavior with a friend should be encouraged to repent and avoid occasions of sin in the future. If they cannot continue the friendship without genital activity, they should end the relationship. See the analysis of the 1973 National Conference on Catholic Bishops document *Principles to Guide Confessors in Questions of Homosexuality*, in Coleman, *Homosexuality*, 86–88.

50. See Coleman, *Homosexuality*, 73–74.

51. See the excellent treatment of these issues provided by Coleman, *Homosexuality*, 70–72, 125–44.

52. See the Congregation for the Doctrine of the Faith, *Non-Discrimination against Homosexual Persons: Some Considerations Concerning the Response to Legislative Proposals*, nos. 12, 15.

tion of the matter reveals the official Catholic position to be a consistent one. The Church's understanding is that, as human beings, homosexual persons have the same dignity and hence the same basic human rights as others. Discrimination against them in regard to these rights is morally evil. At the same time, as an orientation to disordered activity, a homosexual orientation is not comparable to race or ethnicity in matters of discrimination and therefore is not a positive source of new rights or legislative entitlements—including the right to redefine marriage. Marriage in both the biblical tradition and in Western law based upon it has been understood as the lifelong covenant of one man and one woman (excluding certain degrees of blood relation) ordered to the procreation and education of children and the companionship of equal but irreducible persons (male and female). Same-sex partnerships can neither meet this definition of marriage nor achieve either of its ends.[53] Insofar as the family is the basic cell of society in the care and education of its new members, marriage serves society as a whole (not simply the happiness of the couple). As such, the state has a compelling interest in protecting marriage from this kind of diminution, even while protecting the basic human rights of all.

III. Further Questions

Gerald Coleman correctly notes that one of the tasks of those working within Catholic sexual ethics is to honestly admit the "loose ends" within the framework of the Church's teaching.[54] There are clearly many other questions that require further theological reflection on the part of the Church's pastors, theologians, and the faithful as a whole. While a full answer to all of these questions exceeds the scope of this study, it is still valuable to identify them as subjects for further reflection.

While the Church's teaching makes clear that union and openness to procreation in the context of the covenantal gift of self is the basic framework for evaluating the goodness of sexual activity among follow-

---

53. Coleman asks "if one eliminates procreation from the basic definition of marriage, on what legal basis could one stop three people from getting married, or a mother and a son, etc.?"; see *Homosexuality*, 122.

54. Coleman, *Homosexuality*, 74.

ers of Jesus, there is clearly a wide variety of possibilities for specific forms of sexual expression on the part of spouses. Thus while mutual masturbation to the point of orgasm or contraceptive intercourse are clearly proscribed, other sexual practices prior to intercourse are not.[55] The choice of various kinds of sexual expression is a prudential judgment on the part of the couple that must incorporate not only the demands of conjugal chastity, but also respect for one another's health, preferences, and moral sensibility. This requires honesty in communication, patience, and a profound sensitivity to one another over the course of a lifetime.

Many scholars have observed that Catholic sexual ethics has historically been focused upon male experience and now needs to better incorporate the insights and experience of women.[56] There is undoubtedly much truth in this claim. There are clearly aspects of human experience (e.g., pregnancy, childbirth, lactation) that are uniquely accessible to women. A Christian understanding of sexuality and embodiment will be far richer and more complete when such experiences have been subjected to careful reflection and articulation by women. More concretely, it still seems to be the case that the tradition has focused on male experience in defining the terminus of a conjugal act (i.e., male orgasm during vaginal intercourse). With the exception of a few moralists such as Alphonsus Ligouri and Francis Kenrick, much less attention has been paid to the import and ethical status of female orgasm. Yet a case can be made that psychologically and theologically this sexual release within the context of bodily union is not unrelated to the gift of self that intercourse signifies.[57] Furthermore, there is some emerging evidence that

55. Mutual masturbation between spouses should be sharply distinguished from various forms of genital stimulation prior to a conjugal act (i.e., foreplay). This latter practice, in addition to helping both men and women become physically ready for intercourse, can indeed not only express but foster the mutual love of spouses in their bodily gift of self.

56. See, e.g., Barbara Hilkert Andolsen, "Whose Sexuality? Whose Tradition? Women, Experience and Roman Catholic Sexual Ethics," in *Readings in Moral Theology*, No.9: *Feminist Ethics and the Catholic Moral Tradition*, ed. Charles Curran, Margaret Farley, R.S.M., and Richard McCormick, S.J. (New York: Paulist Press, 1996), 207–39.

57. This is not to say that a woman or a man might not occasionally be satisfied merely by having loved or been united with their spouse during intercourse without

orgasm may actually heighten female fertility, thus making it relevant to the procreative meaning of sexuality as well.[58]

Because procreation has been seen as a or the primary purpose of sexual expression by most of the Christian tradition, less attention has been paid to the unitive meaning of sexuality. More attention needs to be devoted to this purpose of sexuality, which is inseperably linked to openness to life within the spouses' sexual self-donation. This means not only paying more attention to offenses against the unitive meaning of sexual expression within marriage along the lines of the previous chapter, but identifying specific practices that can foster and develop the capacity of a couple's sexual relationship to be experienced as a dialogue of love—that is, practices that can foster the virtue of chastity as ordered to self-donation on the part of men and women viewed as integral persons. The remainder of this chapter will focus on one such practice: the periodic continence required by natural means of birth regulation.

IV. A Test Case for Growth in Marital Chastity: The Practice of Periodic Continence

One of the vexing issues for Catholic sexual ethics before and after *Humanae vitae* has been that of specifying the moral difference between natural and artificial means of birth regulation. A virtue-based approach that attends to the recent developments within the Catholic tradition noted above can make a contribution to this difficult question through its identification of the periodic continence required by natural means of birth regulation as a practice that fosters conjugal chastity.

---

themselves experiencing orgasm. In the case of males the tradition has referred to this practice as *amplex reservatus*. See Noonan, *Contraception*, 336–38, 447–50. Nonetheless, if this occurs on a consistent basis there may well be some problem (physical or psychological) in the individual or some manifest insensitivity in his or her spouse.

58. See, e.g., Winifred Gallagher, "The Ecology of Orgasm," *Discover* 7 (February 1986): 51–58.

A. The Problem: Specifying the Moral Difference between
Natural Family Planning and Contraception

Since Catholic moralists and official Catholic teaching began to give cautious approval to natural means of regulating births in the form of the rhythm method in the 1930s and 1940s, it has often been presumed that there is a moral difference between the two approaches.[59] Thus, Pope Pius XII in his allocution of November 26, 1951, "affirmed the legitimacy and, at the same time, the limits ... of a regulation of offspring [i.e., rhythm] which, unlike so-called birth control, is compatible with the law of God."[60] Likewise Pope Paul VI in *Humanae vitae* justified couples having intercourse only during infertile periods for serious motives as licit because in so doing a couple "make legitimate use of a natural disposition," while in contracepting "they impede the development of natural processes."[61] The difficulty of these statements is that they were largely read through the lens of the then dominant physicalist account of natural law which reduced it to the operation of biological process.[62]

Indeed, to many people it seemed that there was no difference at all between natural and artificial means. They were simply different avenues to the same end: avoiding pregnancy. Interestingly, this view has been put forward with equal fervor by those who challenge the Church's ban on contraception and those who see natural family planning (NFP) as a concession to a modern anti-child mentality. This view, especially as articulated by the former group, has been echoed by some theologians.[63]

Some theologians have gone further than arguing for a certain moral equivalence between the two methods. According to them, it is NFP

---

59. On this gradual acceptance, see Shannon, *Lively Debate*, 26–31; and Noonan, *Contraception*, 438–47.

60. Cited in Shannon, *Lively Debate*, p. 28.

61. Pope Paul VI, Encyclical Letter, *Humanae vitae* (1968), no. 16. The citation is from the NC News Service Translation (Boston: Daughters of St. Paul, 1968), p. 13.

62. See the discussion in Chapter 1.

63. Many Catholic moralists have argued that contraception has inherent disvalues (i.e., "ontic evil"), but that its use may not be morally evil in every case. See, e.g., Keane, *Sexual Morality*, 121–28. Cf. Cahill who, without the language of ontic versus moral evil, also arrives at the conclusion that contraception is a sometimes justifiable exception; see *Between the Sexes*, 148–49.

that can be described as "unnatural." This argument can take a number of forms. Some have argued that the method is "unnatural" on biological grounds because it "mutilates" female fertility by wasting ova whereas the pill does not.[64] Others have held that NFP does violence to the values of freedom and spontaneity in a couple's sexual relationship, reducing it to a mechanistic set of calculations based on charts and graphs. In this case, NFP is dismissed as "unnatural" because it is perceived as such in the couple's perceptions and experience.[65] Still other arguments combine biological and experiential considerations and urge that NFP damages a couple's relationship by requiring abstinence precisely when a women's sexual desires are strongest: at the time of ovulation.[66]

While not lacking in rhetorical force, these arguments have substantive problems. The biological appeals made share the same rather physicalist horizon as the neo-Scholastic natural law arguments demolished by the pill—they equate human "nature" with the functioning of biological process. The more experiential appeals reduce the moral meaning of "nature" to that which feels "natural" to the couple. Both kinds of arguments therefore draw their rhetorical force from a basic equivocation. Neither successfully grapples with an understanding of human nature in an existential or ontological sense.

On the other hand, there are also a variety of arguments that attempt to demonstrate a real moral difference between current forms of these approaches to birth regulation. Some focus on the practical differences and consequences of the two approaches. Some of these differences, while significant, are not necessarily moral in themselves. These would include considerations such as the fact that NFP is as effective as any other means of birth regulation short of complete sterilization,[67] that is

64. This was an argument put forward by Louis Janssens at the beginning of the debate over the pill; see his "Morale conjugale," 820–24.

65. Thus Ruether argued in her essay "Birth Control and the Ideals of Marital Sexuality," in *Readings in Moral Theology*, No. 8, *Dialogue about Catholic Sexual Teaching*, 138–52, esp. 144–52. Cf. the findings of John Marshall, *Love One Another: Psychological Aspects of Natural Family Planning* (London: Sheed & Ward, 1995), 23, 31.

66. Cf. the testimonies cited by Marshall, *Love One Another*, 52–53.

67. For comparisons of the effectiveness of natural family planning versus artificial methods and related studies, see Wilson, *Love and Family*, 246–55.

is relatively inexpensive to use,[68] and that it has been successfully learned and effectively used by people from a whole host of economic and cultural backgrounds. Other of these kinds of considerations certainly have moral dimensions, but still do not provide a full-blown articulation of a difference—for example, NFP requires communication and shared decision making by the couple (and hence promotes mutuality)[69]; NFP is the only reversible method of family planning and can aid couples with limited fertility in achieving pregnancy[70]; NFP, unlike contraception, has no medical side effects for women and men[71]; and some forms of contraception, perhaps including oral contraceptives, can actually have an abortifacient rather than a contraceptive action.[72] These factors are certainly important and some will be treated further below, but in themselves none of them provide a larger framework to specify the difference between artificial and natural means of birth regulation.

One significant attempt to articulate such a larger theoretical framework has been put forward by Germain Grisez, Joseph Boyle, John Finnis, and William May.[73] In their view, every act of contraceptive inter-

---

68. On the costs of natural family planning in comparison to artificial methods, see Wilson, *Love and Family*, 256–57.

69. On this point, see the studies cited by Mary Shivanadan, *Crossing the Threshold of Love: A New Vision of Marriage in Light of John Paul II's Anthropology* (Washington, D.C.: The Catholic University of America Press, 1999), 234–51. Cf. Marshall, *Love One Another*, 78–79.

70. See Wilson, *Love and Family*, 264; and Thomas W. Hilgers, *The Creighton Model NaProEducation System*, 3rd ed. (Omaha, Nebr.: Pope Paul VI Institute Press, 1996), 3. Cf. Marshall, *Love One Another*, 39.

71. For an overview of the various health risks associated with different forms of chemical or mechanical contraception as well as surgical sterilization, see Wilson, *Love and Family*, 267–97. Cf. Elizabeta Wójcik, "Natural Regulation of Conception and Contraception," in *Why "Humanae Vitae" Was Right: A Reader*, ed. Janet Smith (San Francisco: Ignatius Press, 1993), 421–43, esp. 440–43.

72. See William F. Colliton, "The Birth Control Pill: Abortifacient and Contraceptive," *Linacre Quarterly* 66 (1999): 26–47; and John Wilks, "The Impact of the Pill on Implantation Factors—New Research Factors," *Ethics and Medicine* 16, no. 1 (2000): 15–22.

73. See Germain Grisez, Joseph Boyle, John Finnis, and William May, "Every Marital Act Ought to Be Open to Life: Toward a Clearer Understanding," *The Thomist* 52 (1988): 365–426, and "NFP: Not Contralife," in *The Teaching of "Humanae Vitae": A Defense*, ed. John C. Ford (San Francisco: Ignatius Press, 1988), 81–92. Cf. Joseph M. Boyle, "Contraception and Natural Family Planning," *International Journal of Natural Family Planning* 44 (1980): 309–13.

course involves a twofold decision on the part of a couple: a decision to have intercourse and a decision (prior to, during, or after intercourse) to negate its procreative potential. It is this second choice in which they locate the malice of contraception because it involves a choice to attack a basic human good—that of life. The will of the couple in this case involves a malice directed against the possible human persons who might result from their union. This explains, in their view, the connection between contraception and abortion in method and in use because the latter merely carries the anti-life decision of the former to its fullest expression. The use of NFP, on the other hand, while it can be used with contraceptive intent, ordinarily involves no such second anti-life choice on the part of the couple.[74]

This view, though not without merit, has been rightly criticized on a number of points. First, in loading all of the evil of contraception into the will of the couple, it seems to neglect the embodied character of human sexuality and of contraceptive choice as a rejection of the person's fertility.[75] Second, there seem to be logical and ontological difficulties in determining the status of "possible persons," and hence of moral acts directed against them.[76] Third, this view does not seem to account for *Humanae vitae*'s understanding of an "inseparable connection" between the unitive and procreative meanings of the conjugal act, given that it grounds its teaching on sexuality in goods that are not only discreet but necessarily incommensurable (i.e., life and friendship).

Thus the debate sparked by *Humanae vitae* continues in the effort to answer the question of the moral difference between NFP and contraception.

74. An important qualification of the Grisez-Boyle-Finnis-May position is offered by William Marshner who holds that while couples can use natural family planning with a bad will, this misuse should not be classified as contraception. See "Can a Couple Practicing NFP Be Practicing Contraception?," *Gregorianum* 77 (1996): 677–704.

75. For a careful analysis and thoughtful critique of the Grisez-Boyle-Finnis-May position, see Janet Smith, *"Humanae Vitae": A Generation Later* (Washington, D.C.: The Catholic University of America Press, 1991), 340–70. But see May's rejoinder in his review of Smith's book in *The Thomist* 57 (1993): 155–61. May asserts that the argument of Carlo Caffarra, which Smith praises, is the same kind of line of reasoning as that of Grisez-Boyle-Finnis-May and is actually based on it.

76. See on this point Moore, *Body in Context*, 166–76.

B. Another Approach: Natural Family Planning as a Practice

Because of the ongoing nature of the disagreement, it may be helpful to approach the problem from a different perspective. One reason it may be difficult to fully discern the difference between natural and artificial means of regulating birth is that the dominance of instrumental reasoning in a scientific and technological culture tends to reduce them to competing methods.[77] In this view, the chief difference between these rival methods is to be found in quantitative measures such as effectiveness, impact on couple communication, health, and so on.[78] But this is to reduce natural methods of regulating birth to mere *techné*, while there is reason to think otherwise.

Even before the revival of interest in virtue theory in the last few decades, Karol Wojtyla offered a number of important but still relatively unexplored observations on this topic in *Love and Responsibility*. First, Wojtyla faces the issue being considered here squarely by asking: "Why should the natural method be morally superior to artificial methods, since the purpose is the same in each case—to eliminate the possibility of procreation in sexual intercourse?"[79] The answer comes in the form of a qualification: "To answer we must rid ourselves of some of the associations of the word 'method.' We tend to approach 'the natural method' and 'artificial methods' from the same utilitarian premises."[80] Understood in this way, the natural method is simply another means to ensure sexual pleasure without the risk of pregnancy. Wojtyla, however, proposes a different understanding:

The utilitarian interpretation distorts the true character of what we call the natural method, which is that it is based on continence as a virtue and this . . . is very closely connected with love of the person . . . Inherent in the essential character of continence as a virtue is the conviction that *the love of man and woman loses nothing as a result of temporary abstention from erotic experiences, but on the contrary*

---

77. On the primacy of instrumental reason in modern Western culture, see Charles Taylor, *The Ethics of Authenticity* (Cambridge, Mass.: Harvard University Press, 1991), 93–108.

78. For a critique of the anthropological presuppositions underlying social scientific research on family planning studies, see Shivanandan, *Crossing the Threshold*, 209–33.

79. Wojtyla, *Love and Responsibility*, 240.

80. Ibid.

gains: the personal union takes deeper root, grounded as it is above all in the affirmation of the value of the persons and not just in sexual attachment. *Continence as a virtue cannot be regarded as a 'contraceptive measure'"* [81]

Wojtyla contrasts calculating and self-interested expressions of continence with its disinterested expression, which is closely bound up with justice—both to the Creator and to one's spouse. [82]

The same view is expressed by Pope John Paul II in his papal teaching. Commenting on the teaching of *Humanae vitae* he writes:

Even though the periodicity of continence in this case is applied to the so-called "natural rhythms" (*HV* 16), the continence itself is a definite and permanent attitude. It is a virtue, and therefore the whole line of conduct acquires a virtuous character. The encyclical emphasizes clearly enough that here it is not merely a matter of a definite technique, but of ethics in the strict sense as a morality of conduct. [83]

In the same audience, the pope notes that "[i]n the case of a morally upright regulation of fertility effected by means of periodic continence, one is clearly dealing with the practice of conjugal chastity, that is, of a definite ethical attitude." [84]

In Wojtyla's analysis continence is one of the components of the moral virtue of chastity that makes possible sexual self-giving. [85] Given this, it is difficult to reduce the whole positive reality of chastity to continence–that is, refraining from intercourse—and to understand this abstinence as virtue in itself. Wojtyla is certainly aware that continence can be practiced from bad motives, in which case it is hardly virtuous. He is also quite clear that chastity does not preclude the embodied gift of self in sexual union—only that it ensures the fully personal quality of this gift. [86] For these reasons, it seems more precise to regard the peri-

81. Ibid., 241; emphasis in original.

82. Ibid.

83. Pope John Paul II, general audience of August 28, 1984, in *Theology of the Body,* 399–401, at 400.

84. Ibid., 401.

85. Wojtyla, *Love and Responsibility,* 166–73. The other, negative component is shame, understood as a reaction that protects the sexual values of the person from exploitation and use. Cf. *Love and Responsibility,* 174–93.

86. "True chastity does not lead to disdain for the body or to disparagement of

odic continence required by NFP not as a virtue in itself, but as a practice integrally related to the acquisition of chastity.

Alasdair MacIntyre in his ground-breaking work *After Virtue* provides a helpful analysis of practices and their relationship to moral virtue. MacIntyre identifies three successive logical stages in his concept of virtue: specific practices, a narrative account of human life, and an account of a moral tradition.[87] It is primarily the first of these that is of interest here. MacIntyre's definition of a practice is rather complex:

By a "practice" I am going to mean any coherent and complex form of socially established cooperative human activity through which goods internal to that form of activity are realized in the course of trying to achieve those standards of excellence which are appropriate to, and partially definitive of, that form of activity, with the result that human powers to achieve excellence, and human conceptions of the ends and goods involved, are systematically extended.[88]

His use of this concept, however, is not as complex. It would exclude rudimentary activities such as tic-tac-toe or activities simply based on natural ability such as throwing a football, but would include more complex games such as chess or the game of football. It would also embrace forms of academic inquiry such as architecture, physics, or history, as well as arts such as painting and music. More to the subject of this analysis, it would include the creation and sustenance of various forms of human community such as nations, cities, and families.[89]

The goods of which MacIntyre speaks can be internal to the practice, such as a recognizable skill or excellence displayed within the practice, or external to it, such as fame or fortune. Virtue in this view can be understood as *"an acquired human quality, the possession and exercise of which tends to enable us to achieve those goods which are internal to practices and the lack of which effectively prevents us from achieving any such goods."*[90] The ability to recognize internal goods depends upon training in perception and truthfulness in regard to the facts of the actual excellence displayed. Hence, "we have to

matrimony and the sexual life. That is the result of false chastity, chastity with a tinge of hypocrisy, or still more frequently, of unchastity"; Wojtyla, *Love and Responsibility*, 171.

87. See MacIntyre, *After Virtue*, 186–87.

88. Ibid., 187.

89. Cf. ibid., 187–89.

90. Ibid., 191; emphasis in original.

accept as necessary components of any practice with internal goods and standards of excellence the virtues of justice, courage, and honesty."[91] Thus, moral practices shape the character of both those who participate in them and those who, through their own experience, evaluate them.

It appears that one can make the case that NFP is a "practice" in MacIntyre's sense of the term. It is a complex activity not based on natural ability. It requires training by those who have acquired a level of proficiency, it calls for careful observation cultivated by experience, it necessitates new levels of cooperation and communication on the part of the couple, and in the process it shapes the character of both couples who use the method and practitioners who teach it in definite ways. As in the case of other practices, this moral impact necessarily involves justice, courage, and honesty. But NFP understood as a moral practice is most directly related to the acquisition and practice of chastity.

C. Marital Chastity and Natural Family Planning

How does the use of NFP as a moral practice serve to shape the character of the couple? As MacIntyre's analysis suggests, NFP, like other moral practices, requires the specific virtues of justice, courage, and honesty. MacIntyre means this in the rather restricted sense that these virtues are the necessary precondition for judging accurately and honestly genuine excellence in a specific practice.[92] This is certainly true for couples who use NFP. They must be honest and accurate in using the method, clear in applying it, willing to seek further information and training when confronting new problems, disciplined in making observations and charting, and committed to avoiding behaviors that compromise the agreed-upon purpose of the method (e.g., genital contact during fertile periods when the method is being used to avoid pregnancy). These same standards are necessary for practitioners to teach the method and evaluate its successful use by couples.

Yet there is a broader sense in which these virtues are required of those who use and teach NFP. Wojtyla makes it clear that the choice to use natural methods is based upon justice and honesty on the part of the couple both toward one another and toward their Creator.[93] If, in fact,

---

91. Ibid.   92. Cf. ibid., 191.

93. Chapter 4 of Wojtyla's *Love and Responsibility* is entitled "Justice towards the Creator." See esp. pp. 222–49 within that chapter.

intercourse is a language that bespeaks the covenantal gift of the whole person to the other, then the deliberate exclusion of fertility is, in fact, a dishonest expression of this gift.[94] Such an act commits an injustice toward the other insofar as it fails to treat him or her as a whole person. The same act is an injustice to the Creator insofar as it disregards the existential values of sexuality that have God as their author.[95] To stand firm for these personal and existential values in sexuality by using or teaching NFP in the face of personal or societal pressure to do otherwise requires the virtue of fortitude or courage. Obviously, these observations revisit some of the personalist and anthropological arguments treated above, now set in the horizon of moral growth and virtue.

The classical tradition of virtue represented by St. Thomas Aquinas understands the moral virtues (or, in the case of a Christian, the moral and theological virtues) to form a unity.[96] Hence justice, honesty, and fortitude require prudence and temperance and their specific forms. Thus a certain level of chastity is necessarily required of the truly just or courageous person—even though it may not be fully developed or expressed in his or her character.

How does NFP understood as a practice enable a couple to acquire the moral virtue of chastity? As noted above, it is misleading to reduce the whole of conjugal chastity to the periodic continence that successful use of NFP requires. But at the same time, it is true that this abstinence is one of the keys to a couple's growth in their freedom to love one another, and hence in their growth in chastity. Continence enables the couple to experience sexual union as a gift given freely to one another rather than as a biological urge that must be obeyed or satisfied.[97] It thus serves as a part of that "apprenticeship in self-mastery" that chastity works within the person in effecting the self-possession that is necessary for genuine love.[98]

---

94. Cf. ibid., 234.   95. Cf. ibid., 54–57, 230.

96. Interestingly, in *After Virtue* MacIntyre rejects Aquinas's understanding of the unity of the virtues (see pp. 179–80), but in more recent works he has accepted and defended this Thomistic position. See, e.g., *Whose Justice? Which Rationality?* (South Bend, Ind.: University of Notre Dame Press, 1988), x, 198.

97. See John Paul II's weekly general audiences of October 24, October 31, and November 7, 1984, in *Theology of the Body*, 408–15.

98. See *CCC*, 2339. Cf. *Familiaris consortio*, 32; and John Paul II's weekly general audience of October 10, 1984, in *Theology of the Body*, 406–8.

It is here that many of the narratives of couples who use NFP or practitioners who work with couples and witness the impact of NFP on them becomes important.[99] Couples very often speak of a deepened respect for one another as a result of the method.[100] Men often report that the method engenders in them a new respect for their wives because of their wonder at the intricate pattern of women's fertility and its impact on the whole of their personality. Women frequently speak of an awareness of their husbands' respect for them as persons engendered in them by their willingness to express love in nongenital forms.[101] Ethically, this is important because it speaks to a deeper perception of the value of one's spouse as a person on the part of the couple and thus to a respect that is the precondition of authentic love.

As noted above, there is significant evidence, both anecdotal and statistical, that NFP helps foster other beneficial practices and moral virtues in the life of the couple. Thus there are indicators that use of the method improves open, honest communication on the part of the couple.[102] Especially if there is shared responsibility for charting, NFP builds a "rhythm" of regular—even daily—communication regarding sexuality into a couple's relationship. The practice of NFP forces a couple to communicate regularly about their fertility, their desire for children, and their sexual relationship. This habituates such couples to talk more openly about these vital issues and may facilitate more open and honest communication throughout their relationship as a whole.

Closely related to deepened communication is deeper intimacy. In-

99. For an individual example of such testimony, see Ruth Lasseter, "Sensible Sex," in *Why "Humanae Vitae" Was Right,* 475–95. For a collection of such narratives addressed to various topics, see Mary Shivanandan, *Natural Sex* (New York: Rawson, Wade, 1979).

100. For an inverse description of the effects of contraception in eroding marital trust and respect see Lasseter, "Sensible Sex," 483–90.

101. See, e.g., Shivanandan, *Natural Sex,* 73. Though practiced for different reasons, commentators have observed that the periodic abstinence enjoined by Jewish law (the *Halakah*) "confines the sexual drive of a man by harnessing it to the sexual rhythms and needs of his wife. Sexual abstention is mandated by the cycle of menstruation. Sexual activity is directed to fulfilling the mitzvah of onah: meeting and responding to the sexual needs of the woman. The 'quiet' introverted sexuality of the woman circumscribes the active, extroverted sexuality of the man. It becomes the center and regulating mechanism of the intimate marital relationship"; Rachel Biale, *Women and Jewish Law* (New York: Schocken Books, 1984), 146.

102. For more anecdotal testimony see Biale, *Womenand Jewish Law,* 77.

deed, communication is merely the verbal form of intimacy. From a psychological perspective, intimacy can be understood as the closeness or sense of connectedness that exists between a couple. Theologically, it can be understood as the quality of a couple's communion with one another. NFP builds intimacy in a marriage because most of the forms in which the method is taught encourage couples to develop physical (but not genital), verbal/psychological, and spiritual forms of intimacy.[103] This instruction is given opportunity and impetus during periods of abstinence when couples are forced to find ways other than genital sex to communicate affection. It is this that creates according to the experience of many couples the "courtship and honeymoon" effect of NFP—the romantic pursuit of the other during times of abstinence that creates a greater appreciation for intercourse during times when a couple can come together sexually.[104] This awareness of other forms of intimacy too creates a heightened perception of the value of the other as a whole person and as a friend that is integral to marital chastity.

Finally, NFP as a moral practice entails shared decision making on the part of the couple, and thus promotes a basic mutuality in the couple's relationship. Unlike the various artificial methods in which the responsibility inevitably devolves upon either the man or the woman, NFP requires not just communication but genuine collaboration on the part of the couple. Ideally, couples together take responsibility for monitoring their shared fertility (women through observation of their signs, men through recording them). But necessarily they must decide together whether or not to have intercourse and whether they are using the method to help achieve or avoid pregnancy. This practice of shared decision making in the realm of decisions regarding their sexual relationship and family planning habituates the couple to communicate and reach decisions together in other areas of their married life. This practice of mutual decision making better reflects the "mutual submission" of men and women in marriage and more closely corresponds to the demands of justice in regard to the equal dignity of the spouses.

The fact that NFP serves to foster greater respect, improved commu-

---

103. See, e.g., Hilgers, *The Creighton Model* 39–45, and Marshall, *Love One Another*, 84–85.

104. Cf. Wilson, *Love and Family*, 263; Shivanandan, *Natural Sex*, 77, 89–104; Marshall, *Love One Another*, 40–41.

nication, deeper intimacy, and mutuality within marriage concretizes the claim that as a moral practice it serves to shape the character of the couple. The method provides a form of moral activity that sensitizes the couple to the demands of justice, honesty, courage, and chastity required by their mutual love. All of these factors together may provide some explanation of the strikingly low divorce rate among couples who use the method (2–5 percent for NFP couples versus a national U.S. average approaching 50 percent).[105] This observation in turn indicates that the impact of NFP as a moral practice is experienced by more than the couple, but within the whole of the family and even the whole of society.[106]

This analysis suggests that a virtue-based approach to the moral life can shed new light on difficult questions of sexual ethics. This chapter has given extensive consideration to one issue: that of identifying a moral difference between natural and artificial means of birth regulation. This choice of subject matter is not accidental given that way in which the controversy over birth control before and after *Humanae vitae* has shaped Catholic consciousness in sexual matters. Still, a method similar to that developed in this "test case" might be more fully applied to other pressing issues of sexual ethics (extramarital sex, reproductive technologies, homogenital activity).[107] This consideration also offers some initial direction as to how one can actually acquire the virtue of chastity rather than simply offering various rules of sexual conduct to which a person is expected to conform. The last chapter of the book will offer some further considerations on how one can foster growth in chastity for oneself and others.

105. See the studies cited in Janet Smith, *Humanae Vitae*, 127; and Jeff Brand, *Marital Duration and Natural Family Planning* (Cincinatti, Ohio: Couple to Couple League, 1995).

106. In this regard, it becomes apparent that the Church's teaching on responsible parenthood is more than a matter of sexual ethics—it is an integral part of its social teaching. See David McCarthy, "Procreation, the Development of Peoples, and the Final Destiny of Humanity," *Communio* 26 (1999): 698–721.

107. For further consideration of the relevance of the infused moral virtues to forms of assisted reproduction, see Romanus Cessario, O.P., "The Meaning of Virtue in the Christian Moral Life: Its Significance for Human Life Issues," *The Thomist* 53 (1989): 173–96.

CHAPTER 7

Teaching Sex
Education, Sexuality, Character

This chapter examines issues of moral education from the standpoint of a virtue-based approach to moral enquiry. How is it that one
can teach moral virtue to others or foster it in onself, particularly in the
often vexing and contentious area of sexuality? The preceding chapters
have made clear that an insistence on particular moral rules is not
enough, though these may well have a place in the interiorization of
moral values and the person's habituation to them through moral action. One must also attend to the larger vision of human sexuality and
its place in the person's call to beatitude realized through the communion of love. Equally important is the identification of concrete practices
that can foster this transformation of the person's character as well as
the concrete social and cultural obstacles to human sexual flourishing
(e.g., the widespread trivialization of sex in contemporary Western culture).

While not purporting to offer an exhaustive treatment, this final
chapter will consider some concrete steps for "teaching" the virtue of
chastity or fostering its acquisition in a variety of settings. First, it will
examine the importance of providing a vision of human sexuality and
human fulfillment that can counteract current cultural ideologies. Continuing the analysis of the previous chapter, it will consider the role of
concrete practices in developing moral virtue. Next, it will consider the
pedagogical role of moral norms in the interiorization of moral values
through action as well as the relation of these norms in regard to the
ongoing conversion to which followers of Jesus are called. It will then
treat the role of community in the acquisition of virtue, particularly the
indispensable role of the family in education in chastity. Also in the
vein of the interpersonal dimensions of the acquisition of virtue, it will

briefly examine the impact of friendship on chastity. The chapter will then offer a brief analysis of the encyclical *Evangelium vitae* as a vital articulation of these various dimensions of education in virtue.

I. Vision and Values

Virtue theorists as far back as Plato have recognized that virtue is first of all a matter of sight—of seeing the good.[1] Vision precedes and shapes character. We must see the good before we can learn to become good. Whether in the form of a great work of literature or a moving piece of art, or in the character of a virtuous person, we need to see and be attracted to the beauty of the good before being moved to pursue it and make it our own. Such impetus can be a form of intellectual and moral conversion that parallels and accompanies the spiritual conversion engendered by the hearing of the gospel message and the fuller vision of the good that it provides.[2]

This larger vision of the good provides a context that makes specific moral rules or norms intelligible. Without this context, rules easily become the focus of moral reasoning and action. This is a tendency against which Western Christian theology has struggled since the fourteenth century. It is also evidenced in many deontological accounts of modern ethics. Certainly, in the West, appeals to various kinds of rules and efforts to establish the authority of those promulgating them has proved singularly ineffectual in countering current dominant cultural ideologies concerning sexuality: sex as secular salvation, sex as mere *techné*, sex as power, or sex as a commodity to be bought and sold. What is needed in this regard is a vision of the meaning and beauty of human sexuality that is more compelling than these shallow and distorted alternatives.

From the perspective of Christian faith, such a vision must be grounded in an understanding of the human person's call to the beatitude of participation in Trinitarian life made possible by the cross of Christ. Human persons are made apt for this end by learning to live in

---

1. See the analysis of Plato's allegory of the cave (*Republic* VII, 514a–517c) provided by Meilaender, *Theory and Practice of Virtue*, 51–53. Cf. the treatment of "visional character" offered by Dykstra, *Vision and Character*, 33–55.

2. On the interconnection of these various dimensions of conversion, see Bohr, *Catholic Moral Tradition*, 104–20; and Conn, *Christian Conversion*, passim.

communion with God and with other human persons—by learning to make "a sincere gift" of themselves.[3] Sexual differences are a tangible indication inscribed within human embodiment of this vocation to communion. Chastity enables this vocation to be realized in a variety of states of life: the single life, religious celibacy, or marriage. Within marriage, chaste sexual union is an embodied form of self-giving that engages, offers, and receives the whole person—including his or her fertility. This union is a gesture that anamnetically recalls and actualizes the irrevocable promise of self made in the marriage covenant. At the same time, it is a proleptic foreshadowing and anticipation of the nuptial union between Christ and the Church in the eschaton already tasted in the Eucharist. Conjugal union is itself sacramental both in the sense that it makes the sacrament indissoluble and in that it serves as an ongoing source of the grace of the sacrament in the life of the couple.

II. Practices Make Perfect

The mere acquisition of information—even if it happens to be true—does not by itself constitute moral virtue. One can have speculative knowledge of the good, but this is not the same as real, experiential knowledge of the good. Genuine moral knowledge involves personal appropriation of goodness and truth such that the appetites and desires of the person are reordered and the person's character is thus transformed. This assimilation of knowledge of the good occurs in a particular way through *praxis*—through concrete moral choices expressed in action by the person.

To make such an assertion is not to reduce the whole of the moral life to individual acts. It is rather to insist that concrete moral actions have a key role in the moral growth and becoming of the person. As noted above, every human action both expresses the character of the person who performs it and reflexively shapes it. While the formation of the *habitus* that is at the heart of moral virtue takes time, this process can be nurtured or subverted by individual choices.

Those who seek to educate others in chastity therefore must attend not merely to the information that they convey, but to the identification

3. Cf. *Gaudium et spes,* no. 24.

and development of practices that support the internalization of this and other forms of moral goodness. In relation to the gift of human sexuality, this would entail fostering a basic respect and reverence for the dignity of other persons that is foundational to justice and love in interpersonal relationships. It would require practices that foster care and respect for the natural world as the work of God entrusted to human stewardship. In particular, it would call for care and respect for the human body as the visible manifestation of the person and his or her uniqueness and transcendent dignity. It would also require the ability to recognize the difference between the friendship and intimacy needed by all persons and genital sex, which is not absolutely necessary to one's happiness and fulfillment.[4]

But because the virtues are ultimately a unity, attention must also be paid to practices that foster other virtues supportive of chastity. Thus forms of moral action such as service to the poor, which inculcates justice and an awareness of the dignity of others; public witness to the value and sanctity of human life in its most vulnerable expressions (i.e., that of the unborn, the elderly, and the handicapped), which fosters courage; friendship with others of high character, which requires prudence in selecting and maintaining these relationships; and continence as the appropriate means of expressing love and friendship outside of marriage (as well as at times within it) are all crucial to the development of chastity. Furthermore, for the Christian, moral virtue is never merely the result of human effort and energy alone. The infused moral virtues and the theological virtues of faith, hope, and love must inform and transform the natural moral virtues through the action of the Holy Spirit.[5] Hence, education in chastity must also encourage the development of a life of prayer—both individual prayer and participation in the liturgical and sacramental worship of the Church.[6]

Because it is the source and summit of the Church's life,[7] participa-

4. This is a distinction not supported by contemporary Western culture. See Dawn, *Sexual Character*, 12–17.

5. On the role of the infused virtues in the moral life, see Cessario *Introduction to Moral Theology*, 200–205.

6. Cf. Dykstra's treatment of the role of disciplines such as repentance, prayer, and service in the formation of character in *Vision and Character*, 89–114.

7. Cf. Second Vatican Council, Dogmatic Constitution on the Church, *Lumen gentium*, no. 11.

tion in the Eucharist is central among the transformative practices lived by Christians. The Eucharist is both food for the journey of moral change and growth and a foretaste of the union with God that this journey makes possible. In the Eucharist the Church becomes "one flesh" with Christ the divine Bridegroom in his act of selfless love on the cross.[8] It therefore signifies in a real way the self-donation to which Christians are called in whatever state of life they live. At the same time, as a sacramental sharing in divine life, it capacitates Christians to realize this self-offering to God and to others in their daily lives. Receiving the Body of Christ enables them to be the Body of Christ given in the world.[9]

III. Moral Norms—Only the Beginning

A conception of the moral life wholly focused on law and obligation is subject to a variety of profound distortions. One cannot reduce the whole of Christian morality to obedience to a set of norms without lapsing back into some stultifying form of the morality of obligation. Nor can one seek escape from this flawed paradigm through the use of a casuistry designed to always find exceptions to whatever moral rule is in question. Ultimately, both the solitary focus on law and the continual effort to seek loopholes in it are two sides of the same voluntarist coin and both share a thoroughly act-centered view of the moral life. The apparent opposites converge in many of their most basic presuppositions in a manner not unlike the barnyard cabals of George Orwell's *Animal Farm*.

Rather, moral norms, such as the prohibitions against extramarital or contraceptive sex, provide a necessary negative minimum for moral growth, but only a minimum. Just because a person refrains from sex outside of marriage does not mean that he or she is chaste or has fully developed the capacity for self-giving love necessary for human flourishing. It may mean nothing more than that such a person is held back from acting on sexual urges by fear or by lack of opportunity. Nonethe-

8. Cf. Hans Urs von Balthasar, *A Theological Anthropology* (New York: Sheed & Ward, 1967), 304–11, and "Ephesians 5:21–33 and *Humanae Vitae*: A Meditation," in *Christian Married Love*, ed. Raymond Dennehy (San Francisco: Ignatius, 1981), 55–73.

9. Cf. *CCC*, 1396.

less, the person who refrains from self-destructive and unchaste behavior for whatever reason is still better off than the person who indulges in it. Such acts, like other offenses against chastity, the Church's tradition has designated as intrinsically evil—that is, bad in their object and incapable of being ordered to God.[10] As such, they are utterly opposed to growth in moral freedom and the attainment of beatitude.

Servais Pinckaers, O.P., offers a very helpful and important contextualization of the role of moral norms in his discussion of the progressive nature of growth in moral freedom. Pinckaers identifies three stages in this process: the stage of discipline, the stage of progress, and the stage of maturity.[11] The *stage of discipline* corresponds to the beginning of education in the moral life—serving as a kind of moral and spiritual adolescence. The beginner is confronted with rules that seem to be imposed from without by various authorities (e.g., parents, teachers). Initially, such rules can be experienced as an infringement upon freedom that is painful as it reorders the person's accumulated habits and desires.[12] Obedience to moral rules such as the Decalogue are the focus of this stage of moral growth.

In the *stage of progress*, the interior reordering effected through repeated action in conformity with moral rules takes root in the formation of a *habitus*, an ontological change within the person that grants a new power to act or perform in accord with genuine moral excellence. The rules that had seemed foreign now arise from within, from the wellsprings of the person's own freedom, as he or she seeks to pursue and practice excellence for its own sake. That is, the person begins to practice virtue in all of its forms. This focus on interior transformation through love and the freedom bestowed by the acquisition of virtue Pinckaers parallels with Jesus' teaching in the Sermon on the Mount.[13]

10. For an analysis of the meaning of intrinsically evil acts as well as the sources of the moral evaluation of human acts (i.e., object, end, and circumstances) see *CCC*, 155–83. Cf. *Veritatis splendor*, nos. 76–81.

11. See Pinckaers, *Sources of Christian Ethics*, 359–71. The same progressive assimilation in excellence may be seen (at least analogously) in the learning of any human art.

12. Pinckaers, in fact, compares it to the purgative way of the spiritual life which is primarily focused upon avoiding sin and being freed of vices; see *Sources of Christian Ethics*, 362–63.

13. See ibid., 355–56. Pinckaers also parallels this stage with the "illuminative way"

The final stage of moral growth Pinckaers terms the *stage of maturity*, which corresponds to the phase of adulthood in the moral and spiritual life. The morally mature person is the one who has achieved mastery in excellent actions, ordering his or her drives, desires, and faculties toward the end of his or her life considered as a whole. In this stage, the individual's freedom reaches its full and optimal expression, enabling the person to stamp each action authored with his or her own spontaneous creativity and personal uniqueness in a manner akin to the imprint left by a great artist on his or her works. In the moral realm, the person is perfected in faith and love through the interior operation of the Holy Spirit, which corresponds to Aquinas's definition of the New Law.[14] The Beatitudes of the Gospel find their realization in the virtues and in the full flowering of these virtues in the gifts of the Spirit.[15]

Moral norms thus provide a foundation for the person's moral growth and development. Yet these norms and obedience to them cannot be equated with the whole of the moral life. Thus moral norms such as those prohibiting extramarital or anti-procreative forms of sexual activity can lay a foundation for a person's growth in freedom. But this only occurs through the interiorization of these norms and the moral goods that they serve to protect through repeated moral choices and the interior work of the Holy Spirit. The capacity to consistently offer onself as a "sincere gift" in a way appropriate to one's state in life and the concrete circumstances of the moment represents the mature spontaneity of the person transformed by love.

---

described by the mystics as the person grows in the life of prayer through the interior work of the Holy Spirit.

14. Pinckaers points to St. Thomas's understanding of the New Law in the *ST* I–II, q. 106, a. 1: "Consequently the New law is chiefly the grace of the Holy Ghost, which is given through faith in Christ . . . we must say that the New Law is in the first place a law that is inscribed on our hearts, but that secondarily it is a written law." The citation is from *ST*, trans. Fathers of the English Dominican Province (New York: Benziger Brothers, 1947), 1:1104. See Pinckears, *Sources of Christian Ethics*, 369. For a longer analysis of Aquinas's understanding of the New Law, see *Sources of Christian Ethics*, 172–78; and Cessario, *Introduction to Moral Theology*, 212–18. Pinckaers parallels this stage of moral growth with the "unitive way" of the spiritual life; see *Sources of Christian Ethics*, 370.

15. See ibid., 178–81, 369. Cf. *ST* I–II, q. 69, a. 3. See also Wadell, *Friends of God*, 121–36; and Cessario, *Introduction to Moral Theology*, 205–12.

IV. An Authentic Gradualism

A virtue-based approach to the moral life regards it as a process of gradual growth and transformation over time. Yet there are varying ways to understand this gradualism, some of which are conducive to fostering further moral growth and some of which are not.

In his Apostolic Exhortation *Familiaris consortio* Pope John Paul II makes a distinction between what he calls "the law of gradualness" and "the gradualness of the law."[16] The "law of gradualness" refers to the fact that conversion is an ongoing process in the life of a Christian. Individuals and couples who are followers of Jesus are called to grow in holiness in the whole of their daily lives, including in the area of their sexuality. Of course, living in a fallen world and subject to their own concupiscence, disciples do fail. When they do so, they need to return to God for his gracious mercy made visible in the cross of Christ and accessible in the sacraments of the Church so as to continue to grow in holiness.

The idea behind the "gradualness of the law" is rather different. In this view, there are "different degrees or forms of precept in God's law for different individuals and situations."[17] Hence if particular groups find some moral norm too burdensome, it ought to be changed or at least accommodated to them in some fashion. Thus some have argued that married couples who find the Church's teaching on contraception onerous or unconvincing should, in some circumstances, be permitted to use such means to avoid pregnancy.[18] Others have urged that persons who have a homosexual orientation who struggle with living chastity in the form of continence should be encouraged to form stable monogamous partnerships with others akin to heterosexual marriages.[19] From the perspective of *Familiaris consortio*, this is an inauthentic expression of

---

16. See no. 34. The citations are from *Role of the Christian Family*, 56. Subsequent references will be to this edition.

17. Ibid.

18. See, e.g., Vincent Genovesi, S.J., who like a number of other theologians argues that while contraceptive use is always a disvalue (i.e., "ontic evil"), it is not in every case a moral evil; see *In Pursuit of Love: Catholic Morality and Human Sexuality*, 2nd ed. (Collegeville, Minn.: Michale Glazier, 1996), 193–206.

19. See, e.g., Farley, "An Ethic for Same-Sex Relations," 93–106.

gradualism based on a faulty conception of the person's capacity for growth in holiness.

Conversion is indeed an ongoing process in the life of the follower of Jesus, but it is not facilitated by lowering the standards or diluting the vision according to which Christians are called to live by attempting to override absolute moral norms through an appeal to circumstances or impediments.[20] As noted above, it is such a vision of the truth in its bracing fullness that often awakens in a person the desire for moral change and growth. And it is negative norms that exclude certain behaviors that provide a foundation for subsequent growth in moral freedom. To undermine these first principles of moral growth is to significantly damage the possibility of the development of virtue that capacitates one for the beatitude of union with God. Followers of Jesus need to continually be challenged to the full measure of excellence and flourishing, even if they fall short of it. The answer to this aspect of the human condition is not to attempt to change norms that flow from the biblical witness and the Church's tradition, but to recall the constant mercy of God that precedes and undergirds the whole of the Christian moral life.[21]

V. The Role of Community

All virtues are inherently interpersonal—that is, they are acquired in and sustained by specific communities and their practices.[22] This is nowhere more evident than in regard to the relational reality that is human sexuality. It follows from this that Christian communities must attend to their practices to see if these enable their members to develop and practice chastity and other moral virtues.[23] This is true of the Church as a whole, of specific Christian communities such as parishes or prayer communities, and of the most basic Christian community of all: the family.

20. Cf. Cessario, *Introduction to Moral Theology*, 108–15, 181–83.

21. On the mercy of God accessible in the sacraments as the foundation of the moral life, see Cessario, *Introduction to Moral Theology*, 218–27.

22. See the insightful discussion of St. Benedict in Cessario, *Introduction to Moral Theology*, 193–95. Cf. Dykstra, *Vision and Character*, 55–58.

23. On the role of Christian communities in forming the character of their members in the area of sexuality, see Dawn, *Sexual Character*, 25–38.

Because of the natural admiration that young children have for their parents and because of the unique love between parents and children, the family provides an ideal setting to impart virtue.[24] As Pope John Paul II notes, the communion of love between spouses ought to pervade the broader community of the family and the education that occurs within it.[25] The family is thus not only a school of love, but a laboratory for virtue.

The Church's teaching and liturgical prayer acknowledges parents to be the primary educators of their children in the faith.[26] This means that they have the primary right and responsibility to evangelize their children, to catechize them in the truths of the faith, and to shape their character by instruction and example. When parents share this role with religious educators, this relationship is governed by the principle of subsidiarity.[27] In regard to education in sexuality, this means that parents have the primary right and responsibility to instruct their children in an authentic human and Christian understanding of sexuality in a manner appropriate to their age and to instill in them the virtue of chastity.[28]

But parents cannot model or instruct their children in qualities of character that they themselves do not possess. Thus for parents to effectively instruct their children in chastity, they must have begun to acquire and practice this virtue themselves. It follows that parents must seek to implement and foster specific practices in their home that can help them develop chastity in themselves and to then foster it in their children.

To continue the example of one specific practice considered in the previous chapter, insofar as the use of NFP contributes to the acquisition of conjugal chastity in the ways described above, it also equips par-

---

24. "The home is well-suited for *education in the virtues*"; *CCC*, 2223, emphasis in original. The citation is from Libreria Editrice Vatican edition (Washington, D.C.: United States Catholic Conference, 1994), 537.

25. See John Paul II, Letter to Families, *Gratissimam sane*, nos. 7–8.

26. See *Familiaris consortio*, nos. 36–39; *CCC*, 2221.

27. Cf. *Familiaris consortio*, no. 40; *CCC*, 2229.

28. See the overviews of the issues here provided by the Sacred Congregation for Catholic Education, in *Educational Guidance in Human Love* (1983), and by the Pontifical Council for the Family, in *Truth and Meaning of Human Sexuality*. Especially note the developmental overview of chastity education in the latter document (nos. 77–111).

ents to be more effective models and teachers in this regard. At the very least, the fact that couples communicate regularly about their sexual relationship and family-planning decisions and have a heightened understanding of the values that ground them, can help to overcome the embarrassment or ignorance regarding the subject that is often a primary obstacle to parents in communicating an authentic understanding of human sexuality to their children. Furthermore, the parents own witness of mutual respect, effective communication, chaste expressions of intimacy, and collaborative leadership powerfully reinforces the words that they address to their children whether these be eloquent or very ordinary.

Within the relationships between parents and children or between children and others who assist their parents in their educational responsibility, it is important to develop concrete forms of moral action that enable moral values such as chastity to be assimilated at a deeper level than that of mere information. For adolescent children and young adults, especially young women, this may well include instruction in some form of NFP as a method for fertility awareness and record of gynecological health. Prudence might suggest reserving aspects of the method necessary for avoiding pregnancy until young adults are engaged to be married. But as noted above, for Christians of all ages, it is necessary to develop a whole range of other practices to make possible an appreciation of the values imparted by NFP as a moral practice as well as to support growth in chastity throughout one's life.

In regard to this range of practices, it is apparent that local churches, parishes, and lay associations provide an indispensable support to families in their mission of moral education. Even if parents are the primary educators of their children in the faith, they are not the only ones. Religious education programs that effectively combine clear catechesis about sexuality with a range of practices that foster growth in moral virtue reinforce and supplement the formation provided within the family.[29] Insofar as the Eucharist orders the Church to the care of the poor and the marginalized,[30] local churches and Christian communities must allow the mystery that they celebrate to move them to concrete

29. Unfortunately, some parents eschew their responsibility of educating their children in the faith altogether, leaving programs of moral education outside the home as the only place of formation.

30. Cf. *CCC*, 1397.

forms of solidarity with the vulnerable around them. Programs of preparation for Eucharist, confirmation, marriage, holy orders, or the rite of Christian initiation for adults are ideal places for Christian communities to foster such a praxis of solidarity among their members.

VI. Friendship

Another indicator of the interpersonal nature of virtue is the indispensable role of friendship in its acquisition. Indeed, for both Aristotle and Aquinas friendship is the primary school for virtue.[31] This is because, more often than not, human persons become what they love. Hence those things that are seen and admired in the character of their friends gradually over the course of time will guide many of a person's actions and in this way shape his or her character.

Friendship is itself a specific form of self-giving between persons, and in this way is formative of a person's sexuality. This does not mean that genital activity is necessary to friendship, rather it indicates that friendship serves to shape the affective and social aspects of sexuality (and hence to some degree the person's masculinity or femininity). All friendships are "sexual" in that they entail mutual love between embodied persons. Chastity ensures that the form this self-gift takes is authentic and true to their respective vocations—continence in the case of persons not married to one another and those living a life of religious celibacy, and fidelity and totality in self-giving in the case of marriage. The bonds of friendship are thus a school and a context for the "sincere gift of self."

Yet there are other virtues that support and sustain chastity within friendships in the midst of or across these various states of life. Friendship is built upon the mutual respect that is the demand of justice. It requires the truthfulness necessary for honesty in communication. A relationship between friends calls for the courage entailed in confronting the one who makes a bad moral decision and the prudence needed to know when to forego such a confrontation. It entails the humility need-

---

31. See the helpful overview provided by Paul Wadell, *Friendship and the Moral Life* (South Bend, Ind.: University of Notre Dame Press, 1989). Cf. Gilbert Meilaender, *Friendship: A Study in Theological Ethics* (South Bend, Ind.: University of Notre Dame Press, 1981).

ed to ask forgiveness and the generosity required to give it. Friendship flourishes in the patience of enduring the other's petty faults and the grace-empowered hope in the power of God to change them. Such virtues and many others are needed in the course of any friendship, particularly that of marriage.[32]

VII. Toward a Culture of Life

The landmark encyclical of Pope John Paul II, *Evangelium vitae*, is remarkable in the way it embodies and draws together many of the various strands of education in virtue considered here. The encyclical does insist on the absolute character of some moral norms, solemnly and authoritatively proscribing the direct killing of the innocent, direct abortion, and euthanasia.[33] Yet these prohibitions are but one aspect of a larger vision of the dignity and value of the life of every human person created in the image of God, redeemed by the blood of Christ, and called to share in the communion of the Trinity.[34] Such a vision is integral to building and sustaining what the encyclical calls "a culture of life." However, this culture is tied to the development of specific practices, particularly the worship of the Author of Life.[35] This is not surprising since the term "culture" is derived from the Latin *cultus* (to worship). Hence evangelization must precede and be the catalyst for such cultural change, since to change a culture one must change what it worships. Also vital in the building of such a culture is age-appropriate catechesis in an authentic understanding of human sexuality for all believers.[36]

From this vantage point, the current cultural ideologies about sex being a form of secular salvation achieved through ecstatic release are simply one more illusory manifestation of the culture of death. For they

32. Cf. the treatment of some virtues needed to sustain the "heroic calling" of marriage in Marva Dawn's reflections on the Pauline fruits of the Spirit (see Gal 5:22) in *Sexual Character*, 61–80.

33. See nos. 57, 62, and 65 of the encyclical for these prohibitions.

34. Cf. the overview of "the gospel of life" in *Evangelium vitae*, nos. 21–51.

35. For some hallmarks of the culture of life and its opposite, see *Evangelium vitae*, nos. 7–21, 78–101.

36. See ibid., no. 97.

strip away the transcendent meaning and mystery of human sexuality, reducing it to its most common and graphic manifestations. Rather than seeing sexual union as a manifestation of the human vocation to the communion of love, such ideologies view it as merely a matter of individual fulfillment for the sake of pleasure. To dispel these shadows cast by the idols of pleasure and self-seeking, the Christian community must offer more than the silence that has characterized many pulpits, parish halls, and homes in recent years. It must offer a real and effective witness of an alternative in the form of effective evangelization, coherent catechesis, and character-shaping praxis.

VIII. Conclusion

This study has argued that a covenantal understanding of sexual fidelity in conjunction with an account of chastity as an integral part of human flourishing can provide a framework for a Christian approach to issues of sexual morality in the present context. This covenantal understanding provides a vantage to critique shallow and distorted views of sexuality in contemporary culture as well as for framing an alternative to them. It is rooted in the mystery of Christ mediated by the biblical witness and the Church's liturgical tradition. It points toward the vocation of followers of Christ to be conformed to him in their capacity to love. Chastity is the virtue that enables this vocation to be realized and lived in a variety of states of life.

Yet for this conceptualization of sexuality to be effective it has to be embodied in personal and communal praxis. A full answer to the crisis of sexuality in the contemporary Church and society can only be found in people who by their lives and practices proclaim a countercultural alternative to its trivialization—people whose masculinity-femininity is a sacramental sign of "the sincere gift of self," whose sexual practices foster authentic human flourishing, whose sexuality is imbued with virtue. This lived witness of the human vocation to communion within marriages, families, religious vocations, and the single life is both a sign and a participation in the One whose very being is Gift and whose life as a Trinity of Persons is an eternal communion of Love.

Works Cited

This list includes recent works of scholarship cited in the notes above. Documents from ancient, patristic, and medieval authors as well as documents from ecumenical councils and magisterial documents are cited fully in the appropriate notes.

Adams, Marilyn McCord. "The Structure of Ockham's Moral Theory." In *The Context of Casuistry*, edited by James Kennan and Thomas Shannon, pp. 25–52. Washington, D.C.: Georgetown University Press, 1995.

Ahlstrom, Sydney. *A Religious History of the American People.* New Haven, Conn.: Yale University Press, 1972.

Allen, Prudence, R.S.M. *The Concept of Woman: The Aristotelian Revolution, 750 B.C.–A.D. 1250.* Montreal: Eden Press, 1985.

———. "Two Medieval Views of Women's Identity: Hildegard of Bingen and Thomas Aquinas." *Studies in Religion* 16 (1987): 21–36.

Altink, Sietske. *Stolen Lives: Trading Women into Sex and Slavery.* London: Scarlet Press, 1995.

Andolsen, Barbara Hilkert. "Whose Sexuality? Whose Tradition? Women, Experience and Roman Catholic Sexual Ethics." In *Readings in Moral Theology*, Vol. 9: *Feminist Ethics and the Catholic Moral Tradition*, edited by Charles Curran, Margaret Farley, R.S.M., and Richard McCormick, S.J., pp. 207–39. New York: Paulist Press, 1996.

Archer, John, and Barbara Lloyd. *Sex and Gender.* Cambridge, U.K.: Cambridge University Press, 1985.

Ashley, Benedict, O.P. *Living the Truth in Love: A Biblical Introduction to Moral Theology.* New York: Alba House, 1996.

Backer, Émile de. "Tertullien." In *Pour l'histoire du mot "Sacramentum,"* edited by Joseph de Ghellinck et al., pp. 66–71. Paris: É. Champion, 1924.

Balthasar, Hans Urs von. *A Theological Anthropology.* Translated by Benziger Verlag. New York: Sheed & Ward, 1967.

———. "Ephesians 5:21–33 and 'Humanae Vitae': A Meditation." In *Christian Married Love*, edited by Raymond Dennehy, 55–73. San Francisco: Ignatius Press, 1981.

———. *The Glory of the Lord*, Vol. 7: *Theology: The New Covenant.* Translated by Brian McNeil, C.R.V. Edinburgh, U.K.: T. & T. Clark, 1989.

Bancroft, John. "Homosexual Orientation: The Search for a Biological Basis." *British Journal of Psychiatry* 164 (1994): 437–40.

Barth, Karl. *Church Dogmatics.* Vol. 3.4. Translated by A. T. Mackay, T. H. L. Parker,

Harold Knight, Henry A. Kennedy, and John Marks. Edited by G. W. Bromiley and T. F. Torrance. Edinburgh, U.K.: T. & T. Clark, 1961.

Bayer, Edward J. *Rape within Marriage: A Moral Analysis.* Lanham, Md.: University Press of America, 1985.

Beal, John P. "Doing What One Can: Canon Law and Clerical Sexual Misconduct." *The Jurist* 55 (1992): 642–83.

Bennett, William J. *Book of Virtues: A Treasury of Great Moral Stories.* New York: Simon & Schuster, 1993.

Biale, Rachel. *Women and Jewish Law.* New York: Schocken Press, 1984.

Blanchette, Melvin, S.S., and Gerald Coleman, S.S. "Priest Pedophiles." *America* 186, no. 13 (April 22, 2002): 18–21.

Bledstein, Adrien Janis. "Was Eve Cursed? (Or Did a Woman Write Genesis?)." *Bible Review* 9, no. 1 (1993): 42–45.

Böckle, Frans. "*Humanae vitae* als Pruefstein des wahren Glaubens? Zur kirchenpolitischen Dimensionen moraltheologischer Fragen." *Stimmen der Zeit* 115 (1990): 3–16.

Bohr, David. *Catholic Moral Tradition: In Christ, a New Creation.* Rev. ed. Huntington, Ind.: Our Sunday Visitor Press, 1999.

Bottomley, Frank. *Attitudes to the Body in Western Christendom.* London: Lepus, 1979.

Bouyer, Louis. *Woman in the Church.* Translated by Marilyn Teichart. San Francisco: Ignatius Press, 1979.

Boyle, Joseph M. "Contraception and Natural Family Planning." *International Journal of Natural Family Planning* 44 (1980): 309–13.

Bowman, A. K. *Egypt after the Pharoahs, 332 B.C.–A.D. 642.* Berkeley and Los Angeles: University of California Press, 1986.

Brand, Jeff. *Marital Duration and Natural Family Planning.* Cincinnati, Ohio: Couple to Couple League, 1995.

Brooke, Christopher N. L. *The Medieval Idea of Marriage.* Oxford, U.K.: Clarendon Press, 1989.

Brooten, Bernadette. *Women Leaders in the Ancient Synagogues.* Chicago and Atlanta: Scholars Press, 1982.

Brown, Peter. *The Body and Society: Men, Women and Sexual Renunciation in Early Christianity.* New York: Columbia University Press, 1988.

Brown, Raymond, S.S. *An Introduction to the New Testament.* New York: Doubleday, 1997.

Brown, Raymond, S.S., and Sandra Schneiders, I.H.M. "Hermeneutics." In *New Jerome Biblical Commentary,* edited by Raymond E. Brown, S.S., Joseph A. Fitzmyer, S.J., and Roland E. Murphy, O. Carm., 1146–65. Englewood Cliffs, N.J.: Prentice-Hall, 1990.

Brueggemann, Walter. "Of the Same Flesh and Bone." *Catholic Biblical Quarterly* 32 (1970): 532–42.

Brundage, James A. *Law, Sex, and Christian Society in Medieval Europe.* Chicago: University of Chicago Press, 1987.

Burtchaell, James, C.S.C. *The Giving and Taking of Life: Essays Ethical.* South Bend, Ind.: University of Notre Dame Press, 1989.

Cahill, Lisa Sowle. *Between the Sexes: Foundations for a Christian Ethics of Sexuality.* Philadelphia: Fortress Press, 1985.

————. *Sex, Gender, and Christian Ethics.* New Studies in Christian Ethics 5. Cambridge, U.K.: Cambridge University Press, 1996.

Carl, Maria. "Law, Virtue, and Happiness in Aquinas' Moral Theory." *The Thomist* 61 (1997): 425–47.

Carr, Anne. *Transforming Grace: Christian Tradition and Women's Experience.* San Francisco: Harper & Row, 1988.

Cessario, Romanus, O.P. *The Moral Virtues and Theological Ethics.* South Bend, Ind.: University of Notre Dame Press, 1991.

————. *An Introduction to Moral Theology.* Catholic Moral Thought Series 1. Washington, D.C.: The Catholic University of America Press, 2001.

Chareire, I. "Les Béatitudes, espace de la vie théologale." *Lumen Vitae* 47, no. 234 (1997): 85–92.

Christen, Yves. *Sex Differences: Modern Biology and the Unisex Fallacy.* Translated by Nicholas Davidson. New Brunswick, N.J.: Transaction Books, 1991.

Cimbolic, Peter. "The Identification and Treatment of Sexual Disorders and the Priesthood." *The Jurist* 52 (1992): 598–614.

Cofino, E., et al. "Transcervical Balloon Tuboplasty: A Multicenter Study." *Journal of the American Medical Association* 264, no.16 (1990): 2079–82.

Coleman, Gerald, S.S. *Human Sexuality: An All-Embracing Gift.* New York: Alba House, 1992.

————. *Homosexuality: Church Teaching and Pastoral Practice.* New York: Paulist Press, 1995.

Collins, Adela Yarbro. *The Apocalypse.* New Testament Message Series 22. Wilmington, Del.: Michael Glazier, 1979.

Collins, Raymond. *Christian Morality: Biblical Foundations.* South Bend, Ind.: University of Notre Dame Press, 1986.

————. *Divorce in the New Testament.* Good News Studies 38. Collegeville, Minn.: Liturgical Press, 1992.

————. "The Beatitudes: The Heart of Jesus' Preaching." *The Living Light* 33, no. 1 (1996): 70–81.

————. *Sexual Ethics and the New Testament: Behavior and Belief.* New York: Crossroad Books, 2000.

Colliton, William F. "The Birth Control Pill: Abortifacient and Contraceptive." *Linacre Quarterly* 66 (1999): 26–47.

Conn, Walter. *Conscience: Development and Self-Transcendence.* Birmingham, Ala.: Religious Education Press, 1981.

————. *Christian Conversion: A Developmental Interpretation of Autonomy and Surrender.* Mahwah, N.J.: Paulist Press, 1986.

Cosgrove, Art. "Consent, Consummation and Indissolubility: Some Evidence from Ecclesiastical Medieval Courts." *Downside Review* 109 (1991): 94–104.

Craven, Toni. "Women in Genesis." *The Bible Today* 35 (1997): 32–39.

Curran, Charles. *Issues in Sexual and Medical Ethics.* South Bend, Ind.: University of Notre Dame Press, 1978.

————. *Toward an American Catholic Moral Theology.* South Bend, Ind.: University of Notre Dame Press, 1987.

D'Antonio, William, James Davidson, Dean Hoge, and Ruth Wallace. *American Catholic Laity.* Kansas City, Mo.: Sheed & Ward, 1989.

Darrieutort, André. "Way." In *Dictionary of Biblical Theology,* 2nd ed., edited by Xavier Léon-Dufour, pp. 647–48. New York: Seabury Press, 1973.

Dawn, Marva J. "The Concept of 'The Principalities and Powers' in the Work of Jacques Ellul." Ph.D. diss., University of Notre Dame, 1992.

————. *Sexual Character: Beyond Technique to Intimacy.* Grand Rapids, Mich.: William B. Eerdmans, 1993.

Dean, Carolyn J. *Sexuality and Modern Culture.* New York: Twayne, 1996.

Deedy, John G. "Five Medical Dilemmas that Might Scare You to Death." *U.S. Catholic* 53 (1988): 6–14.

DeMarco, Donald. *Biotechnology and the Assault on Parenthood.* San Francisco: Ignatius Press, 1991.

Deville, Raymond, P.S.S., and Pierre Grelot. "Kingdom." In *Dictionary of Biblical Theology,* 2nd ed., edited by Xavier Léon-Dufour, pp. 292–95. New York: Seabury Press, 1973.

Diprose, Rosalyn. *The Bodies of Women: Ethics, Embodiment and Sexual Difference.* London: Routledge, 1994.

Dogan, Mattei. "The Decline of Religious Beliefs in Western Europe." *International Journal of Social Science* 47 (1995): 405–18.

Doms, Herbert. *The Meaning of Marriage.* Translated by George Sayer. London: Sheed & Ward, 1939.

Donahue, John R., S.J. "The Challenge of Biblical Renewal to Moral Theology." In *Riding Time Like a River: The Catholic Moral Tradition since Vatican II,* edited by William J. O'Brien, pp. 59–80. Washington, D.C.: Georgetown University Press, 1993.

Dubarle, André-Marie, O.P. "Original Sin in Genesis." Translated by John Higgens. *Downside Review* 76 (1958): 242.

Dulles, Avery, S.J. "'Humanae Vitae' and the Crisis of Dissent." Dallas, Tex., February 4, 1993. Photocopied.

Dykstra, Craig. *Vision and Character: A Christian Educator's Alternative to Kohlberg.* New York: Paulist Press, 1981.

Eichrodt, Walther. *Theology of the Old Testament.* Vol. 1. Translated by J. A. Baker. Philadelphia: Westminster, 1961.

Ellerbee, Linda. "The Sexual Revolution: Well It Seemed Like a Good Idea at the Time. . . ." *New Choices: Living Even Better after 50* 38, no. 3 (1998): 8.

Elliott, Dyan. *Spiritual Marriage: Sexual Abstinence in Medieval Wedlock.* Princeton, N.J.: Princeton University Press, 1993.

Elliott, Peter J. *What God Has Joined: The Sacramentality of Marriage.* New York: Alba House, 1990.

Ellis, L. *Theories of Rape: Inquiries into the Causes of Sexual Aggression.* New York: Hemisphere, 1989.

Elmen, Paul. "On Worshiping the Bride." *Anglican Theological Review* 68 (1986): 241–49.

Erlich, Paul. *The Population Explosion.* New York: Ballantine Books, 1971.

————. *The Population Bomb.* New York: Simon & Schuster, 1990.

Ernst, Wilhelm. "Marriage as an Institution and the Contemporary Challenge to It." In *Contemporary Perspectives on Christian Marriage: Positions and Papers from the International Theological Commission,* edited by Richard Malone and John R. Connery, pp. 39–90. Chicago: Loyola University Press, 1984.

Evdokimov, Paul. *The Sacrament of Love.* Translated by Anthony Gythiel and Victoria Steadman. New York: St. Vladimir's Seminary Press, 1985.

Farley, Benjamin. *In Praise of Virtue: An Exploration of the Biblical Virtues in a Christian Context.* Grand Rapids, Mich.: William B. Eerdmans, 1995.

Farley, Margaret, R.S.M. "An Ethic for Same-Sex Relations." In *A Challenge to Love: Gay and Lesbian Catholics in the Church,* edited by Robert Nugent, pp. 93–106. New York: Crossroad Books, 1983.

Fensham, Frank Charles. "Father and Son as Terminology for Treaty and Covenant." In *Near Eastern Studies in Honor of William Foxwell Albright,* edited by H. Goedicke, pp. 121–35. Baltimore: Johns Hopkins University Press, 1971.

Feuillet, André, P.S.S. "Disciple." In *Dictionary of Biblical Theology,* 2nd ed., edited by Xavier Léon-Dufour, pp. 125–26. New York: Seabury Press, 1973.

Firestone, Shulamith. *The Dialectic of Sex: The Case for Feminist Revolution.* New York: William Morrow and Co., 1970.

Firth, Francis. "Catholic Sexual Morality in the Patristic and Medieval Periods." In *Human Sexuality and Personhood,* pp. 36–52. St. Louis: Pope John XXIII Medical-Moral Center, 1981.

Fortune, Marie. *Sexual Violence: The Unmentionable Sin.* New York: Pilgrim, 1983.

Fuller, A. Kenneth. "Child Molestation and Pedophilia: An Overview for the Physician." *Journal of the American Medical Association* 261 (1989): 602–96.

Gallagher, John, C.S.B. *Time Past, Time Future: An Historical Study of Catholic Moral Theology.* New York: Paulist Press, 1990.

————. "Magisterial Teaching from 1918 to the Present." In *Readings in Moral Theology, No. 8: Dialogue about Catholic Sexual Teaching,* edited by Charles Curran and Richard McCormick, S.J., pp. 71–92. New York: Paulist Press, 1993.

Gallagher, Winifred. "The Ecology of Orgasm." *Discover* 7 (1986): 51–58.

Gallegeo, Epifanio, O.S.A. "La sexualidad. Aporte de los relatos de la creación." *Biblia y fe* 18, no. 52 (1992): 21–36.

Gallup, George, Jr., and Jim Castelli. *The American Catholic People.* Garden City, N.Y.: Doubleday, 1987.

Gardella, Peter. *Innocent Ecstasy: How Christianity Gave America an Ethic of Sexual Pleasure.* New York: Oxford University Press, 1985.

Genovesi, Vincent, S.J. *In Pursuit of Love: Catholic Morality and Human Sexuality.* 2nd ed. Collegeville, Minn.: Michale Glazier, 1996.

Gilbert, Maurice, S.J. "'Une seule chair' (Gn 2, 24)." *Nouvelle Revue Théologique* 100 (1978): 66–89.

Gilligan, Carol. *In a Different Voice: Psychological Theory and Women's Development*. Cambridge, Mass.: Harvard University Press, 1982.

Grabowski, John S. "The Status of the Sexual Good as a Direction for Moral Theology." *Heythrop Journal* 35 (1994): 15–34.

———. "Clerical Sexual Misconduct and Early Traditions regarding the Sixth Commandment." *The Jurist* 55 (1995): 527–91.

———. "Mutual Submission and Trinitarian Self-Giving." *Angelicum* 84 (1997): 489–512.

———. "Person or Nature: Rival Personalisms in 20th Century Catholic Sexual Ethics." *Studia Moralia* 35 (1997): 283–312.

———. "The New Reproductive Technologies: An Overview and Theological Assessment." *Linacre Quarterly* 69 (2002): 100–119.

Graham, Elaine. *Making the Difference: Gender Personhood*. Minneapolis: Fortress Press, 1996.

Grant, George. *Grand Illusions: The Legacy of Planned Parenthood*. Brentwood, Tenn.: Wolgemuth & Hyatt, 1988.

Greeley, Andrew M. *Religious Change in America*. Cambridge, Mass.: Harvard University Press, 1989.

———. *Faithful Attraction: Discovering Intimacy, Love and Fidelity in American Marriage*. New York: Tor Books, 1991.

———. "Sex and the Married Catholic: The Shadow of St. Augustine." *America* 167 (Oct. 31, 1992): 318–23.

———. "Sex and the Single Catholic: The Decline of an Ethic." *America* 167 (Nov. 7, 1992): 342–47.

Grisez, Germain, Joseph Boyle, John Finnis, and William May. "Every Marital Act Ought to Be Open to Life: Toward a Clearer Understanding." *The Thomist* 52 (1988): 365–426.

———. "NFP: Not Contralife." In *The Teaching of Humanae Vitae: A Defense*, edited by John C. Ford, pp. 81–92. San Francisco: Ignatius Press, 1988.

Groeschel, Benedict. *The Courage to Be Chaste*. New York: Paulist Press, 1985.

Grubbs, Judith Evans. "'Marriage More Shameful than Adultery': Slave-Mistress Relationships, 'Mixed Marriages,' and Late Roman Law." *Phoenix* 47, no. 2 (1993): 125–54.

Guardini, Romano. *La realtà della Chiesa*. Brescia: Morcelliana, 1973.

Gudorf, Christine. *Body, Sex, and Pleasure: Reconstructing Christian Sexual Ethics*. Cleveland, Ohio: Pilgrim, 1994.

Gula, Richard, S.S. *Reason Informed by Faith: Foundations of Christian Morality*. New York: Paulist Press, 1989.

Halman, Loek. "Is There a Moral Decline? A Cross National Inquiry into Morality in Contemporary Society." *International Social Science Journal* 47 (1995): 419–39.

Harak, G. Simon. *Virtuous Passions: The Formation of Christian Character*. New York: Paulist Press, 1993.

Häring, Bernard. *Free and Faithful in Christ*, Vol. 1: *General Moral Theology*. New York: Seabury Press, 1978.

Haro, Ramón García de. *Marriage and Family in the Documents of the Magisterium*. 2nd ed. Translated by William E. May. San Francisco: Ignatius Press, 1993.

Harvey, John. *The Homosexual Person*. San Francisco: Ignatius Press, 1987.

Hauerwas, Stanley. *The Peaceable Kingdom*. South Bend, Ind.: University of Notre Dame Press, 1983.

Hauerwas, Stanley, and Charles Pinches. *Christians among the Virtues: Theological Conversations with Ancient and Modern Ethics*. South Bend, Ind.: University of Notre Dame Press, 1997.

Hays, Richard. *The Moral Vision of the New Testament: A Contemporary Introduction to New Testament Ethics*. San Francisco: Harper San Francisco, 1996.

Hellin, Francisco Gil. "El lugar propio del amor conyugal en la estructura del matrimonio segun la 'Gaudium et spes.'" *Annales Valentinos* 6 (1980): 1–35.

Herik, Judith Van. *Freud on Femininity and Faith*. Berkeley and Los Angeles: University of California Press, 1982.

Hiers, Richard H. "Sexual Harassment: Title VII and Title IX Protections and Prohibitions—The Current State of the Law." *Annual of the Society of Christian Ethics* 19 (1999): 391–406.

Hildebrand, Dietrich von. *Marriage: The Mystery of Faithful Love*. London: Longmans Green, and Co., 1942.

———. *In Defense of Purity*. Baltimore: Helicon Press, 1962.

Hilgers, Thomas W. *The Creighton Model NaProEducation System*. 3rd ed. Omaha, Neb.: Pope Paul VI Institute Press, 1996.

Horst, Friederich. "Der Eid im Alten Testament." In *Gottes Recht: Gesammelte Studien zum Recht im Alten Testament*, edited by Hans Walter Wolff, pp. 301–14. Munich: Chr. Kaiser, 1961.

Hossfeld, Frank-Lothar. *Der Dekalog: Seine späten Fassungen, die originale Komposition und seine Vorstufen*. Orbis Biblicus Orientalis 45. Freiburg, Schweiz: Universitätsverlag, 1982.

Hugenberger, Gordon Paul. *Marriage as a Covenant: A Study of Biblical Law and Ethics Developed from the Perspective of Malachi*. Supplements to Vetus Testamentum 52. Leiden: Brill, 1994.

Janssens, Louis. "Morale conjugale et progestgènes." *Ephemerides Theologicae Lovanienses* 39 (1963): 787–826.

Jewett, Paul. *Man as Male and Female*. Grand Rapids, Mich.: William B. Eerdmans, 1975.

Johnson, Elizabeth. "The Maleness of Christ." In *The Special Nature of Women? Concilium* 6 (1991): 108–16.

Johnson, Luke Timothy. *The Writings of the New Testament: An Interpretation*. Philadelphia: Fortress Press, 1986.

Johnstone, Brian V., C.Ss.R. "From Physicalism to Personalism." *Studia Moralia* 30 (1992): 71–96.

Kahn, Charles H. *Anaximander and the Origins of Greek Cosmology*. New York: Columbia University Press, 1960; rpt., Philadelphia: Centrum, 1985.

Kalluveettil, Paul, C.M.I. *Declaration and Covenant: A Comprehensive Review of Covenant For-mulae from the Old Testament and the Ancient New East.* Analecta Biblica 88. Rome: Pontifical Biblical Institute Press, 1982.

Kambic, R., and V. Lamprecht. "Calendar Method Efficacy: A Review." *Advances in Contraception* 12, no. 2 (1996): 123–28.

Kasia, J. M., et al. "Laproscopic Fimbrioplasty and Neosalpingostomy: Experience of the Yaounde General Hospitial, Cameroon." *European Journal of Obstetrical Gynecological Reproductive Biology* 73, no.1 (May 1997): 71–77.

Kasper, Walter. *Theology of Christian Marriage.* Translated by David Smith. New York: Seabury Press, 1980.

———. "The Position of Women as a Problem of Theological Anthropology." Translated by John Saward. In *The Church and Women: A Compendium,* edited by Helmut Moll, pp. 51–64. San Francisco: Ignatius Press, 1988.

Kastner, Patricia Wilson. *Faith, Feminism and the Christ.* Philadelphia: Fortress Press, 1983.

Keane, Philip, S.S. *Sexual Morality: A Catholic Perspective.* New York: Paulist Press, 1977.

Keefe, Donald J., S.J. *Covenantal Theology: The Eucharistic Order of History.* 2 vols. Lanham, Md.: University Press of America, 1991.

Keenan, James, S.J., and Thomas Shannon. "Introduction." In *The Context of Casuistry,* edited by James Kennan and Thomas Shannon, pp. i–xvii. Washington, D.C.: Georgetown University Press, 1995.

Klofft, Christopher. "Moral Development, Virtue, and Gender: A Comparison of the Differing Accounts of Lisa Sowle Cahill, Servais Pinckaers, and Paul Evdokimov." S.T.D. diss., The Catholic University of America, 2000.

Klopfenstein, Martin A. "Was heisst 'Macht euch die Erde untertan?' Überlegungen zur Schöpfungsgeschichte der Bibel in der Umweltkrise heute." In *Leben aus dem Wort: Beiträge zum Alten Testament,* Beataj 40, edited by Walter Dietrich, pp. 275–83. Bern: P. Lang, 1996.

Kottackal, Joseph. "Family Life in Pentateuchal Traditions." *Bible Bhashyam* 20 (1994): 267–79.

Kurz, William, S.J. *The Acts of the Apostles.* Collegeville Bible Commentary 5. Collegeville, Minn.: Liturgical Press, 1983.

Kraft, William F. *Sexual Dimensions of the Celibate Life.* Kansas City, Mo.: Andrews & McNeil, 1977.

———. "A Pyschospiritual View of Masturbation." *Human Development* 3 (1983): 79–85.

———. *Whole and Holy Sexuality: How to Find Human and Spiritual Integrity as a Sexual Person.* St. Meinrad, Ind.: Abbey Press, 1989.

Kratz, Reinhard Gregor. "Der Dekalog im Exodusbuch." *Vetus Testamentum* 44 (1994): 205–38.

Laaser, Mark. *Faithful and True: Sexual Integrity in a Fallen World.* Grand Rapids, Mich.: Zondervan, 1996.

Landau, I. "On the Definition of Sexual Harassment." *Australasian Journal of Philosophy* 77, no. 2 (1999): 216–23.

Lasseter, Ruth. "Sensible Sex." In *Why Humanae Vitae Was Right: A Reader*, edited by Janet Smith, pp. 475–95. San Francisco: Ignatius Press, 1993.

Laumann, Edward O., John H. Gagnon, Robert T. Michael, and Stuart Michaels. *The Social Organization of Sexuality: Sexual Practices in the United States.* Chicago: University of Chicago Press, 1994.

Lawler, Michael. *Secular Marriage, Christian Sacrament.* Mystic, Conn.: Twenty-Third Publications, 1985.

Lawler, Ronald, O.F.M., Cap., Joseph Boyle, and William E. May. *Catholic Sexual Ethics: A Summary Explanation and Defense.* 2nd ed. Huntington, Ind.: Our Sunday Visitor Press, 1998.

LeBlanc, Marie, O.S.B. "Amour et procréation dans la théologie de saint Thomas." *Revue Thomiste* 92 (1992): 433–59.

Lehmann, Karl. "The Sacramentality of Christian Marriage: The Bond between Baptism, Faith and Marriage." In *Contemporary Perspectives on Christian Marriage: Positions and Papers from the International Theological Commission*, edited by Richard Malone and John R. Connery, pp. 91–115. Chicago: Loyola University Press, 1984.

Léon-Dufour, Xavier. "Body." In *Dictionary of Biblical Theology*, 2nd ed., edited by Xavier Léon-Dufour, pp. 53–55. New York: Seabury Press, 1973.

Levin, Michael. *Feminism and Freedom.* New Brunswick, N.J.: Transaction Books, 1987.

Lienhard, Joseph T., S.J. *The Bible, the Church, and Authority: The Canon of the Christian Bible in History and Theology.* Collegeville, Minn.: Liturgical Press, 1995.

Lohfink, Norbert. *Die Landverheissung als Eid: Eine Studie zu Gn. 15.* Stuttgarter Bibel-Studien 28. Stuttgart: Verlag Katholisches Bibelwerk, 1967.

MacIntyre, Alasdair. *After Virtue.* 2nd ed. South Bend, Ind.: University of Notre Dame Press, 1984.

———. *Whose Justice? Which Rationality?* South Bend, Ind.: University of Notre Dame Press, 1988.

Mackin, Theodore. *What Is Marriage?* New York: Paulist Press, 1982.

———. *The Marital Sacrament: Marriage in the Catholic Church.* New York: Paulist Press, 1989.

MacNamara, Vincent. *Faith and Ethics: Recent Roman Catholicism.* Washington, D.C.: Georgetown University Press, 1985.

Mahoney, John, S.J. "Human Fertility Control." In *Readings in Moral Theology*, No. 8: *Dialogue about Catholic Sexual Teaching*, edited by Charles E. Curran and Richard A. McCormick, S.J., pp. 251–66. Mahwah, N.J.: Paulist Press, 1993.

———. *The Making of Moral Theology: A Study of the Roman Catholic Tradition.* Oxford, U.K.: Clarendon Press, 1987.

Marcia, Colish. *The Stoic Tradition from Antiquity to the Early Middle Ages.* 2 vols. Leiden: Brill, 1990.

Marietta, Don. *Philosophy of Sexuality.* Armonk, N.Y.: M. E. Sharpe, 1997.

Marshall, Marshall. *Love One Another: Psychological Aspects of Natural Family Planning.* London: Sheed & Ward, 1995.

Marshall, Robert, and Charles Donovan. *Blessed Are the Barren: The Social Policy of Planned Parenthood.* San Francisco: Ignatius Press, 1991.

Marshner, William. "Can a Couple Practicing NFP Be Practicing Contraception?" *Gregorianum* 77 (1996): 677–704.

Martelet, Gustav. "Sixteen Christological Theses on the Sacrament of Marriage." In *Contemporary Perspectives on Christian Marriage*, pp. 275–83. Chicago: Loyola University Press, 1984.

Martin, Francis. "Male and Female He Created Them: A Summary of the Teaching of Genesis Chapter One." *Communio* 20 (1993): 240–65.

———. "St. Matthew's Spiritual Understanding of the Healing of the Centurion's Boy." *Communio* 25 (1998): 160–77.

———. "Family Values in the First Century." Unpublished manuscript.

Martinez, German. "Marriage as Worship: A Theological Analogy." *Worship* 62 (1988): 332–53.

Matera, Frank. *New Testament Ethics: The Legacies of Jesus and Paul.* Louisville, Ky.: Westminster John Knox Press, 1996.

May, William E. *An Introduction to Moral Theology.* Huntington, Ind.: Our Sunday Visitor Press, 1990.

———. "Review of *Humanae Vitae: A Generation Later.*" *The Thomist* 57 (1993): 155–61.

———. *Marriage: The Rock on Which the Family Is Built.* San Francisco: Ignatius Press, 1995.

McCasland, S. V. "The Way." *Journal of Biblical Literature* 77 (1957): 220–30.

McCarthy, David. "Procreation, the Development of Peoples, and the Final Destiny of Humanity." *Communio* 26 (1999): 698–721.

McCarthy, Dennis J. "Notes on the Love of God in Deuteronomy and the Father-Son Relationship between Yahweh and Israel." *Catholic Biblical Quarterly* 27 (1965): 144–47.

———. *Old Testament Covenant: A Survey of Current Opinions.* Richmond: John Knox, 1972.

———. *Treaty and Covenant.* 2nd ed. Analecta Biblica 21A. Rome: Pontifical Biblical Institute Press, 1978.

McKenzie, John, S.J. *Dictionary of the Bible.* New York: Macmillan, 1965.

Meier, John. *The Vision of Matthew: Christ, Church and Morality in the First Gospel.* Theological Inquiries. New York: Paulist Press, 1979.

Meilaender, Gilbert. *Friendship: A Study in Theological Ethics.* South Bend, Ind.: University of Notre Dame Press, 1981.

———. *The Theory and Practice of Virtue.* South Bend, Ind.: University of Notre Dame Press, 1984.

———. *Faith and Faithfulness: Basic Themes in Christian Ethics.* South Bend, Ind.: University of Notre Dame Press, 1991.

Melina, Livio. "Moral Theology and the Ecclesial Sense: Points for a Theological 'Re-Dimensioning' of Morality." *Communio* 19 (1992): 67–93.

———. *Sharing in Christ's Virtues: For a Renewal of Moral Theology in Light of Veritatis Splendor.* Translated by William E. May. Washington, D.C.: The Catholic University of America Press, 2001.

Michael, Robert T. "Why Did the U.S. Divorce Rate Double within a Decade?" *Research in Population* 11 (1988): 361–99.

Miletic, Stephen F. *"One Flesh": Ephesians 5:22–24, 5:31. Marriage and the New Creation.* Analecta Biblica 115. Rome: Pontifical Biblical Institute Press, 1988.

Miller, Donald, O.F.M. "A Critical Evaluation and Application to Various Situations in the United States of the Official Roman Catholic Position on Family Life from Vatican II through *Christifideles laici*." Ph.D. diss., The Catholic University of America, 1995.

Miller, Jo Ann L. "Prostitution in Contemporary American Society." In *Sexual Coercion: A Sourcebook on Its Nature, Causes and Prevention*, edited by Elizabeth Grauerholz and Mary Koralewski, pp. 45–57. Lexington, Mass: Lexington Books, 1991.

Miller, John W. *Biblical Faith and Fathering: Why We Call God Father.* New York: Paulist Press, 1989.

Monteleone, James A. "The Physiological Aspects of Sex." In *Human Sexuality and Personhood*, pp. 71–85. St. Louis: Pope John XXIII Medical-Moral Center, 1981.

Moore, Gareth, O.P. *The Body in Context: Sex and Catholicism.* London: SCM Press, 1992.

Moran, William L. "The Scandal of the 'Great Sin' at Ugarit." *Journal of Near Eastern Studies* 18 (1959): 280–81.

Motte, René, O.M.I., and Michel Join-Lambert. "Moses." In *Dictionary of Biblical Theology*, 2nd ed., edited by Xavier Léon-Dufour, pp. 368–70. New York: Seabury Press, 1973.

Murphy, Cornelius F., Jr. *Beyond Feminism: Toward a Dialogue on Difference.* Washington, D.C.: The Catholic University of America Press, 1995.

Nelson, James. *Body Theology.* Louisville, Ky.: Westminster John Knox Press, 1992.

Nicholson, Ernest W. *God and His People: Covenant and Theology in the Old Testament.* Oxford, U.K.: Clarendon Press, 1986.

Nolan, Michael. "Aquinas and the Act of Love." *New Blackfriars* 77, no. 92 (1996): 115–30.

Noonan, John T. *Contraception: A History of Its Treatment by the Catholic Theologians and Canonists.* Rev. ed. Cambridge, Mass.: Harvard University Press, 1986.

———. "Development in Moral Doctrine." *Theological Studies* 54 (1993): 662–77.

O'Connell, Timothy E. *Principles for a Catholic Morality.* Rev. ed. San Francisco: Harper, 1990.

Ong, Walter, S.J. *Fighting for Life: Contest, Sexuality and Consciousness.* Ithaca, N.Y.: Cornell University Press, 1981.

Örsy, Ladislas, S.J. "Married People: God's Chosen People." In *Christian Marriage Today*, edited by Klaus Demmer and Aldegonde Brenninkmeijer-Werhahn, pp. 38–54. Washington, D.C.: The Catholic University of America Press, 1997.

Palmer, Paul F., S.J. "Christian Marriage: Contract or Covenant?" *Theological Studies* 33 (1972): 617–65.

Parrella, Frederick J. "Towards a Spirituality of the Family." *Communio* 9 (1982): 127–41.

Patrick, Anne E. "Sexual Harassment: A Christian Ethical Response." *Annual of the Society of Christian Ethics* 19 (1999): 371–76.

Pedersen, Johannes. *Der Eid bei den Semiten, in seinem Verhältnis zu verwandten Erscheinungen sowie die Stellung des Eides im Islam.* Studien zur Geschichte und Kultur des islamischen Orients 3. Strassburg: Trübner, 1914.

Pedersen, Larry R., and Gregory V. Donnenwerth. "Secularization and the Influence of Religion on Beliefs about Premarital Sex." *Social Forces* 75 (1997): 1071–88.

Pellauer, Mary D. "A Theological Perspective on Sexual Assault." *Christianity and Crisis* 44 (1984): 250–55.

Perkins, Pheme. "Marriage in the New Testament and Its World." In *Commitment to Partnership: Explorations in the Theology of Marriage,* edited by William P. Roberts. New York: Paulist Press, 1987.

Perlitt, Lothar. *Bundestheologie im Alten Testament.* WMANT 36. Neukirchen-Vluyn: Neukirchener Verlag, 1969.

Perniola, Mario. "Between Clothing and Nudity." In *Fragments for a History of the Human Body,* part 2, edited by Michel Feher with Ramona Naddaff and Nadia Tazi, pp. 237–65. New York: Zone, 1989.

Peterson, John. "Natural Law, End, and Virtue in Aquinas." *Journal of Philosophical Research* 24 (1999): 397–413.

Philips, Anthony. *Ancient Israel's Criminal Law.* Oxford, U.K.: Blackwell, 1970.

Pieper, Josef. *The Four Cardinal Virtues.* South Bend, Ind.: University of Notre Dame Press, 1966.

Pinckaers, Servais, O.P. "La question des actes intrinsèquement mauvais et le 'proportionalisme.'" *Revue thomiste* 82 (1982): 181–212.

———. *The Sources of Christian Ethics.* Translated by Mary Thomas Noble, O.P. Washington, D.C.: The Catholic University of America Press, 1995.

Plé, Albert. *Chastity and the Affective Life.* Translated by Marie-Claude Thompson. New York: Herder & Herder, 1966.

Population Division of the Department of Economics and Social Affairs of the United Nations. "World Population Monitoring 2001." Available at http://www.un.org/esa/population/unpop.htm.

Porter, Jean. *Moral Action and Christian Ethics.* New Studies in Christian Ethics. New York: Cambridge University Press, 1995.

———. "What the Wise Person Knows: Natural Law and Virtue in Aquinas' *Summa Theologiae.*" *Studies in Christian Ethics* 12 (1999): 57–69.

Potterie, Ignace de la. "'Reading Scripture in the Holy Spirit': Is the Patristic Way of Reading the Bible Still Possible Today?" *Comunio* 4 (1986): 308–25.

———. "The Spiritual Sense of Scripture." *Communio* 23 (1996): 738–56.

Price, Richard. "The Distinctiveness of Early Christian Sexual Ethics." *Heythrop Journal* 31 (1990): 257–76.

Provost, James H. "Some Canonical Considerations Relative to Clerical Sexual Misconduct." *The Jurist* 55 (1992): 615–41.

Quell, Gottfried. "*Diatheke.*" In *Theological Dictionary of the New Testament,* edited by Gerhard Kittel, Gerhard Friedrich, and Geoffrey W. Bromiley, 2: 114. Grand Rapids, Mich.: William B. Eerdmans, 1964.

Rabinowitz, Jacob J. "The 'Great Sin' in Ancient Egyptian Marriage Contracts." *Journal of Near Eastern Studies* 18 (1959): 73.

Rad, Gerhard von. *Genesis: A Commentary.* Translated by John H. Marks. Philadelphia: Westminster Press, 1961.

————. *Old Testament Theology.* Vol. 1. Translated by David M. G. Stalker. New York: Harper, 1965.

Readings in Moral Theology, No. 1: Moral Norms and Catholic Tradition. Edited by Charles Curran and Richard McCormick, S.J. New York: Paulist Press, 1979.

Readings in Moral Theology, No. 2: The Distinctiveness of Christian Ethics. Edited by Charles Curran and Richard McCormick, S.J. New York: Paulist Press, 1980.

Readings in Moral Theology, No. 3: The Magisterium and Morality. Edited by Charles Curran and Richard McCormick, S.J. New York: Paulist Press, 1982.

Reynolds, P. Lyndon. "Marriage, Sacramental and Indissoluble: Sources of the Catholic Doctrine." *Downside Review* 109, no. 375 (1991): 105–50.

Riley, Patrick. *Civilising Sex: On Chastity and the Common Good.* Edinburgh, U.K.: T. & T. Clark, 2000.

Ritzer, Karl. *Le mariage dans les églises chrétiennes du Ier au XIe siècle.* Paris: Les Éditions du Cerf, 1970.

Robinson, John A. T. *The Body: A Study in Pauline Theology.* Philadelphia: Westminister Press, 1952.

Rock, John. *The Time Has Come.* New York: Alfred A. Knopf, 1963.

Rossetti, Stephen J. *A Tragic Grace: The Catholic Church and Child Sexual Abuse.* Collegeville, Minn.: Liturgical Press, 1996.

————. "The Catholic Church and Child Sexual Abuse." *America* 186, no. 13 (April 22, 2002): 8–15.

Roth, Catherine P. "Introduction." In *On Marriage and Family Life*, edited by Catherine P. Roth, pp. 7–24. Crestwood, N.Y.: St. Vladimir's Seminary Press, 1986.

Rouche, Michel. "The Many Changes in the Concept of Christian Marriage and the Family Throughout History." In *Christian Marriage Today*, edited by Klaus Demmer and Aldegonde Brenninkmeijer-Werhahn, pp. 25–37. Washington, D.C.: The Catholic University of America Press, 1997.

Rousselle, Aline. "Personal Status and Sexual Practice in the Roman Empire." Translated by Janet Lloyd. In *Fragments for a History of the Human Body*, edited by Michael Feher et al., pp. 301–33. New York: Zone, 1989.

Ruether, Rosemary Radford. "Can a Male Savior Save Women?" In *To Change the World: Christology and Cultural Criticism*, pp. 45–56. London: SCM, 1981.

————. *Sexism and God-Talk: Toward a Feminist Theology.* Boston: Beacon Press, 1983.

————. "Birth Control and the Ideals of Marital Sexuality." In *Readings in Moral Theology, No. 8: Dialogue about Catholic Sexual Teaching*, edited by Charles Curran and Richard McCormick, S.J., pp. 138–52. New York: Paulist Press, 1993.

Russell, Diana E. *Rape in Marriage.* Rev. ed. Bloomington: Indiana University Press, 1990.

Schillebeeckx, Edward, O.P. *Marriage: Human Reality and Saving Mystery.* Translated by N. D. Smith. 2 vols. New York: Sheed & Ward, 1965.

Schnackenburg, Rudolph. *The Moral Teaching of the New Testament.* Translated by J. Holland-Smith and W. J. O'Hara. New York: Seabury Press, 1979.

Schrage, Wolfgang. *The Ethics of the New Testament.* Translated by David E. Green. Philadelphia: Fortress Press, 1988.

Searle, Mark, and Kenneth W. Stevenson. *Documents of the Marriage Liturgy.* Collegeville, Minn.: Liturgical Press, 1992.

Secretariat for Family, Laity, Women and Youth. *Marriage Preparation for Cohabiting Couples: An Informational Report on New Realities and Pastoral Practices.* Washington, D.C.: United States Catholic Conference, 1999.

Selling, Joseph. "Magisterial Teaching on Marriage, 1880–1986: Historical Consistency or Radical Development?" In *Readings in Moral Theology,* No. 8: *Dialogue about Catholic Sexual Teaching,* edited by Charles Curran and Richard McCormick, S.J., pp. 93–97. New York: Paulist Press, 1993.

Seubert, Xavier John, O.F.M. "The Sacramentality of Metaphors: Reflections on Homosexuality." *Cross Currents* 42 (1991): 52–68.

Shannon, Thomas. "Method in Ethics: A Scotistic Contribution." In *The Context of Casuistry,* edited by James Kennan and Thomas Shannon, pp. 3–24. Washington, D.C.: Georgetown University Press, 1995.

Shannon, William H. *The Lively Debate: Response to "Humanae vitae."* New York: Sheed & Ward, 1970.

Shivanadan, Mary. *Natural Sex.* New York: Rawson, Wade, 1979.

———. *Crossing the Threshold of Love: A New Vision of Marriage in Light of John Paul II's Anthropology.* Washington, D.C.: The Catholic University of America Press, 1999.

Sharp, Donald B. "A Biblical Foundation for an Environmental Theology." *Science et Espirit* 47 (1995): 305–13.

Simon, Yves. *The Definition of Moral Virtue.* Edited by Vukan Kuic. New York: Fordham University Press, 1986.

Slattery, Joseph A. "The Catechetical Use of the Decalogue from the End of the Catechumenate through the Later Medieval Period." Ph.D. diss., The Catholic University of America Press, 1980.

Smith, Janet. *"Humanae Vitae": A Generation Later.* Washington, D.C.: The Catholic University of America Press, 1991.

Speyer, Wolfgang. "Zu den Vorwürfen der Heiden gegen die Christen." *Jahrbuch für Antike und Christentum* 6 (1963): 129–35.

Stanley, Stanley, Daniel Trathen, Savanna McCain, and Milt Bryan. *A Lasting Promise: A Christian Guide to Fighting for Your Marriage.* San Francisco: Jossey-Bass, 1998.

"Statement by Catholic Theologians Washington, D.C., July 30, 1968." In *Readings in Moral Theology,* No. 8: *Dialogue about Catholic Sexual Teaching,* edited by Charles Curran and Richard McCormick, pp. 135–7. New York: Paulist Press, 1993.

Stevens, Clifford. "The Trinitarian Roots of Nuptial Community." *St. Vladimir's Theological Quarterly* 35 (1991): 351–59.

Sueoka, K., et al. "Falloposcopic Tuboplasty for Bilateral Tubal Occlusion: A Novel Infertility Treatment as an Alternative to In-Vitro Fertilization?" *Human Reproduction* 18, no. 1 (January 1998): 71–74.

Taylor, Charles. *Sources of the Self: The Making of Modern Identity.* Cambridge, Mass.: Harvard University Press, 1989.

———. *The Ethics of Authenticity.* Cambridge, Mass.: Harvard University Press, 1991.

Tosato, Angelo. *Il matrimonio israelitico: una teoria generale.* Rome: Pontifical Biblical Institute Press, 1982.

Touhey, John. "The Correct Interpretation of Canon 1395: The Use of the Sixth Commandment in the Moral Tradition from Trent to the Present Day." *The Jurist* 55 (1995): 592–631.

Trible, Phyllis. *God and the Rhetoric of Sexuality.* Overtures to Biblical Theology 2. Philadelphia: Fortress Press, 1978.

Tsirpanlis, Constantine N. "Saint Gregory the Theologian on Marriage and Family." *Patristic and Byzantine Review* 4 (1985): 33–38.

Tucker, Gene M. "Covenant Forms and Contract Forms." *Vetus Testamentum* 15 (1965): 487–503.

Uehlinger, Christopher. "Nicht nur Knochenfrau. Zu einem wenig beachteten Aspect der zweiten Schöpfungerszählung." *Bibel und Kirche* 53 (1998): 31–34.

Vogels, Walter. "The Human Person in the Image of God (Gn 1, 26)." *Science et Espirit* 46 (1994): 189–202.

———. "The Power Struggle between Man and Woman (Gen 3, 16b)." *Biblica* 77 (1996): 197–209.

Wadell, Paul, C.P. *Friendship and the Moral Life.* South Bend, Ind.: University of Notre Dame Press, 1989.

———. *Friends of God: Virtues and Gifts in Aquinas.* American University Studies, Series 7, Vol. 76. New York: Peter Lang, 1991.

Weiner, Neal O. *The Harmony of the Soul: Mental Health and Moral Virtue Reconsidered.* Albany: State University of New York Press, 1993.

Weippert, Manfred. "Tier und Mensch in einer menschenarmen Welt. Zum sog. *Dominium terrae* in Genesis 1." In *Ebenbild Gottes—Herrscher über die Welt,* pp. 35–55. Biblisch-Theologische Studien 33. Neukirchen-Vluyn: Neukirchener Verlag, 1998.

Weitzer, Ronald. *Sex for Sale: Prostitution, Pornography, and the Sex Industry.* New York: Routledge, 2000.

Welch, Michael R., David C. Leege, and James C. Cavendish. "Attitudes toward Abortion among U.S. Catholics: Another Case of Symbolic Politics?" *Social Science Quarterly* 76, no. 1 (1995): 142–57.

Westermann, Claus. *Genesis 1–11: A Commentary.* Translated by John J. Scullion, S.J. Minneapolis: Augsburg, 1984.

Wilks, John. "The Impact of the Pill on Implantation Factors: New Research Factors." *Ethics and Medicine* 16, no. 1 (2000): 15–22.

Wilson, Mercedes Arzú. *Love and Family: Raising a Traditional Family in a Secular World.* San Francisco: Ignatius Press, 1996.

Witherington, Ben. *Women in the Earliest Churches.* Society for New Testament Studies 59. Cambridge, U.K.: Cambridge University Press, 1988.

Wójcik, Elizabeta. "Natural Regulation of Conception and Contraception." In *Why*

"Humanae Vitae" Was Right: A Reader, edited by Janet Smith, pp. 421–43. San Francisco: Ignatius Press, 1993.

Wojtyla, Karol. *Love and Responsibility.* Translated by H. T. Willets. New York: Farrar, Straus and Giroux, 1981; rpt., San Francisco: Ignatius Press, 1993.

Woodall, George John. "The Principle of the Indissoluble Link between the Dimensions on Unity and Fruitfulness in Conjugal Love: A Hermeneutical Investigation of Its Theological Basis and of Its Normative Significance." S.T.D. diss., Gregorian University, 1996.

Yip, Andrew K. T. "Dare to Differ: Gay and Lesbian Catholics' Assessment of Official Catholic Positions on Sexuality." *Sociology of Religion* 58 (1997): 165–80.

Index

Sex and Virtue: An Introduction to Sexual Ethics was designed and composed in Centaur by Kachergis Book Design, Pittsboro, North Carolina, and printed on 60-pound Sebago 2000 Eggshell and bound by The Maple-Vail Book Manufacturing Group of York, Pennsylvania.